Polanyi in Times of Populism

The rise of populism across Europe and the US – first in the wake of the 2008 global financial crisis and then in the shape of Donald Trump's presidential campaign and the Brexit vote in 2016 – are indicative of a seismic shift in the terrain of economic ideas in public discourse. Settled liberal norms concerning ever-increasing international market expansion, and the political integration required to sustain it, have been decisively upset by political forces that, whilst once on the fringes, now dominate economic debate. How might we make sense of this ideological breakdown and what might we hope for next?

This book turns to the work of Karl Polanyi for answers, developing the expansive, historicised approach to political economy that Polanyi pioneered. Holmes provides a wide-ranging history of economic ideas read in terms of a series of hopeful theoretical visions of order, in which political, social and ecological contradictions could be transcended in one way or another. Through this, the book demonstrates that the failing utopian visions of pre-2008 economic orthodoxy, which have formed the backdrop to the rise of populism today, are only the latest in a series that stretches across economic thought in Western modernity as a whole.

This book will interest students and scholars of international political economy, political science, sociology, anthropology, law and history.

Christopher Holmes is a Lecturer in Political Economy at King's College, London. He works on various topics including the history of economic ideas, financial and monetary politics and alternatives to GDP in policymaking. He has published in a variety of leading journals including *Economy and Society*, *New Political Economy*, *Review of International Political Economy* and the *British Journal of Politics and International Relations*.

RIPE Series in Global Political Economy

Series Editors: James Brassett (*University of Warwick, UK*), Eleni Tsingou (*Copenhagen Business School, Denmark*) and Susanne Soederberg (*Queen's University, Canada*)

The RIPE Series published by Routledge is an essential forum for cutting-edge scholarship in International Political Economy. The series brings together new and established scholars working in critical, cultural and constructivist political economy. Books in the RIPE Series typically combine an innovative contribution to theoretical debates with rigorous empirical analysis.

The RIPE Series seeks to cultivate:

- Field-defining theoretical advances in International Political Economy
- Novel treatments of key issue areas, both historical and contemporary, such as global finance, trade, and production
- Analyses that explore the political economic dimensions of relatively neglected topics, such as the environment, gender relations, and migration
- Accessible work that will inspire advanced undergraduates and graduate students in International Political Economy.

The *RIPE Series in Global Political Economy* aims to address the needs of students and teachers.

For more information about this series, please visit: www.routledge.com/RIPE-Series-in-Global-Political-Economy/book-series/RIPE

Securing Finance, Mobilizing Risk
Money Cultures at the Bank of England
John Hogan Morris

Affective Politics of the Global Event
Trauma and the Resilient Market Subject
James Brassett

Transnational Capital and Class Fractions
The Amsterdam School Perspective Reconsidered
Edited by Henk Overbeek and Bob Jessop

Polanyi in Times of Populism
Vision and Contradiction in the History of Economic Ideas

Christopher Holmes

LONDON AND NEW YORK

First published 2018
by Routledge
2 Park Square, Milton Park, Abingdon, Oxon OX14 4RN

and by Routledge
711 Third Avenue, New York, NY 10017

Routledge is an imprint of the Taylor & Francis Group, an informa business

© 2018 Christopher Holmes

The right of Christopher Holmes to be identified as author of this work has been asserted by him in accordance with sections 77 and 78 of the Copyright, Designs and Patents Act 1988.

All rights reserved. No part of this book may be reprinted or reproduced or utilised in any form or by any electronic, mechanical, or other means, now known or hereafter invented, including photocopying and recording, or in any information storage or retrieval system, without permission in writing from the publishers.

Trademark notice: Product or corporate names may be trademarks or registered trademarks, and are used only for identification and explanation without intent to infringe.

British Library Cataloguing in Publication Data
A catalogue record for this book is available from the British Library

Library of Congress Cataloging in Publication Data
Names: Holmes, Christopher, 1983- author.
Title: Polanyi in times of populism : vision and contradiction in the history of economic ideas / Christopher Holmes.
Description: New York : Routledge, [2018] | Series: Ripe series in global political economy | Includes bibliographical references and index.
Identifiers: LCCN 2017050158| ISBN 9781138226708 (hardback) | ISBN 9781315396989 (e-book)
Subjects: LCSH: Polanyi, Karl, 1886-1964. | Economists–Hungary–Biography. | Economic policy–20th century. | Economic policy–21st century.
Classification: LCC HB102.P64 H65 2018 | DDC 330.15–dc23
LC record available at https://lccn.loc.gov/2017050158

ISBN: 9781138226708 (hbk)
ISBN: 9781315396989 (ebk)

Typeset in Times New Roman
by Taylor & Francis Books

for Edith

Contents

Acknowledgements   viii

PART I
Polanyian perspectives   1

1   Polanyi in times of Brexit and Trump   3
2   Towards a post-Polanyian approach   18

PART II
Contradiction and transcendence   41

3   Property, order and commerce   43
4   Justice, price and power   57
5   Transcendence and the disembedding of economic ideas   69

PART III
Marketised social protection   81

6   Money and finance   83
7   Nature and climate change   99
8   People and welfare provision   116

PART IV
Contradiction without transcendence   135

9   Habitation versus improvement today   137

Bibliography   150
Index   169

Acknowledgements

This book is the result of a decade of wrangling with Karl Polanyi's ideas. Over this period, I have had the pleasure of working with a fascinating range of scholars, first at the Department of Politics and International Relations at the University of Southampton, then at the Department of Politics and International Studies at the University of Warwick and most recently at the European and International Studies Department at King's College, London. I would therefore like to collectively thank my colleagues at these departments for providing consistently interesting, challenging and varied intellectual environments to think, talk and write in.

Beyond that, various individuals deserve special thanks. At the top of the list is Matthew Watson, who initially nurtured my interest in Polanyi's work and the history of economic ideas more generally. His intellectual and moral support has been essential to me over the years and, without it, I would not have started on the path to writing this book in the first place. James Brassett also deserves special mention. I have always been able to talk about ideas completely freely with James, and that is a freedom I have relied on many times in thinking through the arguments developed here. I also thank the following people for their thoughts, comments, critique and encouragement at various points along the way: David Bailey, Fred Block, Ben Clift, Gareth Dale, Nancy Fraser, Colin Hay, David Owen, Lena Rethel, Ben Rosamond, Magnus Ryner, Len Seabrooke, Kate Weaver and David Yarrow. I also specially thank Chris Clarke for taking the time to read through an early draft and for making a variety of valuable suggestions for tightening things up. Needless to say, responsibility for contents remains solely mine.

In terms of institutional support, I am grateful to the Leverhulme Trust. Their provision of a twelve-month Research Fellowship (RF-2014–656) during the 2014–2015 academic year was critical to allowing me the time and mental space to develop my thoughts properly. Without it, completing this book would simply not have been possible. I also wish to thank the editors at Routledge, both past and present, who have been a pleasure to work with. In particular, I thank RIPE series editors Jacqueline Best and Eleni Tsingou and commissioning editor Rob Sorsby for their input. Thanks also to Claire Maloney for her assistance in preparing the book for publication. I also thank the two anonymous reviewers tasked with reviewing a partial draft. Their suggestions were important in helping to finesse the direction of the argument as the book approached completion.

Some of the arguments presented here can be traced back to journal articles that I have written. Early and partial forms of the overall argument can be found in 'Ignorance, denial, internalisation and transcendence: A post-structural perspective on Polanyi's double movement' published in 2012 in *Review of International Studies* 39:2 pp.271–290 and 'A post-Polanyian political economy for our times' published in 2014 in *Economy and Society* 43:4 pp.525–540 and Chapter Six is derived, in part, from 'Seeking alpha or creating beta?' published in 2009 in *New Political Economy* 14:4, available online at www.tandfonline.com/doi/abs/10.1080/13563460903287231. I thank the editorial teams at these journals as well as the anonymous reviewers of each article, who all helped me to hone various ideas developed in this book.

My greatest debts of gratitude are owed, of course, to my family. I especially thank my parents, Richard and Patricia, who, beyond providing a rock of love and support, have proofread various iterations of the manuscript, often at unreasonably short notice. Above all, I thank my wife Emma, who has weathered the ups and downs of the writing process with me from the beginning. Without Emma, nothing is possible. Finally, I thank our baby daughter, Edith, to whom this book is dedicated. Her recent arrival opened up a wonderful new chapter in our lives and, in the process, provided me with the perfect reason to put the pen down and finally send this manuscript off.

Part I
Polanyian perspectives

1 Polanyi in times of Brexit and Trump

Karl Polanyi's book *The Great Transformation* (2001) has become a canonical text in international political economy (IPE). Various concepts, ideas and theories have been drawn from it and brought to bear on all manner of contemporary issues: from the 'big' questions – the nature of neoliberalism, the trajectory of globalisation and the changing role of the state – to a host of more specific areas, including financial market practices, central banking, civil resistance movements, the European Union, climate change politics, international organisations and economic development amongst many others. *The Great Transformation* (hereafter *TGT*) has also provided a conceptual language for a variety of key theoretical arguments about the nature of markets, society, economy and politics: Does it make sense to think of economy as distinct from polity? Are the ends of society in tension with those of the market? How important are economic ideas *vis-à-vis* political practice? Polanyi was notoriously ambiguous on these issues, but that ambiguity has been productive, spurring many fascinating and thought-provoking analyses, amongst those who raise his ideas only to reject them, as much as amongst committed Polanyians. I will present my position on these issues in full later, but if we for a moment block out all the noise of seventy years of commentary and debate on *TGT* and park the theoretical ambiguity in the text to one side, it becomes clear that Polanyi's thesis is relevant more so today than ever before.

At surface level, *TGT* provides a novel analysis of the collapse of international society in the 1930s, tracing that collapse in part back to the failures of an economic theoretic view of people, nature and productive organisation in general in market terms only, that is to say as the commodities labour, land and money respectively. This 'economistic fallacy' (Polanyi 1977: 6), Polanyi argued, had been centuries in development, but reached its apotheosis in the conflicted ideology surrounding the Gold Standard monetary system. In the liberal economic theory of the time, the Gold Standard was presented as the real-world, global expression of the idea of market equilibrium: the balance of payments should have functioned automatically in response to global trade without any 'political' interference by participating states. By facilitating global economic integration, the system should have helped propel humanity towards ever higher productivity and wealth *ad infinitum*. But Polanyi argued

4 *Polanyian perspectives*

that this view was conceptually blind to the role states had in creating, sustaining, manipulating and resisting the automatism of the Gold Standard in the defence of national interests. This was problematic in itself, but more importantly it occluded the fact that, as well as being the foundation of international economic productivity, the Gold Standard had also grown to become the foundation of international political order too. It had become a fabric through which states related to one another on the global stage.

Thus, when the wheels of productivity ceased to turn as depression gripped participating nations in the 1930s, different national economies did not simply rebalance against each other automatically via currency movements as trade dried up. Rather, states tended to draw inwards and pursue policies which increasingly undermined the ability of the Gold Standard to function at all, leading to the eventual collapse of the system. According to Polanyi, this inward turn then led quickly to a concomitant collapse in international political co-operative sentiments, making room for non-liberal ideologies – amongst them fascism – to take a hold of popular consciousness in various countries. By virtue of its marketised view of international relations and of humanity in general, economic liberalism was unable to see this breakdown of international society coming, and unable to provide the intellectual resources to do anything about it when it arrived. The only way that the collapse could be conceptualised from a liberal perspective, for Polanyi, was in terms of a combination of the undue machinations of power hungry politicians, undying imperialist passions and sheer economic irrationality (2001: 220–221).

To spell out the obvious parallels, the finance-led growth model that became increasingly critical to the continued reproduction of Western international economic order in the late twentieth and early twenty-first centuries represented a form of economic integration similar to that of the Gold Standard (see Silver and Arrighi 2003 for a Polanyian comparison). Although the gold peg no longer featured, international financial and monetary flows increasingly connected diverse nations deeply, shaping the economic and political fortunes of people, firms and nations across borders in myriad ways. And with the coming of the global financial crisis in 2008, that model failed spectacularly: in the same way that the Gold Standard helped to transmit the effects of the 1929 stock market crash across the world, the money, stocks, bonds and derivatives markets of the twenty-first century enabled the collapse of a segment of the US mortgage market to trigger a global liquidity crisis, global recession, several sovereign debt crises and the near collapse of the world's most important currency bar the dollar: the euro. Since then, analogies between the Western political economy of the post-2008 period and that of the 1930s – often specifically the connection between economic crisis and political fallout – have become common (Elliott 2017; Judis 2016). The global financial crisis itself was regularly described as 'the worst since the great depression' by economists, commentators, journalists and politicians. Angela Merkel described the crisis of the euro as an 'existential test' with 'incalculable' consequences for Europe and the world. The director of the International

Monetary Fund, Christine Lagarde, warned of a 'nineteen thirties moment' in which countries would turn against one another.

Financial crises occurring since 2008 were not the same as 1929, though. In most countries, Keynesian automatic stabilisers kicked in and governments swiftly enacted massive programmes of intervention in order to support their financial systems. These measures were often deeply problematic to the extent that they worked to defend the interests of some of the wealthiest and most powerful people in society (financiers and those with financial interests), but they did prevent the horrors of the great depression from repeating themselves in full. Nevertheless, a widely felt sense of economic insecurity, coupled with stagnant wage growth, growing inequality and many years of punishing austerity policies, sometimes with little democratic legitimacy to back them up, once again made room for political ideologies which rejected central precepts of international political and economic order in various ways. What came to be known as 'populism' swept across Europe in the shape of a variety of insurgent movements and political parties, including the French Front National, Alternativ für Deutschland, the Austrian Freedom Party, the UK Independence Party, the Five Star Movement in Italy, the True Finns party, Jobbik in Hungary, Podemos in Spain, the Swedish Democrats and both the Golden Dawn party and Syriza in Greece.

The picture is not black and white, of course. Syriza's radical opposition to the economic dictates of the EU powers, which was for a time the most powerful expression of this new populism, have receded recently. And there has been some resurgence of the kinds of liberal-centrist 'third way' political ideologies that were so dominant before 2008. In 2017, Mark Rutte's defeat of Geert Wilders in the Dutch elections and Emmanuel Macron's defeat of Marine Le Pen have prompted speculation that we may have reached the high watermark of the tide of populism in Europe. On top of this, although the future of her chancellorship is now uncertain, Angela Merkel's constant presence has provided a steadying backdrop to European politics in general.

But the two biggest international relations events of 2016 – the British referendum vote to leave the European Union and the election of Donald Trump to the US presidency – were indicative of a shift in the ideological terrain of Western political economy that would have been difficult to imagine even just a few years earlier: each represented in part the rejection of a broad consensus on the virtues of international economic integration and of the political cooperation required to sustain it. In the case of the 'Brexit' vote, whilst calls for deeper trading ties with non-EU nations were in the background of the campaign, the headline messages revolved around the repatriation of sovereignty over economic and political decision-making and the ability to more freely turn away economic migrants from abroad. Likewise, Trump's 'America First' campaign was thick with protectionist rhetoric, openly hostile to trading partners, and also marked by promises to 'tear up' international economic agreements, to leave the World Trade Organisation (not to mention NATO) and to fortify borders against migrants. Both events abundantly demonstrated that economic nationalism, demands for protectionism and the rejection of mainstream economic thought had acquired newfound political legitimacy and electoral capital.

In reading Part III of *TGT*, where some sharp and often neglected commentary on the politics of the nineteen thirties takes place, Polanyi's analysis seems remarkably apposite at points. In his characterisation of the breakdown of market society and the rise of fascism during this period, he remarks that 'important signs were the spread of irrationalistic philosophies, racialist aesthetics, anticapitalistic demagogy, heterodox currency views, criticism of the party system, widespread disparagement of the "regime"' (2001: 246). In the Brexit and Trump campaigns, anti-migrant sentiments often sat uncomfortably close to – or plainly overlapped with – bigotry, received economic wisdom on the benefits of economic integration was rejected, and both campaigns emerged from outside of the existing structures of two party politics, pitching themselves as 'anti-establishment', 'anti-elite', 'anti-political'. Prominent Brexit campaigner Michael Gove captured the mood in his famous remark in an interview with Faisal Islam on Sky News in 2016: 'people ... have had enough of experts' (see Mance 2016).

Polanyi's reflections on the kinds of arguments made by those from within 'the regime' seeking to admonish the rise of protectionism and later fascism are also prescient. He notes, for example, a German scholar surveying the rise of anti-internationalism in 1933:

> Can a policy, he asked, be right which is being unanimously condemned by all experts as utterly mistaken, grossly fallacious and contrary to all principles of economic theory? His answer was an unconditional 'No'. But in vain would one seek in liberal literature for anything in the nature of an explanation for the patent facts. An unending stream of abuse of the governments, politicians, and statesmen whose ignorance, ambition, greed, and shortsighted prejudice were supposedly responsible for the consistently followed policies of protectionism ... was the only answer.
> (2001: 220)

This passage captures much of the thrust of the arguments that were, and continue to be, pitched against Trump and Brexit. Both sitting prime minister, David Cameron and then economic secretary to the treasury, Harriet Baldwin, had described a vote for Brexit as 'economic self-harm' (see Press Association 2016). Donald Trump's protectionist and insular rhetoric on economic matters – immigration, the abandonment of free trade deals, the prospect of openly hostile trading relations with China – were almost universally derided by economists, the financial press and by international economic organisations. In both the British and American cases, the benefits of inward migration in terms of aggregate economic growth and governmental tax income were repeatedly cited. Standard international economic theory suggests that free movement of labour on the basis of the search for higher wages can only increase the allocative efficiency of the global labour market, and both Britain and America could be shown to have benefitted substantially from that dynamic.

The same applied to trade. In the 2017 International Monetary Fund (IMF) *World Economic Outlook April 2017*, Maurice Obstfeld (chief economist) argued that, in a number of 'advanced economies', politicians were 'capitulating' to political pressures to raise protectionist barriers in a way that would lower productivity, ultimately reducing domestic economic benefits and undermining multilateral cooperation (2017: xiii-xiv). In the face of overwhelming evidence of the apparent economic irrationality of these ideas, the sense was that democracy must have got it wrong, or, in the words of one economist writing in the *Financial Times* '[capitalism] can no longer afford the financial demands that full-blown democracy is placing upon it' (Power 2017). These arguments all vividly recall Polanyi's observation of the 1930s that, as popular governments increasingly hostile to the existing international economic order were elected to power, 'there was not a militant liberal who did not express his conviction that popular democracy was a danger to capitalism' (2001: 234).

It is impossible to know how Brexit will turn out, how long Trump will last, or how nationalist and insular political movements will fare in the future. For decades now, the usual strategy for teaching the recent history of economic ideas in IPE has been to divide the post-World War II period into one of more or less Keynesian 'embedded liberalism' (Ruggie 1982) stretching from the 1940s to the 1970s, then an ongoing period of Washington consensus neoliberalism underpinned by norms of ever-increasing international economic integration through the globalisation of markets. Could the populist tide be washing us towards a new, as yet unnamed, period in the history of political economic ideas, to be summarised for students in fifty minutes in the lecture theatres of the future? We can at least say that a major disruption in the discursive field of Western capitalism has been underway, forged in the experience of financial crisis in 2008 and coming of age in the divisive politics of 2016. And, on the strength of the most cursory reading of *TGT*, we can say that that disruption has evinced an obviously Polanyian character.

To draw simple analogies, however, is not enough. The resonances with Polanyi's analysis are indeed striking, but there are all sorts of ways in which our current situation differs from the period he was concerned with. The very fact that people have reflected on the analogy between then and now introduces a hermeneutic quality to the relationship between the two periods, and beyond this, so much of the structure of the global economy and its ideological terrain differs. States function in different ways today, as do markets; neoliberalism is not the same ideology as classical liberalism and economic theory has developed and changed since Polanyi's time. This means that we have to think carefully about why the Polanyian resonances exist: what is it about *TGT* that produces an analysis that seems so freshly relevant today? What does it mean to think through current times of populism from a Polanyian perspective? This book is an attempt to answer these questions, and so it is worth spending a bit of time defining what it might mean to do Polanyian political economy.

Thinking like Polanyi

The casual reader of secondary literature on Polanyi in IPE can justifiably feel rather bewildered by the variety of interpretations of his work on offer and the variety of schools of thought his theses have been read through. For some, Polanyi is 'quintessentially constructivist' (Abdelal 2009: 69), whilst for others, he is first and foremost an institutionalist (Blyth 2002) providing inspiration for the study of capitalism in different national and cultural contexts (van der Pijl 2009: 133). There has also been a long-running debate over the extent to which Polanyi's analytical categories should be interpreted from a Marxian perspective in which the analysis is geared towards the complete rejection of commodity logic and the overthrow of market society (Clark 2014; Lacher 1999) or from a social democratic, quasi-Keynesian one where the aim is to moderate the harshest edges of market society via political interventions of one sort or another (*e.g.* Caporaso and Tarrow 2009). There are grains of truth in all these interpretations which can be traced to the variety exhibited in his own work: Polanyi's influences were various, including Austrian economists, British Marxists, American institutionalists, his own conservative brother, Michael, and socialists of one sort or another including not least his radical revolutionary wife, Ilona Duczyńska. These different threads can all be picked up at different points in Polanyi's writing, often blended together, and sometimes in ways that scholars in each tradition individually might have deemed problematic. The result, as Dale has demonstrated in his extensive studies of Polanyi's life and work, is that, although much of his output can be explained in terms of one or other of his theoretical influences and practical life experiences, the net result is a number of theses which combine all those influences and experiences in a way unique to him (Dale 2016a; 2016b).

In amongst all this heterogeneity, there is something rather special about *TGT*, which is rightly regarded as Polanyi's *magnum opus*. The book offers a rich intellectual toolbox of concepts and ideas which have been mined and deployed to great effect by generations of scholars of international political economy: the idea of a 'double movement' of capitalism, the 'embeddedness' or 'disembeddedness' of economic interactions in a deeper social level of human experience, the critique of *laissez-faire* ideology and the idea of market society. The book also offers a variety of penetrating insights into the international politics and economics of the inter-war period and before – on colonialism, the monetary system, the role of global finance and the effect of economic change on international relations and domestic policy-making – as well as providing a novel history of economic ideas stretching back to the seventeenth century and a variety of anthropological insights to boot. The range and ambition of the relatively slim volume is astounding.

There are costs to this polymathic, sweeping style, though. Data – if it can even be called as such in a book like *TGT* – is scanty at points, methodology – ditto – is mixed and unclear, concepts are not as precise as one would like, due respect for alternative literatures is sometimes absent. All this has provoked substantial debate amongst those interested in his work, and most major parts of his conceptual and empirical scheme have been shown to be problematic in one way or another over the years. As one scholar remarked to Margaret Lewis early on in the revival of interest in his political economy: 'why do Polanyi's emotions seem clear, but his reasoning cloudy?' (Lewis 1991: 475). In encompassing such a wide variety of historical periods, schools of thought, analytical approaches and in traversing so many academic disciplinary lines, the book has often been found wanting in the details.

To focus on the parts of *TGT* only – to treat it as an intellectual toolbox – is, however, to miss the benefits of the whole: the value of the book comes precisely from its breadth and scope. In a time when the social sciences are increasingly measured by the yardsticks of their natural science cousins, Polanyi's social science strikes one with some of the feel of a novel, full of twists, turns, metaphor and leaps of imagination. The remarkable style of writing propels the analysis along, engages the reader and manages to make its wide diversity hang together in a way few writers could pull off. The historical range of it is also long, shifting from the 1930s to the early seventeenth century and back again, interspersed with various detours into ancient economic systems and societies. The book suggests that understanding the collapse of international relations before World War II requires understanding the economics of Ricardo. Understanding the evolution of the free market idea means reflecting on the decline of organised religion. Being socially responsible in an economically complex world means thinking hard about what freedom means philosophically. Probing any of these questions, much less all of them together, necessitates taking the long and wide-ranging view that Polanyi adopts. As I read it, the political economy of the book emerges from no less than an engagement with the physical, psychological and spiritual condition of humanity in Western modernity.

Wresting the full value of Polanyi's political economy for understanding the current era of economic and political turmoil will not be achieved by isolating specific concepts or by hastily drawing analogies between the market society of classical liberalism and the market society of neoliberalism today. Neither will it be achieved by asserting or denying the validity of this or that Polanyian concept in the abstract. Much of the literature on Polanyi seeks to position 'for' or 'against' him on the contents of *TGT*, but it's not as if he would have written the book out again verbatim were he alive today, examining contemporary issues. Rather, I think one has to try and think like Polanyi, meaning that one must be willing to do the kind of political economy that he did: to take a wide-angle, long-range view of the present. But one must also be willing to develop, upend or transfigure his analysis as necessary. The world has changed, and political economy has developed as an academic pursuit. Moreover, despite the manifest relevance of Polanyi's thesis in *TGT*, we can hardly ignore the barrage of critique – sometimes penetrating, sometimes not – that it has attracted over the years. Dogmatic applications of canonical texts are not likely to be interesting at all, and so instead of trying to find ways to dismiss Polanyi's critics, my approach in this book is to try and learn from them: to see what ephemera they have whittled away, and what remains of value underneath. With these two aims in mind, then, let us peel back another layer of analysis in *TGT* to get a fuller picture of how Polanyi's theoretical outlook drives his analysis of the 1930s, and what the potential problems with that analysis are.

Polanyi's critique of economism

Polanyi had a very particular definition of what the economy is, rooted in a rejection of the precepts of neoclassical thought that were coming to define the scope of economics as a distinct academic pursuit during his lifetime. For Polanyi, the neoclassical definition of the economy as, to use Lionel Robbins's famous words, 'the science which studies human behaviour as a relationship between ends and scarce means which have alternative uses' (1932: 15), was too restrictive in that it limited any understanding of what the economy is to the extent of the existence of markets. Polanyi thought it better to think of the economy as the 'livelihood of man' (1977: title) by which he meant the way in which people provide for their material needs and wants, and this in the context of each person's relationships with other persons in the context of institutions (since hardly anyone makes a living on their own). Some of these institutions might well be markets, but they might also be nations, tribes, classes, communities, professions, kith and kin. The economy was, for Polanyi, a part of the fabric of society more generally, seamlessly joined to culture, politics, law and environment. This meant that any attempt to measure the economy in terms of a simple, abstract idea such as Robbins's was inherently suspect, since to do so was to do an injustice to the way in which it is 'embedded' (2001: 60) in the infinite variety of persons, their experiences and their relationships with others.

The liberal economic understanding of the Gold Standard developed in the nineteenth century was one of these abstract ideas, but Polanyi argued that the principle of automatism embodied in that idea was only a particularly advanced version of a deeper economistic fallacy hatched a century earlier. This was the utilitarian notion that all people are, at base, identical in that they respond only to the two master-motives of the pursuit of gain and the avoidance of pain. From this view of all people as materially self-interested, Polanyi argues, the idea that the entire economy could and should be run as a market emerged, since only the market could effectively deliver the right incentives to that type of person. This was not just excessive parsimony, but a powerful promise of economic order based on an abstract 'vision of perfectibility' (Polanyi 2001: 88): if the principle of market self-regulation could be applied completely to the economy, then a true economic order could be reached, with social and political order following behind. In later formal economic theory, this promise would be embodied in anodyne concepts such as 'equilibrium', 'efficiency' and 'optimality', but for Polanyi, this abstract mode of thought was nothing less than a secular religion (2001: 191) which could give intellectual reason both to explain the brute contingency of history past and to give a sense of inevitability to developments in the present.

The problem was that attempts to model society according to any such vision were doomed to failure. However inevitable processes of marketisation were depicted to be, there were some human needs which were in fact adversely effected by the rapid economic change that characterised life in market societies. Beyond rising standards of material welfare, workers also needed some stability of livelihood, the economy as a whole needed to be stable enough to allow production and development, and the physical environment needed to be managed sufficiently well that it continued to provide human sustenance over the long-term. Markets had indeed proven to be the best possible mechanism for driving economic growth, but growth was not the only economic need people have. In Polanyi's words, people living in market society need the means for 'habitation' as well as the opportunity for 'improvement' (2001: 36).

It is not difficult to find contemporary analogues to the value of improvement and the costs to habitation that Polanyi discusses. The potential for automation delivered by microprocessors, robots and the internet continues to drive growth and raise standards of living on one hand, but also to transform employment, destroy jobs and create new ones in just the same way that the harnessing of steam or the invention of the spinning jenny did. Labour market insecurity has become an increasingly visible issue recently, with growing recognition of how financial incentives, outsourcing, flexibilisation and increasingly poor wage contracts might drive productivity in some ways, but also come together to produce more precarious forms of livelihood (Standing 2011). All the while, financial markets continue to drive growth, but yet financial crises appear unpreventable, and the growing global economy continues to exploit natural resources, including breathable air, habitable land and ploughable soil.

For Polanyi, the need for human habitation was not well addressed by the market. And so, he argues, non-market institutions grew to serve those needs, often in ways that contradicted the principle of market self-regulation: the formal recognition of trade unions, the growth of labour standards legislation, factory regulations, livestock grazing controls, the raising of the minimum working age, the provision of welfare and the evolution of central banking were all, by Polanyi's reading, moments of 'social protection' against the new problems of market society. For the early marginalist and *laissez-faire* economists whom he sought to challenge, this social protectionism as practised by the state could be understood as nothing more than a conspiracy working against the natural order of the market economy, whereas for Polanyi, it was a reflection of the economic need for habitation.

In this way, Polanyi provided one of the first coherent analyses of the paradox between the ascendancy of *laissez-faire* economic ideas, in which states and political authority generally are admonished, and the ongoing practices of increasingly sophisticated and intricate forms of governance and control that characterise capitalist state development (for varied examples of this thesis see Foucault 2008; Levy 2006; Gamble and Wright 2004; Robison 2006). As such, the failure to see the Gold Standard as a political system, as well as an economic system, was only one example of a broader failing in economic liberalism, which laid in the way in which it presented the economy as an independent sphere to the political. Economic liberalism suffered from a cognitive dissonance between the actual practices of political economic governance in market society, in particular the role of the state, and the idealism of the *laissez-faire* view. And when things go wrong in markets, as they did so profoundly in 1929, the conceptual resources and institutional cognisance required to think through and manage events were not available in liberal thought, hence the turn to non-liberal ideologies.

We have already seen that there are some very strong resonances between Polanyi's analysis of the 1930s and our current political situation, but how much of this argument that led him to that analysis is still relevant? The inadequacies of market economism in providing an adequate representation of economic life are now well appreciated across academic disciplines, if perhaps not always so much in the discipline of economics itself. Sociologists, geographers, anthropologists, political scientists, psychologists, philosophers, neuroscientists and evolutionary biologists have all parked their tanks on the economists' lawn and demonstrated in myriad ways that the assumption of individual economising rationality and the market-centrism that that assumption produces is either logically flawed, misleading, myopic, a-moral, immoral or empirically inaccurate. And modern mainstream economics itself can hardly be described as *laissez-faire*. The notion of 'market failure' is these days a standard trope in mainstream economic textbooks, implying a role for state intervention on the management of environmental resources, the regulation of market structure and the provision of certain public goods. All but the most ardent libertarian-capitalists appreciate some role for state and civil society in counteracting the less desirable effects of free market systems upon people, society and environment.

Relatedly, the institutional layout of the economy has got a lot more complex since the time in which Polanyi wrote. Markets and non-market institutions have come to manifest themselves in a far more complicated and diverse range of relationships than the neat state/market, society/economy split that Polanyi framed his thesis within. Today, states sometimes pursue policies through market mechanisms; market actors sometimes have such power as to exhibit state-like qualities. The line between private and public power is often very difficult to draw at all, as is the line between business practice and regulatory oversight (Graeber 2015). In sum, state and market are so deeply imbricated in the modern economy that it doesn't make sense to see them as monolithic, opposed forces, if indeed it ever did (Underhill 2000).

This is an issue particularly when thinking about the dividing lines that have characterised the political economy of Brexit and Trump. Whilst the parallels between the discourses in evidence in Polanyi's case and our own are clearly there, the ideological cleavages cannot be said to fall along Polanyi's marketisation/social protectionism lines. Whilst some elements of the Brexit campaign were protectionist, for example promises to curb the free movement of labour, it was also founded on the idea that European regulation was stifling British business and that it should be removed in order to 'unleash' productivity in the private sector. And whilst Trump was elected on some protectionist promises, such as the threat to apply tariffs to Chinese imports in order to shield American business from competition, he too was elected on the back of other promises to reduce taxation and social spending and to remove regulations, particularly financial ones, from business. Both campaigns were a blend of rhetorics of market, nation, society and economy all at once – a blend which isn't captured well in the market/society opposition.

So, if Polanyi's critique of economic ideas hinges on a rejection of *laissez-faire* thought, and if that *laissez-faire* has increasingly been rejected in contemporary scholarship, and is difficult to identify in the modern economic practice or discourse anyway, what is left of Polanyi's thesis? As I will explore in Chapter Two, these are key issues for any Polanyian political economy for good reason. But I will come to the conclusion that when considering Polanyi's work as a whole, one comes to recognise that his critique of the economistic outlook and his description of a pathological relation between market and society is an expression of a broader set of ideas about ideal reasoning in general and its role in the way that we think about the world. It is in this broader set of ideas, I will argue, that the greatest relevance of Polanyi's work today lies.

Visions of perfectibility

For Polanyi, the visions of perfectibility that early political economy offered made promises of order rooted in the infinite application of the market idea, which paid little deference to the lived experience of particular people and the institutions within which they might sit. But more general critiques of rationalism, essentialism, universalism and hopes of order and perfectibility crop up throughout his work in different guises. For example, Polanyi was of the opinion that central economic planning was impossible and undesirable on precisely the same basis: it relied on the notion of a unity of values and motivations amongst those being planned for that did not exist and should not be engineered. Consequently, his main input into the debate about how a just, socialist society might be achieved was to emphasise that such a society would have to operate through bargaining between diverse institutions and through a plurality of motivations and units of account, aims which neither profit-oriented free-marketism or central planning alone could achieve (Rosner 1990).

This way of thinking is also evident in his admonishment of totalitarian ideology. For example, in an essay entitled 'The Essence of Fascism', published in 1935, Polanyi challenged fascist appropriations of Nietzschean and Hegelian thought on the basis that they lost sight of the autonomous morality of the individual that was so important to the original thought of Nietzsche and Hegel, in the process generating unwarranted caricatures of their intellectual schemes (Polanyi 1935). By this reading, fascism, communism and *laissez-faire* ideology were all problematic in that they generated universal ordering principles from abstract systems of thought. None were sensitive to the creative role of human agency in changing, transforming and resisting their conditions of existence autonomously, and none had any way to account for cultural or social particularities. Each vision extended to infinity both temporally, through the fulfilment of some essence of human nature, and spatially, through the globalist narratives that they shared (Holmes 2014b).

This glimpse into the philosophy of Polanyi's approach is enough to establish the analytical thrust of my take on Polanyi's critique of economism presented in this book. Whilst it is most often read in IPE – whether to reject it or to accept it – as a critique of *laissez-faire* ideology (see Inayatullah and Blaney 1999 for one particularly valuable exception), to my eyes it has a much more postmodern character. By the account I present, the highest levels of analysis are not market and exchange, but rather all ways of thought which tend to universalise, to make truth claims about the nature of economy and society and which suggest the potential for human life to be ordered according to those claims. In light of this, Polanyi's sweeping style in *TGT* starts to make more sense: his analysis of economism stretches across Western modernity in a historical sense because his thesis is a reflection of a critique of Western modernity in an intellectual sense.

In Chapter Two, I will draw out as much as possible from Polanyi's own work to substantiate my reasons for taking this approach, drawing parallels with other critiques of modernity in mid-twentieth century thought. With this in hand, I will suggest that we can think of Polanyi's approach to economic ideas as a history of economic problematisations (Foucault 1984). As Michel Foucault argued, the way in which problems are posed 'develop[s] the conditions in which possible responses can be given' (Foucault 1984) and therefore a history of problematisation concerns itself with trying 'to see how the different solutions to a problem have been constructed [and] how these different solutions result from a specific form of problematisation' (Foucault 1984). Within that broad gambit, Polanyi appears to have been most interested in how, as 'the economy' became identified as a distinct sphere of human existence, the new economic problems of market society came to be presented in terms of a series of logical contradictions: between the needs of industry and the stewardship of the environment, between the provision of welfare and the productivity of the workforce, between the principle of sound money and the demands of national economic management, and so on. Rather than accepting the existence of plurality in what ends the economy is required to serve, the idea of 'the market', for Polanyi, amounted to an attempt to transcend those contradictions with recourse to modernist tropes of universalism and biological essentialism. The result was a series of overly hopeful visions of the potential for social and economic order to be realised through the self-regulating logic of price. By this account, Polanyi's critique of economic ideas is an account of a certain type of modernist idealism as applied to the economic dimensions of human life.

Having identified the underlying character of the critique in *TGT*, I become free to think more creatively about how the problematisation of economy in terms of contradiction has been manifest in economic thought past and present. In Part Two of the book, therefore, I extend Polanyi's fledgling history of economic ideas backwards and outwards to identify in greater detail the origin and subsequent development of that way of thinking. What we will see is that the suggestive hints that Polanyi drops about the quasi-religious nature of some aspects of economic thought are telling: a fairly straightforward story can be told about how the contradiction that late-medieval scholars saw as existing between the divine order and a fallen humanity transformed into the central conceptual contradictions that underpinned later secular economic thought. The specific logical problem scholars sought to address changed over time, but the underlying mode of problematisation in terms of contradiction and the potential for transcendence has remained a consistent theme in many of the most significant interventions in modern Western political economic thought.

I break down this history of ideas into three chapters, each examining different moments of economic problematisation. The first is exhibited in the natural law tradition and the way in which scholars in it handled the contradiction between the existence of private property and the scriptural notion of property held in common before God. The second concerns the Enlightenment problematisation of economy in terms of the opposition of freedom and power and how that shaped the political economy of the nineteenth century. In the third, I look at how neoliberal thinkers in the early- to mid-twentieth century resurrected the Enlightenment problematisation of economy in terms of freedom and power, but set within a more theoretically developed theory of price. In all three chapters, I show how scholars tussled with these fundamental contradictions, finding various ways to navigate paths through them as moral problems. However, concluding the section in Chapter Five, I suggest that, in the long run, it was often ways of thought which promised to transcend the terms of each contradiction altogether which proved to be the most enduring and influential, coming in the shape of simplistic appropriations of Locke's account of private property, the distillation of the moral economy of Smith and his contemporaries into various 'principles of political economy' in the nineteenth century and the degeneration of early neoliberal thought into a pure faith in the self-regulating properties of price. In all cases, I show how the moral ambiguity of the initial form of problematisation receded, replaced by transcendent visions of economic perfectibility, before summarising how this analysis informs the subsequent chapters.

In Part Three I move on to apply this approach to a range of more recent policy issues, focusing on financial market regulation, climate change policy and attempted innovations in welfare delivery by the British government, each intended as examples of the trajectory of economic thought on the three factors of the economy that Polanyi described as 'fictitious commodities' (2001: 76): money, the natural environment and people. In each case I argue that, over the course of the twentieth century, the notion of a Polanyian contradiction between the desire for improvement (economic growth and profitability) and the need for habitation (stability and security of livelihood and the economy as a whole, broadly speaking) came to be the fundamental problem that economic theorists sought to 'solve'. Whether expressed in terms of the relationship between productivity and environmental stewardship, between credit creation and financial stability or between the provision of welfare and the pressures of globalisation, economic theory increasingly searched for ways to suggest that these fundamental tensions could be transcended once and for all. I call this ideology 'marketised social protection'. This was not *laissez-faire* liberalism re-hashed in the shape of neoliberalism, but rather a complex overlapping of market-regarding and society-regarding priorities which were made to fit together in a new vision of perfectibility necessary to garner political legitimacy as a set of internally coherent policy ideas. In the decades leading up to 2008, policy on these key issues thus increasingly came to be sold in utopian, 'win-win', terms, abnegating the difficult choices and trade-offs between the fundamentally different ends of improvement and habitation.

Finally, in Part Four, I consider the period since 2008 as one in which the marketised social protection vision failed. Financial crisis may have provided the trigger for the failure, but I will argue that it was a failure of a paradigm of thought about the nature of the economy as a whole, which in turn led to a new sense of opposition between the ends of improvement and of habitation in public economic debate. The nakedness with which financial crisis response measures prioritised the ends of improvement were the first expression of this: whatever one thinks of it morally, the austerity that has so defined European political economy since the crisis has certainly not been underpinned by a win-win philosophy. But only in 2016, nearly a decade out from the crisis, have we really begun to see the true scale of the ideological breakdown that has taken place. I argue that the debates surrounding the political economy of the Trump campaign and the Brexit referendum reflected the new politics of habitation *versus* improvement in full. Whilst ambivalent about the role of market and state in building the new societies that each envisioned, both Brexit and Trump campaigns consistently played upon an imaginary of economic habitation which proved to be electorally successful. Each event established a new language of the economy which was unassailable by the barrage of counter-arguments rooted in the imaginary of improvement.

By the end of the book, I hope to have demonstrated that Polanyi's analysis in *TGT* is indeed more important today than ever before, but that its importance comes from the way in which it forces the reader to think philosophically and morally about the nature of the economy and what ends it ought to serve. To the extent that the breakdown of the marketised social protection ideal has provoked reflection of this sort in the time since 2008, I argue that it might be a good thing. By my reading, Polanyi's thesis shows how the production of economic knowledge has been marked by attempts to solve the unsolvable and how those attempts reflect a desire for coherence, order and conceptual unity that is deeply embedded in the fabric of Western modernity. Yet, as we will see, there are often moments when that desire is resisted, in which conflict, moral ambiguity and uncertainty – in short, politics – are recognised as fundamental to the way in which we think about the economy. I therefore conclude in the hope that the divisive political economy of Brexit and Trump are only 'first parries' in a longer period of debate over the fundamental questions of what the economy is and what its purpose is *vis-à-vis* human life.

2 Towards a post-Polanyian approach

In IPE, scholarship taking Polanyi's theoretical scheme as a starting point to understand contemporary issues has often been characterised as 'neo-Polanyian' (Block 2007). In this chapter I want to make the case for a particular reading of Polanyi's understanding of market society which might be termed 'post-Polanyian', differentiating it from the neo-Polanyian approach on a number of counts. Where neo-Polanyian political economy is typically critical or constructivist in theoretical orientation, the thesis presented in this book brings Polanyi's ideas into conversation with postmodern and poststructural thought. The critical opposition in neo-Polanyian scholarship is that between the economic and the social, which tends, problematically, to take for granted the existence of each as separate and autonomous realms of human experience (Konings 2015, see also de Goede 2003). As we shall see, variants of this problem have captivated the critical literature on Polanyi, but I argue that it is only really relevant if we think about Polanyi's critique of economic ideas as a critique of commodification, on a par with Karl Marx's account of economic alienation.

After taking some time to explore the neo-Polanyian literature in IPE and examining its characterisation of the market/society distinction, I move on to explore some alternative points of entry to understanding Polanyi's thesis. Firstly, I explain and develop the tension between habitation and improvement in Polanyi's work. I suggest that it is a much better starting point for understanding the analytical thrust of *TGT* than the market/society couplet, highlighting themes of change, transformation, livelihood and individuality and the way in which these themes are set against the principle of reasoning in universalised terms. Then, I move on to Polanyi's parallel critique of economic ideas, developing the Foucauldian theme of problematisation discussed in Chapter 1.

Where neo-Polanyian literature typically treats economism, or market fundamentalism, as a self-contained ideology, I argue that one can think of Polanyi's understanding of economism as a critique of broader trends in the development of systems of thought in Western modernity as a whole. As such, modernity, understood as an intellectual paradigm supposing certain modes of problematisation and reasoning – broadly what Foucault called an 'episteme' (2002: xxiii) – becomes important as an empirical focus. To that end, I bring together fragments of Polanyi's analysis from various sources and put them in the context of other contemporaneous critiques of ideas which sought to problematise the promises of universalised reasoning, including for example the English liberal philosophy of Isaiah Berlin and the French absurdism of Albert Camus. From there, I proceed to flesh out a full interpretation of Polanyi's critique of economic reason specifically as a critique of modernism, which establishes the methodological basis of the history of ideas presented in the rest of the book.

'Double movement' then and now

In IPE, the opposition of market economy and (non-market) society is often the basic starting point for engagement with Polanyi's thought, and for good reason: it does seem to permeate many of his most important political economic conceptual terminologies. For example, let us unpick the notion of econo-mistic fallacy a little more. The fallacy, in Polanyi's view, was to think of economy in formal terms as the ontic expression of market logic, rooted in the assumption of economising, self-interested behaviour by individuals, and to think of these assumptions as universal to human economic interaction. Such assumptions were fallacious for Polanyi to the extent that they defined the factors of the economy in a certain way: people, nature and economic structure became understood as labour, material resources and the monetary system, respectively, obscuring the extent to which each of these 'fictitious commodities' served non-commodity functions (Polanyi 1968: 32). The monetary system provided social stability within and between capitalist nations, the natural world served as a habitat within which humans exist and people were not atomised utility maximisers, but morally autonomous, creative individuals, who make economic decisions in the context of their relationships with others. In his celebrated terminology, the economy is 'embedded' in society, and to see it as separate, as the expression of market logic only, was to think of it as disembedded from society (Polanyi 2001: 60).

This was, in essence, a critique of marginalist, early neoclassical economic thought, particularly the version espoused by Carl Menger. But in *TGT*, this critique gets blended with a historical analysis of the increasing prevalence of markets in the economic organisation of human affairs over the nineteenth century. Polanyi argues that the growth of the economistic worldview over this period could be traced back at least as far as Thomas Malthus and David Ricardo, and that it had served to make contingent processes of marketisation – the enclosure of farmland (Polanyi 2001: 37), the replacement of feudal economic organisation by labour markets (Polanyi 2001: 86) and the establishment of the Gold Standard as the pillar of international economic and political integration (Polanyi 2001: 204) – seem like a part of the inevitable march of history. By imputing market-based assumptions as rational and universal (Polanyi 1947; 1968: 26) – often at the level of human nature

(Polanyi 2001: 119) – any policy designed to inhibit the power of the market as the institutional basis for growing portions of human activity seemed either morally suspect, doomed to failure or pointless.

The irony, for Polanyi, was that the economistic assumptions that made these processes of marketisation of the economy look inevitable flew in the face of ever-increasing amounts of social and political control of the economy by society – most often the state – during the same period. Although their spread had facilitated hitherto unknown degrees of productivity and growth, the invention of markets had also generated new types of social harm: fluctuating employment levels and worker insecurity, environmental degradation, problems of monetary coordination and new types of economic and financial crisis, as well as the general disruptive effects of continual economic development upon societies not used to rapid change. In result, from regulation of land use, the development of trade unions and worker legislation through to systems of welfare and on towards trade protectionism and currency controls, a tide of legislation and political control over the economy swelled with, and in proportion to, the growth of the market. Polanyi argues that the economistic view of Menger and others obscured the new role of society in containing and countering harms arising from the marketisation of life. It legitimated the harm caused by rapid capitalist development – 'movement' – but also simultaneously denied the legitimacy of its mostly state-led opposite – 'counter-movement', the latter of which could not be assimilated from within the economistic perspective (Polanyi 2001: 151).

At the domestic level, states secure some degree of success in managing the tension between market and society in Polanyi's narrative. Workers are protected via legislation, systems of public credit are developed to even out business cycles and the environment is protected somewhat from exploitation by industry. It is, if not an ideal form of political economy in Polanyi's eyes, one in which the state is able to reconcile economy and society to a sufficient degree for both to reproduce themselves. But it is when the market/society relationship breaks across national/international lines that the tensions really come to bear. The increasing integration of nations through expanded global trade and, especially, through the strictures of the Gold Standard monetary system, had made each domestic economy dramatically more sensitive to changing economic fortunes elsewhere. And so, when depression gripped in the 1930s, the economic integration that had propelled fortune before now spread crisis and deprivation. With no state-like authority to exert social control over the growing tension between countries, resistance to the international market order fused with nationalist and protectionist sentiment, turning an economic contradiction into a political one, propelling the collapse of international society.

This is Polanyi's story of 'double movement' as told over the pages of *TGT*. The story has not gone unchallenged, with a variety of authors having picked holes in his analysis at empirical and theoretical levels (*e.g.* Hejeebu and McCloskey 1999; Konings 2015; Rothbard 1961; Zelizer 1988). Even those sympathetic to Polanyi's work admit that he sometimes overstates his evidence and makes his claims about the relationship between market and society in either a too generalised or a conceptually confused way (*e.g.* Hart and Hann 2009: 9; Jessop 2001: 215). Nevertheless, during the past two decades, it is a story which has had a profound impact upon the community of political economy scholars, with a great many people seeking to understand the relationship between economy and society and between market and state using Polanyi's observations. Following Fred Block, these research programmes can be labelled 'neo-Polanyian' in that they adopt Polanyi's account of double movement but are more systematic and specific in their empirical focus (Block 2007: 11). All observe in contemporary international political economy the same problematic market fundamentalism (Hart and Hann 2009: 9; Block and Somers 2014) that Polanyi took issue with, and all seek to map the contradictory outcomes resulting from its influence upon political economic life today. But each transposes Polanyi's observation of the tension between market and society into new geographical contexts, new institutional settings, new types of policy and governance.

The neo-Polanyian narrative sits against the background of a familiar periodisation of post-World War II international political economy in state-market terms. Contemporary authors who invoke the double movement tend to see the post-war settlement through John Ruggie's eyes as a period of 'embedded liberalism' (Ruggie 1982: 393), where the Polanyian contradiction between markets and social protection was temporarily resolved through the power of the national welfare state and an implicit international agreement on the need to allow space for countries to balance domestic and international obligations, thus preventing a repeat of the 1930s. The collapse of that system – *i.e.* the 1970s oil crises and the breakdown of the Bretton Woods architecture – is understood as the turning point when extreme *laissez-faire* policies return to the stage, giving Polanyi's analysis a new lease of life (see Randles 2003: 416). By this account, neoliberalism – under banners of globalisation, Chicago School economics, Thatcherism, Reaganomics, the 'Washington consensus', and through policies of privatisation, the lowering of trade barriers and the abandonment of capital controls – is understood as representing the latest attempt to revive the self-regulating market mechanism in a way comparable to the experience of the European societies of the nineteenth century that Polanyi studied (Block and Somers 2014; Polanyi-Levitt 2005, 2006; Raffer 2011; Sandbrook 2011; Silver and Arrighi 2003). In this vein, Mark Blyth describes Polanyi's account of market-state dynamics as the 'motor of institutional change', such that 'the contemporary neo-liberal economic order can be seen as merely the latest iteration of Polanyi's double movement' (Blyth 2002: 4).

If globalisation and neoliberalism are analogous to the marketisation of the economy that Polanyi detailed in earlier periods of history, then authors have also been drawn to search for plausible accounts of anti-market 'countermovement' today. Some have looked towards the role that states continue to play (or fail to play) in containing and countering market forces (*e.g.* Block and Somers 2014; Silver and Arrighi 2003; Scharpf and Schmidt 2000). Others have looked towards international organisations including the EU (*e.g.* Jones 2003; Taylor-Gooby 2003; Caporaso and Tarrow 2009; van Apeldoorn and Horn 2007) and global institutions like the World Bank and the International Monetary Fund (IMF) (Best 2003; Kirby 2002). Others still have looked towards civil society and resistance movements of one type or another (Hettne 2006; Kim 2010; Munck 2006; Palaciaos 2001; Sandbrook 2011; Stiglitz 2001; Streeck 2011: 8). In varying ways, all reflect the idea that, in the face of the growing marketisation of the global economy, society's 'inevitable self-protection against the commodification of life' (Mendell and Salée 1991: xiii) is, will or should be taking place.

The sense is thus that Polanyi's diagnosis of the ills befalling the global economy in the early twentieth century became relevant again thanks to a second rise of market fundamentalism in the shape of neoliberalism. This fits in, as Dale argues, to a 'pendular' (Dale 2010: 220) approach to international political economic history, in which 'great oscillations' (Dale 2010: 230) take place between periods in which economies are explicitly socially embedded, usually through state management of some type, and periods in which markets are ascendant, cowing both state and society. In turn, marketisation produces instability and crisis which provoke state and/or society to resist and to re-embed economic relations within social ones. Within this narrative, nineteenth century *laissez-faire* and late twentieth/early twenty-first century neoliberalism stand out as periods of market ascendancy whilst post-war embedded liberalism and contemporary resistance to neoliberalism represent their respective social antitheses.

Prima facie, the pendular narrative seems reasonable enough, chiming with our loose sense of the ideological ebb and flow of the twentieth century. But there are many ways in which that narrative does not fit. As much as post-war Keynesian welfare capitalism was a state-led 'embedded liberal compromise' (Ruggie 1982) at the international level, it was also a period of intensive commodification of labour, nature and knowledge in Western economies as industrial economies grew (Dale 2010: 228). And the neoliberal period since the 1970s has, if anything, been marked by an upswing in the volume of state interventions into market processes in terms of protecting big financial institutions and corporations, marshalling an increasingly complex labour market and responding to economic crises (ibid.). What we think of as neoliberal marketisation has more often than not involved the instantiation of new forms of public-private partnership (Kay 2004: 74) in which, rather than simply allowing the market to 'do its own thing', new patterns of regulation and institutional control over the economy by government have emerged (see Gamble and Wright 2004; Robison 2006; Levy 2006). It would be difficult to describe these changes as the 'self-protection of society', in Polanyian terms. Rather, they are indicative of an increasing degree of hybridity between state and market in the organisation of capitalism. As such, to equate neoliberalism with marketisation risks occluding as much political economy as it reveals in terms of concrete descriptions of how capitalism functions.

This is a reflection of a deeper conceptual weakness in Polanyi's work which has become a standard trope for those seeking to position against it: he seems to adopt a restrictive account of what constitutes 'the economic' in general and 'a market' in particular. As Martijn Konings has recently argued (2015), this seems only to accentuate the idea of an independent and autonomous realm of human experience as distinctively economic, consisting of utilitarian, possessive individualist, instrumentally rational postulates, which must be reined in by a separate sphere of humanity which is in some way distinctively ethical and social. For Konings, this overlooks the extent to which market and economy are themselves produced and sustained by 'morality, faith, power, and emotion' (2015: 15). In effect Konings's is the latest of many complaints that, whilst Polanyi put so much effort in to developing an institutionalist methodology which sought to reveal the essentially social, cultural and political nature of economic interaction in pre- and non-capitalist societies – the embeddedness of economy in society (2001: 48) – he wilfully chose not to apply that methodology to the market, preferring instead to see it as somehow genuinely 'disembedded', that is to say, absented from social control (Granovetter 1985; Jessop 2001; Lie 1991; Mitchell 2008; Zelizer 1988). As such, Polanyi appeared to adopt exactly the same restrictive definition of economy as that of the marginalists whom he sought to challenge.

On one hand, Polanyi's advocation of 'substantivist' economics is designed to recognise precisely the social and cultural nature of economic interaction. In pre-modern societies at least, a person's economic life is, for Polanyi, a practical reflection of all the particular institutions in which a person exists (Polanyi 1977: 11). As he describes,

> [H]uman beings will labor for a large variety of reasons so long as they form part of a definite social group. Monks traded for religious reasons, and monasteries became the largest trading establishments in Europe. The Kula trade of the Trobriand Islanders, one of the most intricate barter arrangements known to man, is mainly an esthetic pursuit. Feudal economy depended largely on custom or tradition. With the Kwakiutl, the chief aim of industry seems to be to satisfy a point of honor. Under mercantile despotism, industry was often planned so as to serve power and glory. Accordingly, we tend to think of monks, Western Melanesians, villeins, the Kwakiutl, or seventeenth-century statesmen as ruled by religion, esthetics, custom, honor, or power politics, respectively.
>
> (Polanyi 1977: 11)

Yet in *TGT* and elsewhere, Polanyi speaks of the coming of market society in the nineteenth century as having reversed this social embeddedness such that, from then on, 'social relations are embedded in the economic system'

(1947; 2001: 60). And this does seem to directly contradict his methodological claims about the social embeddedness of economic interaction in general.

If we are charitable towards Polanyi, we might argue that the disembedded market is an unobtainable ideal type which never actually becomes real, but provides ideological cover for the extension of markets over society and the dismantling of mechanisms of social control over the market (*e.g.* Block 2007). For Konings, however, this view of the disembedded market as a social construction leaves the same idealisation of the market, and its distinction from some other putatively social realm of existence, intact:

> It is only when we switch into a critical mind-set that we lose our appreciation of the constructive role that economy plays: we now come to view things that are constructed as 'merely constructed,' as possessing only a low level of facticity, and we begin to see the tendency to attribute reality to such things as a cognitive mistake or limitation, akin to fetish-ism or idolatry. Suddenly we become concerned that economy is a process whereby mere conventions and fictions acquire a life of their own and, owing to the way in which people literally lose track of their own role in constructing them, become disembedded.
>
> (Konings 2015: 17)

Konings is surely right on this point. 'The economy' is as social a realm of human existence as any other, and in that it encourages us to think of it as otherwise, the embedded/disembedded couplet is analytically suspect. A view of the economy as an arena of self-interest only, set against a somehow separate arena of 'ethical goodness' diminishes, rather than augments, our understanding of the lived experience of political economy (Brassett and Holmes 2010).

This is a perennial issue which has been discussed extensively in the literature on Polanyi, but suffice to say, the idea of an actually existing, fully disembedded market has been variously explained as a mere lack of analytical clarity on Polanyi's part (Jessop 2001: 215); as an unnecessary 'overdrawn ideal type' (Hann 2009: 9) or as a theoretical reflection of Polanyi's haphazard engagements with Marx's early work – particularly the theory of alienation as developed in the *Paris Manuscripts* – at the time of writing *TGT* (Tomasberger 2003: 5). The latter of these seems particularly pertinent. Drawing on Hegel's rendition of the subject/object divide (*e.g.* Hegel 1930: 251), Marx's philosophical critique of capitalism developed in his early work hinged on the idea that commodity relations were unreal, objectifying humans, and that, whilst a person's human affairs were conducted through them, they were alienated from their true subjective nature, their 'species being' (Marx 1963: 31). In Polanyi's narrative, the embedding of society in economy is, by this reading, analogous: it disconnects people from their social being and enslaves them to the logic of the commodity.

This seems to leave the Polanyian political economist with a choice. On one hand, we can accept the methodological principle that all economies, including market economies, are socially embedded, and just ignore Polanyi's double movement critique, implicitly or explicitly dismissing it as bogus due to its reliance on a reification of market logic. This is the route, established initially by economic sociologists (Lie 1991; Zelizer 1988; 1989) now taken by Konings and other international political economists interested in questions of culture (Best and Paterson 2010). On the other hand, we can simply choose to embrace the critique of market society in *TGT* as a more or less Marxist critique of commodification, re-expressed in terms of a critique of market fundamentalism. This is the route taken by neo-Polanyians, and that which has been more dominant in IPE. This is perhaps in part because of the long-standing dominance of Marxist thought in critical international political economic thought in general, but also particularly because of the way in which Polanyi's work has often been adopted alongside that of Gramsci in publications widely read in IPE (Birchfield 1999; Burawoy 2003; Silver and Arrighi 2003).

Both routes are intellectually legitimate and both have produced fascinating work, but the choice is a false one in that it reduces Polanyi's approach to economic ideas down to its Marxist variant. True, Polanyi's attitudes towards Marxism are critical to understanding some of the key twists and turns that his thought took at various points in his life, but as I have discussed, a big part of the appeal of his work is the way in which it reflects the many different intellectual influences that he came under. Hence there is a third route which this book takes. We can try instead to re-think Polanyi's critique of market society outside the confines of the Marxist orbit, picking out and developing the aspects of Polanyi's theory of economy which are not captured well in the existing debate over the merits and limitations of the embeddedness or double movement concepts. This is the task of the remainder of this chapter. We will see that the philosophy that underpins Polanyi's critique of economism emerges from a certain attitude to modernity which has a great deal in common with other theories of modernity emerging during his lifetime. In short, whilst Polanyi clearly saw the idea of market self-regulation, and the underlying view of humans as utility maximisers only, as an important one, his point, I want to suggest, was less the veracity or otherwise of that view itself, but rather the modes of reasoning in general terms which allowed such claims to make sense. As such, the most important arena of problematisation is not that between the economic and the social but between reality and abstraction, the way in which that opposition is stabilised, mediated or breaks down.

Habitation, improvement and livelihood

The core issue in *TGT* is, as the title implies, transformation, or change, and the problem with a focus on the market/society opposition that characterises much Polanyian literature is that it risks not speaking sufficiently well to this central concern. Fortunately, Polanyi provides an alternative way of presenting the tensions in market society that he seeks to depict in *TGT*: between habitation and improvement. Quoting an English parliamentary document from the early seventeenth century, he writes:

> An official document of 1607 ... set out the problem of change in one powerful phrase: 'The poor man shall be satisfied in his end: Habitation; and the gentleman not hindered in his desire: "Improvement"' This formula appears to take for granted the essence of purely economic progress, which is to achieve improvement at the price of social dislocation.
> (Polanyi 2001: 36)

The conceptual opposition of habitation and improvement is much less well-appreciated in IPE (for an exception see Watson 2009a), but nevertheless captures something distinct in Polanyi's work, something broader and more substantial than the market/society couplet. It speaks of a tension between two different visions of the economy: a vision of economic growth, progress and transformation on one hand and of stability and security of livelihood – both physically and psychologically – on the other.

Although, as we shall see, the invention of market ideology at the hands of figures like Joseph Townsend and Thomas Malthus is indeed a critical turning point in the analysis for Polanyi, he tended to think of industrial transformation – the background of exponentially increasing productivity – as the bedrock of any understanding of political economy. This 'improvement', as he puts it elsewhere, is the 'fundamental fact' (Polanyi 1977: xlviii). The invention of the machine is a decisive development in the narrative, producing demand for a network of merchants capable of shifting the increased volume of goods, a division of labour capable of producing all the different types of labour at the right scale and volume and standardised money to facilitate transactions.

In *TGT*, the term habitation sits within the double movement matrix at points, as for example when Polanyi argues that market-resisting legislation in the eighteenth century was designed to protect the habitation of the poor 'against the juggernaut, improvement' (2001: 191). Again, though, the focus is not on 'society' in an abstract sense, but rather on some of the economic requirements of humans not captured in the imaginary of improvement: the practical concern Polanyi had with the development of market society was the disruptive effects of such developments upon people's livelihoods in an everyday sense. For example, in discussing the rationalisation of agriculture in seventeenth-century England, the point is that it produced great material benefits, but took away the economic security afforded by a plot held in common by a family or village, which could support a person if market trade was not forthcoming (2001: 96). This era of agricultural improvement was, moreover, a radical transformation in the whole structure of English economic and political order: as well as upending the manorial system of land ownership, it also rapidly destroyed the integrating aspects of rural community and village life (see Comninel 2000). Read in this way, the problem with all this was not that people were alienated or disembedded from their social being, but, more prosaically, that the conditions of life were transformed at a rate of knots by forces of improvement, which had the effect of transforming people's lived realities at a rate which they were unable to accommodate.

These were social harms, but also economic harms if one thinks of economy as livelihood, as Polanyi often did. In more anodyne formulations, Polanyi described livelihood as the institutionalised interaction between persons and their environment in satisfaction of 'a continuous supply of want-satisfying means' (1968: 147; see also 1977: 32). On this basis, Polanyi and his early followers in economic anthropology developed an account of possible patterns of livelihood which included redistribution, reciprocity and householding alongside market exchange as all equally 'economic' forms of human interaction (see Polanyi 1966, 1968, 1977; Bohannan 1955).

There are two key components to the description of economy of livelihood, therefore, which are missed out in a description of economy in improvement terms. Firstly, the 'continuous supply' element implies the means towards economic security and stability rather than towards rising material welfare in aggregate terms. Anthropologists developing Polanyi's substantivist economics more recently have recognised this in regard to non-market economic practices such as the sharing of household labour, local work co-operatives, informal credit provision and localised lending and borrowing of goods and services. As Hillenkamp et al. note, such 'informal' economic practices have been widely shown to 'proceed from people's demands for [individual or social] security rather than for growth or capital accumulation per se' (2013: 5). Secondly, the institutional nature of economic interaction: livelihood was, for Polanyi, a practical reflection of all the particular institutions in which a person exists, and all the associated sediments of custom, rule and power which comprise them, from family and kinship circles through the workplace, associations and unions up to social orders, legal systems and religions (Polanyi 1977: 11). True, in 'Marxist mode', Polanyi argues that the coming of market society reverses this 'embeddedness', but we can easily park that exposition to one side and consider the nature of livelihood and habitation within market society.

At root, the notion of livelihood implies some sense of continuity between one moment and the next. The security of a way of making a living, but also the security of the sense of identity that comes from that way of making a living too. There is some form of intrinsic worth in a person's economic way of life in its complexity and particularity because it is a material reflection of personhood. The psychologist Jerome Kagan hits upon this value and its emergence in various more or less identifiably economic patterns of human behaviour:

> Humans require rituals, be they the routines of the workplace, shopping, caring for children, weekend recreations, prayers, writing books, checking the stock prices, attending conferences, or conversations with one's immediate family at dinner or with the extended family on holidays.

None can claim a rational foundation that is more secure than the others, but each dilutes the threat posed by uncertainty and imposes a form on what would otherwise be perceived as a shapeless and endlessly flat expanse of time.

(Kagan 2009: 91)

In part, Polanyi's analysis of the history of market society centres on the disruption caused to people's livelihoods understood in this way. The relative material benefits of exponential economic development during the eighteenth, nineteenth and twentieth centuries – of enclosure, of industrialisation, urbanisation and the growth of global trade – are never disputed. The problem was more specific: the *rate* at which that development took place compared to that ability of people to accommodate the changes to their livelihood. The critical question in *TGT* is economic transformation and so it is not the direction of changes to the conditions of livelihood (through processes of marketisation, communisation, socialisation or whatever else), but the *velocity* of change, which is the important variable.

For Polanyi, the instability and insecurity produced by economic development invoked a very particular role for political authority in managing the rate of economic change so as to allow individuals and society to cope with changes to their livelihood, something he describes as an 'elementary truth of political science and statecraft' (2001: 35). For example, in discussing the enclosures movement, he writes:

In retrospect nothing could be clearer than the Western European trend of economic progress which aimed at eliminating an artificially maintained uniformity of agricultural technique, intermixes strips, and the primitive institution of the common. ... Yet, but for the consistently maintained policy of the Tudor and early Stuart statesmen, the rate of that progress might have been ruinous, and have turned the process itself into a degenerative instead of a constructive event. For upon this rate, mainly, depended whether the dispossessed could adjust themselves to changed conditions without fatally damaging their substance, human and economic, physical and moral.

(Polanyi 2001)

Throughout *TGT*, Polanyi describes how governors of society fulfilled this function with varying degrees of success, by slowing down the industrialisation of agriculture, by regulating the labour market and by finding ways to control the money supply. He notes how these moves often reflected the partial class interests of their day, whether aristocratic, royal, capitalist or other, but argues – departing from class-based analysis – that in each case, the substantive economic effect was the defence of livelihoods in the face of the momentous changes wrought by industrialisation and the globalisation of trade.

Read through the lens of the embeddedness/disembeddedness metaphor, the habitation/improvement couplet could be seen merely as an alternative way of phrasing the distinction between society and economy, state and market. By this reading, the critical angle emerges from there being too much improvement/ economy/market and too little habitation/society/state, with economism acting as ideological subterfuge. But to do so is to compress all the different levels of analysis at work in *TGT*. In Polanyi's narrative, the distinction between habitation and improvement precedes and predates both the emergence of the institutions of market and state, and the discursive distinction between economy and society. The latter two oppositions are essentially effects, or institutional manifestations, of the underlying tension between economic improvement and economic livelihood, or habitation.

Technological progress and the need for some security of livelihood are presented as being utterly fundamental to the condition of humanity in industrialised modernity, but, critically, as of *fundamentally different type*. This does give us a yardstick by which to form critical judgments on questions of political economy, but it is not a yardstick rooted in a rejection of market for state, or a rejection of a thin understanding of economy-as-self-interest for society-as-ethical-goodness. Rather, it is a yardstick rooted in the recognition of the heterogeneous nature of habitation and improvement as social goods. One does not lead to the other in any automatic way, and neither can be substituted for by the other, and so a responsible political authority has to find ways to bargain and trade off between these differing goals. The important point is therefore the underlying assumption that there are qualitatively different types of social good which cannot be drawn under one uniform analytical umbrella, which evinces a strongly pluralist vein in Polanyi's thought. The social value of habitation and improvement are, in Polanyi's account, simply incommensurable, so the question is how we make room for that incommensurability: how do we make room for a plurality of human needs and desires in our understanding of the economy?

This question is never fully addressed by Polanyi in *TGT*, but is reflected in his engagement with the language of functional theory which was circulating amongst guild socialist scholars in the inter-war period. As Dale has discussed, for guild socialists the institutions in their vision of a socialist society – the church, the state, unions, cooperatives *etc.* – could be understood as expressions of a plurality of distinct human purposes and values (Dale 2011: 11). Polanyi was attracted to this model, developing it in order to argue that the function of an organisation should determine the realm of its activity (Dale 2008: 511), on the basis of which he developed his own positive vision of what a functional socioeconomic order might look like, including democratic representation within the context of particular associations of trade, all with the aim of making the social and political nature of conducting one's livelihood as transparent and visible as possible (Mendell 2007: 85).

This strikes one as a direct precursor of more recent, formalised pluralist political philosophy. For example, in *Spheres of Justice* Michael Walzer argued for a variety of pluralism in relation to how we think about the distribution of different things in society – health, money, free time, love, security, welfare *etc.* – arguing that 'different social goods ought to be distributed for different reasons, in accordance with different procedures, by different agents; and that all these differences derive from different understandings of the social goods themselves' (Walzer 1983: 6), producing a situation where 'all distributions are just or unjust relative to the social meanings of the goods at stake' (1983: 9). This is a theme which I will return to later. For now, however, it is the critique implicit in this theme which is important. As I read it, Polanyi's understanding of economism is a critique of various attempts to resist the plural nature of human socioeconomic needs and desires in favour of a view that all types of social goods are commensurable at some deeper level. Market logic may be one such view, but I want to suggest that, for Polanyi, commodity logic is not 'ideology' in the Marxist sense. Rather, his understanding of market logic emerges from a critique of modernity, understood as faith in universal reason in the light of a decline in faith in God. It is important that we get a sense of his attitude at this broad level if we are to understand how it conditions his approach to political economic ideas.

Polanyi and modernity

Polanyi's story in *TGT* begins by noting how the last 200 or so years have been characterised by an exponential rate of economic progress unknown to any earlier epoch, yet he is careful to note that his aim is not to *explain* this phenomenon. As he argues both in *TGT* and more explicitly in later work, the Industrial Revolution's transformative impact was a result not of technological change only, but of that change in combination with changes in economic organisation and science, each of which had unique, *sui generis* origins (Polanyi 2001: 42; 2014: 31). Is it possible to in any way explain the unique and extreme upswing in the rate of economic development produced by the advent of industrial capitalism? Theories of growth proffered by economists fail on this score because they only seek to explain varying rates of growth within capitalism and not in comparison with previous or alternative economic systems (Baumol 2002). One might instead map the various empirical causes in great detail as for example Eric Hobsbawm did (1988). Or one might pick up on particular parts of the story – the influence of particular ideas and moral dispositions (*e.g.* McCloskey 2006), innovations, class interests, demographic changes or, as in Jared Diamond's popular account, the conditioning effects of geography on development (Diamond 1997). But the story is so complex and so all-encompassing that one cannot move far beyond description without succumbing to reductivism of one sort or another.

The question of how we can make sense of industrial capitalism might not have been worth asking if it had brought only positive outcomes. But, for its early scholars, as much as for us today, the existence of poverty amidst such huge productive advances – the 'wound of wealth' (Blaney and Inayatullah 2010) – was an issue that loomed large. Over the seventeenth and eighteenth centuries, economic improvement entailed processes of enclosure, mass urbanisation and industrialisation, which came together to produce a nascent free market for labour which was marked by a lack of security of employment. The new phenomenon of the economic cycle, as engendered by the increasingly interconnected system of global trade in the late eighteenth century, was producing new fluctuations in the quantity of work available at any one time and in the levels of wages to be paid on that work. The upshot of all this was a situation in which the means of livelihood could not be assured in the same way that they could under previous economic orders.

It is against this background that the first tension between economic development and the security of livelihood – improvement and habitation – emerges in Polanyi's narrative. In an effort to act against the new risks and insecurities of market society, Polanyi discusses the famous Speenhamland system of poor relief, which subsidised workers' wages when they fell below a particular level. This amounted to a self-defence by society, in Polanyi's view, which 'protect[ed] labour from the dangers of the market system' (2001: 84). Yet its impact was swamped by the new structure of incentives presented by the nascent market for labour emerging at the time: employers soon realised that they had no incentive to pay wages if those wages would be paid by the state anyway. In their study of the period, Block and Somers demonstrate that the picture was a lot more complex than historians usually account for (2003). There were many conflicting economic forces at work and many regional particularities in the English economy that meant that the apparent moral hazard conundrum could not have been read straightforwardly from events at the time. The important thing, however, is less the moral hazard problem itself, and more the fact that there was no overall paradigm of thought within which to situate these developments, and the fact that later authors imputed such a framework in terms of the incompatibility of a free market and interference with it by political authority.

As Polanyi writes: 'contemporaries did not comprehend the order for which they were preparing the way ... the complicated economics of Speenhamland transcended the comprehension of even the most expert observers of the time' (2001: 85–86). In the parishes of late-Tudor England, Polanyi notes that the question 'where do the poor come from?' elicited a great variety of theories in response, from the prosaic to the ridiculous: from concerns for wages or rents being too high or too low to poor diet, drug habits, excessive consumption of tea, insufficient consumption of beer and many other reasons besides (2001: 94). It is from this confusion, Polanyi argues, that the ideology of economism emerges to provide a paradigm to make sense of it all. In perhaps the most spectacular paragraph to appear in *TGT*, and one which is foundational to the approach I am taking to Polanyi's work in this book, he describes the situation thus:

> The form in which the nascent reality came to our consciousness was political economy. Its amazing regularities and stunning contradictions

had to be fitted into the scheme of philosophy and theology in order to be assimilated to human meanings. The stubborn facts and the inexorable brute laws that appeared to abolish our freedom had in one way or another to be reconciled to freedom. This was the mainspring of the metaphysical forces that secretly sustained the positivists and utilitarians. Hope – the vision of perfectibility – was distilled out of the nightmare of population and wage laws, and was embodied in a concept of progress so inspiring that it appeared to justify the vast and painful dislocations to come.

(Polanyi 2001: 120)

Out of the bewilderment, Polanyi charts the rise of economism as an ideology which sought to explain this new world in all of both its productive wonder and immiserating horror in a magnificently simple way: by imputing market-like, self-interested characteristics to the biological essence of human nature, from which all social outcomes could be inferred.

To demonstrate this thesis, Polanyi presents a very short history of economic thought. This history begins with Adam Smith, who Polanyi regarded as the 'founder of [the] new science [of] economics' (2001:116). Polanyi suggests that, although Smith was the first exponent of the possibilities of a market economy, he also regarded it as a human-made, contingent institution. He imputes to Smith the view that '[p]olitical economy should be a human science; it should deal with that which was natural to man, not to nature' (Polanyi 2001: 117). In consequence, any economistic rationality implied by Smith's market economics was tightly circumscribed by social concern for 'civic order', 'reason and humanity' and 'the dignity of man' (Polanyi 2001: 117; on these themes in Smith, see also Hont 2015; Tribe 2015). Polanyi then places a great deal of emphasis upon a treatise written by the scholar and vicar Joseph Townsend in 1786, one decade after the publication of the first edition of Smith's *Wealth of Nations*. In this treatise, entitled *Dissertation on the Poor Laws*, Townsend argued against the provision of welfare payments to the rural poor in England on the basis that such provision interfered with the natural incentives of hunger and pain that a genuinely free market for labour provided. The important thing, for Polanyi, was the allegory upon which Townsend based this argument:

The scene is Robinson Crusoe's island in the Pacific Ocean, off the coast of Chile. On this island, Juan Fernandez landed a few goats to provide meat in case of future visits. The goats had multiplied at a biblical rate ... In order to destroy them, the Spanish authorities landed a dog and a bitch, which also, in the course of time, greatly multiplied, and diminished the number of goats on which they fed. 'Then a new kind of balance was restored', wrote Townsend. 'The weakest of both species were among the first to pay the debt of nature; the most active and vigorous preserved their lives'. To which he added: 'It is the quantity of food which regulates the number of the human species'.

(Polanyi 2001: 118)

Then, the critical conclusion comes:

> 'Hunger will tame the fiercest animals, it will teach decency and civility, obedience and subjection, to the most perverse. In general it is only hunger which can spur and goad them [the poor] on to labour, yet our laws have said they shall never hunger'.
>
> (2001: 118)

One may well find Townsend's conclusions reprehensible, and Polanyi did, but the important thing was the method of reasoning as much as the answer in itself. In short, the social naturalism that Townsend apparently originated presented a way of looking at the human world in which economy was distinct from polity, subject to its own timeless, abstract laws (Polanyi 2001: 120). The argument against market-inhibiting welfare legislation via poor relief was made on the basis that it was an interference with the laws of nature, or indeed of God, as in Edmund Burke's formulation of the same basic idea (Burke 1795).

As with any period of history, Townsend's was a time in which competing and heterogeneous demands were being placed upon the body politic. Political authority will always have to negotiate between differing interests, whether labour and capital, parliamentarians and lords, or between internal factions of the court, notwithstanding the interests of the sovereign itself. It has to navigate and compromise between different aims, whether, its own prestige and reputation, national security, religious observances, economic productivity and a hundred other things besides. In the throes of industrial revolution, new social forms – mass pauperism for some, exponential growth and riches for others – were giving rise to new constellations of classes and interests which could be interpreted in a number of ways. What was new was that this particular set of demands – the habitation needs of the poor and the new forces of economic improvement – were crystallised in the form of a *logical* contradiction arising from characteristics of human nature posited as *universal*. And by problematising the issue in terms of logical contradiction, it could only apparently be resolved through the adumbration of a single, all embracing mode of thought which transcended the opposition altogether. In Townsend's vision of the economy, there is no room for heterogeneity or a pluralism of economic interests or needs. All the messy reality of life is swept away and replaced by a transcendent vision rooted in the animalistic view of the human being.

It would be difficult to overstate the importance Polanyi assigns to Townsend's rather obscure tract. It is, for Polanyi, the beginning of economism and a 'new starting point for political science' (2001: 119). In contrast to the socially circumscribed and contingent market relations of Smith presented a decade earlier in *The Wealth of Nations*, Townsend argued in an essentialising manner that self-interest was a human master motive pre-conditioned by biological essence. Polanyi charts the influence of the story, noting how it influenced contemporaries such as the Marquis de Condorcet, as well as, critically, Thomas Malthus, who's 'Iron Law of Wages' was to have such a large impact upon the way in which Victorian England thought about the poor and about the economy in general. From here, Polanyi draws straight lines to figures as diverse as Ricardo, Bentham and Burke, arguing that, despite their differences, all more or less consciously adopted Townsend's naturalistic approach to the economy, Ricardo in his law of diminishing returns, Burke through his view of labour as a commodity and Bentham through his all-encompassing utilitarian psychology. These all worked as systems of thought by addressing the economy as a sphere of social relations separate to society and polity, with its own immutable laws.

This moment in the history of ideas is thus critically important to Polanyi's critique, yet it occupies only a few short pages of *TGT*. Townsend's intervention is presented by Polanyi as a watershed moment (Dale 2016: 230), a cliff edge off which the history of economic ideas falls. All at once, fully fledged Enlightenment rationalism comes to bear on the economy conceived of as an independent realm. In Chapter 3, I will dig further into this issue, arguing that the Townsendian view was only one iteration of a longer-lived desire to see economic life in abstract terms. But for now, we need to bring more diverse fragments of Polanyi's thought together in order to see why he might have seen this as the defining moment in the history of economic ideas.

Polanyi's thesis as postmodern

The biologically essentialist economistic fallacy that Polanyi identified was not a self-contained ideology dreamed up in the minds of Townsend and Malthus and then foisted upon the masses, and, equally, the naturalistic mode of their theses was not merely a rhetorical prop. The type of idealism that underpins Polanyi's imputation of economistic fallacy is not something unique to economism, but is rather a reflection of the tendency to think about the world through the prism of idealised visions that is so characteristic of Western modern political economic thought in general. Given this, my argument here is that the market ideology that Polanyi critiques was not fallacious in the sense that it represented the true nature of people or of the economy incorrectly, but rather in the sense that it was an attempt to impute a single essence to people and economy at all. It is the *formalism* itself, of the economistic view – that is to say, the aspiration to conceptualise the economy in universalised terms (Dale 2016a: 48) – rather than its market content, that is at issue fundamentally.

Despite the brevity of Polanyi's actual history of ideas in *TGT*, we do get some sense that, for him, market ideology is only one example of a larger set of attempts to cope with a lack of authoritative foundations for knowledge, that characterise Western modernity. In particular the relationship posited between *laissez-faire* economic theory and the decline of theocentric knowledge is explicit throughout the book: economic liberalism 'turned almost into religion' (2001: 145), evolving into 'a veritable faith in man's secular salvation through a self-regulating market' (2001: 141). The economic question of poverty 'began to reflect philosophical outlook, very much as theological questions had before' (2001: 110). As he put it in a later unpublished manuscript, 'Man believes in development as he once believed in God' (cited in Polanyi-Levitt and Mendell 1987: 22). The fullest realisation of economic liberalism in his narrative, the Gold Standard, was not just any old economic policy, but the 'faith of the age' and a 'creed' (Polanyi 2001: 141). At the end of *TGT*, we get a most far-reaching statement of this mode of exposition, informed by the importance Polanyi assigned to the Bible (see Dale 2016: 60–61) in constituting the moral nature of humanity:

> We invoked what we believed to be the three constitutive facts in the consciousness of Western man: knowledge of death, knowledge of freedom, knowledge of society. The first, according to Jewish legend, was revealed in the Old Testament story. The second was revealed through the discovery of the uniqueness of the person in the teachings of Jesus as recorded in the New Testament. The third revelation came to us through living in an industrial society.
>
> (2001: 267–268)

This framing is little reflected upon in the secondary literature on Polanyi, and it is unclear whether it held any purchase amongst his readers at the time of publication of *TGT*, but as a critique of economism, it does clearly fit into the framework of later postmodern approaches to the history of ideas, as summarised by Roland Bleiker:

> [M]odern debates all have a distinctive character. They are all well framed. The contours of the modern framing process have to a large extent been drawn by the recurring unwillingness to deal with what Nietzsche called the death of God, the disappearance, at the end of the medieval period, of a generally accepted worldview that provided a stable ground from which it was possible to assess nature, knowledge, common values, truth, politics – in short, life itself. When the old theocentric world crumbled, when the one and only commonly accepted point of reference vanished, the death of God became the key dilemma around which modern debates were waged. Yet, instead of accepting the absence of stable foundations and dealing with the ensuing responsibilities, many prominent modern approaches embarked on attempts to find replacements for the fallen God.
>
> (Bleiker 1998: 475)

Rather than accepting the lack of fully objective, and therefore fully authoritative, foundations for knowledge – 'thinking without a bannister', as Tracy Strong puts it (2012) – the history of modern thought has, by this account, been marked by a series of attempts to erect new foundations to underpin knowledge claims through reason and rationality.

Kant's system of ethics is the paradigmatic case for political philosophy. Instead of lamenting the apparent limitations of a lack of external foundation to human understanding, Kant celebrated the new centrality of human understanding itself as the foundation: the human as both subject and object of knowledge (Foucault 2002). And this way of thinking took on the same universalist hue as its theological predecessors. For Kant, ethics could be derived completely from nothing more than the notion of rational agency, and as such suggests itself as universally applicable to all people in all places and in all times (Geuss 2008: 7). From there, one can extrapolate towards later thinkers who have sought to build moral universes through idealised abstraction, including John Rawls's system, which sought to produce a universal set of ethical precepts upon which any reasonable person 'ought' to be able to agree.

Polanyi was firmly ensconced in the socialist tradition and most of the formative influences on his work came from various shades of the left, traditionally conceived, but in another sense, the continually deepening suspicion of the promises of modernity, understood in terms of the power of reason and abstraction, were clearly a part of the tenor of the times in which he wrote. For authors in other traditions, these suspicions sometimes manifested themselves in a critique of 'rationalism'. For example, Isaiah Berlin, harangued 'modern' political philosophies of all colours in an essay which first appeared in *Foreign Affairs* in 1950 entitled 'Political Ideas in the Twentieth Century':

> Conservatives, liberals, radicals, socialists differed in their interpretation of historical change. They disagreed about what were the deepest needs, interests, ideals of human beings ... They differed about the facts, they differed about ends and means, they seemed to themselves to agree on almost nothing. But what they had in common ... was the belief that their age was ridden with social and political problems which could be solved only by the conscious application of truths upon which all men endowed with adequate mental powers could agree.
> (Berlin 1969: 12–13)

For Berlin, the historical sources for this tendency stretched back to Spinoza and Grotius and were reflected in Leninist Marxism and Benthamite social reform. In the case of the latter two at least, Polanyi seemed to be in tacit agreement, being both deeply suspicious of the deterministic elements of Marxist thought (*e.g.* Polanyi 2014: 40) and of course of Bentham's brand of social rationalism, which he traced back to Malthus and Townsend before.

Berlin saw in rationalism of all types the seeds of great oppression of 'the infinite variety of persons' (Berlin 1969: 39) and a hostility towards the things that make people human, including idle curiosity and the practice of all arts 'not obviously useful to society as being at best forms of social frivolity' (1969: 28). In turn, he implored scholars of society to adopt 'less Messianic ardour, more enlightened scepticism, more toleration of idiosyncrasies ... less mechanical, less fanatical application of general principles, however rational or righteous' (Berlin 1969: 40). Polanyi's work expresses similar sentiments in relationship to market economic practices and theory. The abandonment of the market idea meant an abandonment not just of the principle itself in practice, but of any idea of organising social life through any single, infinitely applicable, rationally derived scheme of order. It meant recognising that there can be no final 'unity of motivations and valuations' (Polanyi 1977: 10), as suggested by the economistic view.

Sometimes, Polanyi's concern for an overly unified conception of economy is revealed in practical terms, as a resistance to the 'paralyzing division of labor, standardisation of life, supremacy of mechanism over organism and organization over spontaneity' (Polanyi 1968: 59) – the factories, mines, call-centres, sweatshops, and delivery depots *etc.* that are so central to capitalism today for example – but it is more often pitched in a philosophical way revolving around the different possible meanings of freedom. In one lecture delivered just after the publication of *TGT*, he argues that the negative and universal account of freedom should be replaced by '*freedoms* (in the plural) – the capacity to follow one's personal convictions in the light of one's conscience: the freedom to differ, to hold views of one's own, to be in a minority of one, and yet to be an honoured member of the community in which one plays the vital part of the deviant' (Polanyi 2014: 39). In an essay written shortly before, he talks in terms of 'civic liberties', arguing that 'freedom finds its institutional expression in the prize set on personality, integrity, character, and nonconformity' (2014: 38). In a later typescript, he extends this mode of thinking to the international level, arguing that the very principle of universalism was and should be in decline, to be replaced by 'separate and distinct cultures ... based on *incommensurable* core values' (2014: 32, italics added). It is similarly in this light that Polanyi's enthusiasm for a functional theory of society makes sense. Economic institutional heterogeneity could provide the space for individual difference to flourish.

Interesting parallels can also be drawn between Polanyi's critique of economism and the work of contemporary existentialist authors. For example, in *Le Mythe de Sisyphe*, first published in 1942, Albert Camus characterised the condition of life in modernity without authoritative knowledge bestowed by 'the fallen God' as one of absurdity. For Camus, any person who became aware of this lack of possibility of a rational foundation for meaning in life had the most serious of all choices to make: whether to go on living regardless or to end one's life in despair at the lack of a fundamental scheme of meaning. To avoid the latter, Camus saw only two possible options. Firstly, one can take a 'leap of faith' (2005: 31), by ignoring the implications of the absurd and to live as though ultimate truths and rational foundations existed nevertheless. This 'escape' (2005: 34) was delusional for Camus, indicative of a desire to cling to a way of thinking and being which the coming of modernity had disavowed. Better to take the second option, which was to accept the lack of absolute truth: 'There is ... a metaphysical honour in enduring the world's absurdity ... It is a question of breathing with it, of recognising its lessons and recovering their flesh' (2005: 90). Or as he puts it elsewhere: 'The important thing is not to be cured, ... but to live with one's ailments' (2005: 37). There is no permanent resolution, no definitive choice, for Camus. Rather, the gap between these two possible choices – the desire for absolute knowledge and reason on one hand and the acceptance of contingency and loss of meaning on the other – characterises the experience of modernity in general:

> I can negate everything of that part of me that lives on vague nostalgias, except this desire for unity, this longing to solve, this need for clarity and cohesion ... I do not know whether this world has a meaning that transcends it. But I know that I do not know that meaning and that it is impossible for me just now to know it. I can understand only in human terms. What I touch, what resists me – that is what I understand. And these two certainties – my appetite for the absolute and for unity and the impossibility of reducing this world to a rational and reasonable principle – I also know that I cannot reconcile them.
>
> (2005: 49)

This critique of modernity in terms of a choice between a leap of faith and acceptance bears immediate familiarity to Polanyi's critique of the pristine abstraction of economism and its disavowal of the contingent, messy 'reality of society'. Society was, for Polanyi, complex (2001: 266), consisting of multiple types of value, varied means of livelihood and social engagement and infinite varieties of power and compulsion as the necessary corollary of life lived in communities of people (2001: 268). Above all, the world was full of irreducibly autonomous and creative individuals capable of transforming their social context in any number of different ways (Baum 1996). This meant that society, and therefore economy, is not reducible to any scheme of ultimate meaning or any rationally derived set of principles or rules. Economism attempted precisely this by universalising the market idea and conceptually subsuming all livelihoods within it.

Although not much discussed in contemporary applications of Polanyi's ideas (see Cangiani 2012 for an exception), the final chapter of *TGT*, 'Freedom in a complex society', makes it clear that definitional questions around the nature of freedom itself are indeed the underlying issue. Polanyi argues that economism relied on a particular 'liberal' view of freedom and power where freedom meant only freedom from interference and power only unjust and arbitrary compulsion of one by another. Thinking about freedom in this way led to perversity for Polanyi since the vision of an economy of negatively free people engaged with one another purely through contractual relations – in short market fundamentalism – promised a type of rational and just social order which was never attainable in practice. This opened a permanent gap between the 'nightmare' reality of power, complexity and contingency in real world political economy, and the 'vision of perfectibility' promised by 'a market view of society which equated economics with contractual relationships, and contractual relations with freedom' (2001: 266). The wise move for Polanyi, as for Camus, was to abandon the fundamentalism of this account and instead to accept the tension – to accept the 'reality of society' (2001: 267) – and so to abandon the absolutised philosophy of freedom and contract:

> Man accepted the reality of death and built the meaning of his bodily life upon it. He resigned himself to the truth that he had a soul to lose ... and founded his freedom upon it. He resigns himself, in our time, to the reality of society which means an end to that freedom. Uncomplaining acceptance of the reality of society gives man indomitable courage and strength to remove all removable injustice and unfreedom. This is the meaning of freedom in a complex society.
>
> (2001: 278)

To uphold the negative account of freedom and the principle of contractualism as absolute goods manifest in the institution of the market, despite continual evidence of the limitations and perversities of free markets in practice, was to engage in a 'leap of faith'. But where Camus's leap was primarily indicative of an individual's psychological weakness, Polanyi's leap had major social consequences by obscuring the need for social integration and political negotiation over the tensions inherent in a rapidly technologically developing social context. Fundamentalism allowed space for only two possible positions: 'either to remain faithful to an illusionary idea of freedom and deny the reality of society, or to accept that reality and reject the idea of freedom. The first is the liberal's conclusion; the latter the fascist's' (2001: 266). Read in this way, the object of *TGT* is to uncover systems of thought that seek to transcend the tension between the desire for improvement and the need for habitation through idealised visions of how economy and society should operate. The social naturalism of Townsend and Malthus was one such attempt, but the same idealism also underpinned the prejudice against state action in later economic thought.

As an empirical observation, the notion of a tension between society and market was banal. As Polanyi himself notes (2001: 147–148), many commentators had recognised the sweep of social protectionism concomitant with the rise of the free market during the nineteenth century – from the recognition of trade unions, pervasive legislation on working standards, parliamentary acts preventing the worst excesses of environmental destruction all the way to the installation of nationalised central banks and political control over the money supply. The key point was not the intervention itself, but the discursive frame within which it was cast. Polanyi argues that 'liberal' political economy could not understand social protectionism, in all its forms, as anything other than a 'collectivist conspiracy' (2001: 151) which could not be 'assimilated' (Polanyi 2001) from the economistic perspective. As he writes elsewhere,

> Honour and pride, civic obligation and moral duty, even self-respect and common decency, were ... summed up in the word 'ideal'. Hence man was believed to consist of two components, one more akin to hunger and pain, the other to honour and power. The one was 'material', the other 'ideal'; the one 'economic', the other 'non-economic'; the one 'rational', the other 'non-rational' ... He who would have refused to imagine that he was acting for gain alone was thus considered not only immoral, but also mad.
>
> (Polanyi 1968: 70)

In the same way that Foucault argued that reason was defended through the construction of madness as its other (1988), the economistic fallacy required that 'non-economic' behaviour be understood as deviant in some way.

The desire to maintain the Gold Standard in the wake of the First World War and Great Depression was, in Polanyi's narrative, the high-water mark of this form of prejudice. Making a show of handing over the stability of both the global financial system and subscribing nations' domestic economies to a supposedly self-regulating system of exchange rate pegs had, *ipso facto*, deemed state interference in currency issues to be illegitimate. This logic was held despite the fact that states were *constantly* manipulating the mechanism in various ways (see Knafo 2005). This cognitive dissonance reflected the fact that the desire to stay 'on gold' was not a simple, rational policy choice from a menu of possible exchange rate systems that might be read from a textbook. Rather, it was a part of the long story of 'man's secular salvation through a self-regulating market' (Polanyi 2001: 141). Faith in the Gold Standard was so deeply ingrained because it was entwined with deep-seated moral beliefs about the proper nature of the economy, with distant roots in Townsend's allegory. To deviate from the Gold Standard was to challenge the 'faith' and to therefore challenge sedimented beliefs about what humans were like and how, society and economy ought to function. Rather than being recognised as a necessary counterweight to the new risks and dangers of the globalising economy, state resistance against market self-regulation through gold was, by virtue of thought experiment, cast as something unnecessary and to be eliminated.

Part II
Contradiction and transcendence

3 Property, order and commerce

Beyond economism as light switch

So far, we have seen that Polanyi's critique of economic formalism is not only a statement about methodology, but also a critique of abstract and universalising modes of thought that Polanyi saw in various descriptions of life. Market society is marked by a set of tensions – the existence of poverty amongst plenty, conflicting desires for stability and progress, ideals of freedom and the reality of society and power – which are all transcended through the vision of perfectibility offered by Townsendian economism. However, the details of this thesis are not clear in Polanyi's work due to his history of economic ideas being rather undeveloped. Despite what we have teased out so far, his coverage is limited to Townsend, Malthus and later utilitarianism, and even here it is extremely brief, considering the importance he assigned to those ideas in shaping the trajectory of future thought on the nature of the economy.

As Matthew Watson has noted, whilst Polanyi was a keen student of the classical political economists, he had a marked tendency to characterise all economic theory, from whatever time and place, as *laissez-faire* economic theory, with the result that the intricacies of all preceding, and indeed later economic theory become 'flatlined' around a principle of market self-regulation appropriate to Ricardo and Malthus only (Watson 2014: 607). Under the influence of Townsend's pamphlet, economism appears fully formed under the pen of these two scholars, and thus 'Economic society … emerge[s] as distinct from the political state' (Polanyi 2001: 120) all at once. *Laissez-faire* economism is presented as something like a light switch, turned on by Malthus, or perhaps Townsend before, in response to the unusual conditions in the period between the establishment of the Speenhamland system of poor relief in 1795 and its abolition in 1834, with no nuance or subtlety along the way.

This lack of detail prevents the development of any more than a binary conception of the history of economic thought around the pivot of Townsend and Malthus. It is, in turn, not hard to see how this inadequacy becomes reflected in the overly caricatured nature of the embeddedness/disembeddedness couplet. A theoretical argument about the perils of transcendent modes of thought is mapped directly on to a historical juncture such that 'the market' as an institutional manifestation of pure self-interest becomes posited as an empirical reality. The rhetorical power of this combination of different 'voices' (Watson 2014: 604) at work in Polanyi's analysis comes at the expense of clarity on what, precisely, the problem with economism is, leaving his thesis open to the many critiques that highlight the undue veracity he assigns to the visions of *laissez-faire* economic theory as an accurate description of life in market society. As we have seen, this problem has become the central playing field for debate over the merits and de-merits of Polanyi's political economy.

In the following three chapters I seek to present a different history of economic ideas which speaks more directly to the postmodern aspects of Polanyi's thought. The critical issue about economism, in my reading of Polanyi's narrative, is the way in which it problematised market society in terms of contradictions which could be transcended, and so my aim is to put that contradiction/transcendence mode of thought on questions surrounding the nature of the economy into a broader historical context in two ways: firstly by showing how it emerged from earlier iterations of thought concerning private property, and secondly by showing how it continued to condition later iterations of thought on the economy in ways that cannot be read directly from early nineteenth century *laissez-faire* economism. From this, it becomes clear that the framework of early-Victorian economic thought, which Polanyi so much made the centre of his critique of market society, was only one example within a series.

This process of contextualisation begins with an examination of how scholars in the natural law tradition thought about the economy through discourses on the nature of private property. The essence of the natural law approach was the attempt to derive – by means of scriptural guidance and the application of reason – universal, or 'natural' truths of existence. What is important here is the specific way in which the natural law problematised the economy in terms of the contradiction between a biblical conception of property as a gift from God, held in common by mankind, and the reality of private, or enclosed, property existing on earth. I trace how the two key economic virtues which natural lawyers propounded in order to resolve this contradiction – order and productivity – were articulated in different ways, and with varying degrees of sophistication, in the work of Aquinas, Grotius, Pufendorf and Locke. Partially through Locke, but more significantly in the work of Hume in Chapter Four, I then examine how this mode of problematisation was translated into a non-theistic context, where the central contradiction was instead between property as an individual right and property as a means of social coercion.

In making this part of the argument, I am taking cues from the repeated analogies that Polanyi draws between theological and economic forms of knowledge, but the analysis is analytically closer to Weber's argument (2001) that the shifting doctrines of the church over the course of the Protestant Reformation had the effect of establishing some of the conceptual resources necessary to conceive of the economy in individualised and capitalistic terms. Weber argued that the Lutheran emphasis on the soul of the individual as the fundamental source of moral and spiritual guidance developed into a faith in the individual's capacity for economic self-improvement through hard work – the 'protestant ethic' (Weber 2001). This allowed an important translation of theological imperative into economic imperative, which, whilst forgotten down the ages, furnished capitalism with an initial theological basis which was critical to establishing its legitimacy. Weber's point was that there was no hard edge dividing the apparently secular modernity and the theism that had gone before. Rather, Protestantism provided a way to fit these different ideas together into a conceptually unified system. Although the object of analysis is different here – the way in which the economy as a whole has been problematised – it is similar insofar as it attempts to map a similar process of translation. This moves us away from the light-switch-like reading of modern economic ideology provided by Polanyi, and more towards an appreciation of the 'constant transformation of the conceptualisation of economic activity' (Tribe 2015: 29) over history.

In examining this new problematisation of property in the Enlightenment in Chapter Four, I show that the new theoretical paradox between the visions of property as an individual right and as a means of social coercion represented a new problematisation of the economy in general, which offered up a new continuum of possible positions one could take in order to resolve it. Hume and Rousseau marked the extremes of this continuum, emphasising property as right and property as coercion respectively. From there, we are able to see how this problematisation became embodied in Smith's conception of market society and specifically in his understanding of price. After tracing the nineteenth century lineages of the positions of these three scholars, I finally consider the development of neoliberalism through the activities of the Mont Pelerin Society (MPS) as a translation of the Enlightenment form of problematisation in Chapter Five. The MPS represented an eruption of political economic idea-making which contrasted markedly from the work of *laissez-faire* devotees before them, but did so by reviving precisely the same set of dualisms – political/economic, freedom/power – which had animated Hume, Smith and Rousseau. What these scholars did was to bring a sense of intellectual extremism to the more fluid debate of their forbears.

In all cases, my aim is to recover some of the complexity and ambiguity of these great debates over the nature of the economy. As the analysis moves further towards the present, I observe how those complexities and nuances often dissipated with the passing of time, particularly as economic ideas became more directly applied to questions of economic governance. The tensions within Locke's account of private property, Smith's cautious particularism, the ambivalences of Enlightenment thought in general and even the conflicted set of positions adopted by members of the MPS in its early days, all gradually receded, leaving much more simplistic and transcendent 'solutions' to the problems of market society to take root.

Property and divine order

In *Summa Theologiae,* Thomas Aquinas put forth the first defence of explicitly private property since the classical period which, whilst occupying a relatively small place in the huge volume of his writings, clearly expresses the central problematiques which would continue to shape thought on property in the work of later natural lawyers. This defence represents the first of a series of points of translation between theological and non-theological forms of reasoning on the economy thanks to the way in which he combined precepts of early Christian thought with Aristotle's system of natural philosophy. Although Aristotle's works on natural philosophy had been available to European scholars for some time, most before had seen them as incompatible with the tenets of Christianity. Aquinas's decision to instead synthesise the two marks him out as a good starting point for our analysis.

Appointed as a professor of theology at the University of Paris in 1256, Aquinas's main responsibility was to provide comment and elaboration upon Christian scriptures and to transmit it through writings, lectures and sermons. Most often, this commentary took the form of the presentation of a question, of objections and responses to those objections, often alternating between sources from the Bible and Christian theologians such as Augustine and Ambrose on one hand, and those from Aristotle on the other. Aquinas's defence of private property proceeds in that manner, beginning with the question of 'whether it is natural for man to possess external things?' (Aquinas 1920: IIaIIae 66 Article 1). He starts by presenting quotes from the Book of Psalms, of Luke and from Ambrose which object to this suggestion on the basis that God has complete dominion over all material things. For example, from Psalms: '"The earth is the Lord's", therefore it is not natural for man to possess external things' (Aquinas 1920: Objection 1). To reply to this objection, Aquinas, drawing on Aristotle, makes a distinction between the nature of a thing and the use to which it is put in order to argue that private property is justified by human reason as manifest in productivity:

> External things can be considered in two ways. First, as regards their nature, and this is not subject to the power of man, but only to the power of God Whose mere will all things obey. Secondly, as regards their use, and in this way, man has a natural dominion over external things, because, by his reason and will, he is able to use them for his own profit, as they were made on his account: for the imperfect is always for the sake of the perfect.
> (Aquinas 1920: Article 1 Response)

But 'reason and will' is not reason enough. In the following article (Aquinas 1920: IIaIIae 66 Article 2), a similar argument is replayed, this time counterposing the Christian view of external things as held in common with the existence of private ownership. Here, the emphasis on productivity is maintained, but critically, the prospect of *social order* enters his justification on three counts:

> [E]very man is more careful to procure what is for himself alone than that which is common to many or to all: since each one would shirk the labor

and leave to another that which concerns the community, as happens where there is a great number of servants. Secondly, because human affairs are conducted in more orderly fashion if each man is charged with taking care of some particular thing himself, whereas there would be confusion if everyone had to look after any one thing indeterminately. Thirdly, because a more peaceful state is ensured to man if each one is contented with his own. Hence it is to be observed that quarrels arise more frequently where there is no division of the things possessed.

(Aquinas 1920: Article 2 Response)

As Giorgio Agamben has shown, the concept of *oikonomia* – the progenitor of 'economy' – provided a way for early Christian scholars to rationalise the distinction between the human and the divine in that it suggested that the divine could be reproduced through the immanent ordering of human populations, rather than through the direct power of God (2011). As such, Agamben argues, the concept of order became the 'fundamental paradigm' of thought in the medieval period (2011: 99). Aquinas's approach to property clearly evinces this spirit. The question is framed in terms of how an inherently imperfect humanity can tend towards a perfect Godliness, in this case through productivity on the land. Since God is understood by Aquinas to have made society to work harmoniously together, mirroring God's own infinite harmony, private dominion is understood to assist in maintaining that order.

In the *Summa,* it appears that this discussion is little more than a way to set up the more substantial discussion of the rights and wrongs of theft and robbery that follows it. Nevertheless, this kernel of reasoning on the relationship between private property, productivity and order was to prove influential. For example, John of Paris (1255–1306), an immediate follower of Aquinas, also argued that a system of ownership of material things by individuals was a good state of affairs in that it would promote peace and order (Wood 2008: 215). In John's hands, this argument would provide the central intellectual justification for the temporal authority of nation states in the conflict between Pope Boniface and the French and English kings in the late thirteenth century, which was of course a critical episode in the Protestant Reformation. But for our purposes, the important issue is the structure of the argument: the presentation of private property in terms of contradiction between the divine and earthly realms, and the use of motifs of order and productivity in order to solve it. It is this form of problematisation which we can now trace through later thought in the natural law tradition.

Variations on the theme

Over the course of the seventeenth century, the major scholars in the natural law tradition made concrete advances towards a notion of economy as a distinct sphere of human engagement, incorporating more explicitly the idea of privately agreed contracts between independent actors. But the Thomistic framework of analysis was retained to a greater or lesser degree: understanding of the economy was framed by the underlying view that absolute, Godly, truth, could be accessed by means of reason. For example, the most influential natural lawyers before Locke, Hugo Grotius and Samuel Pufendorf, consciously sought to recast natural law as a matter for lawyers and philosophers rather than moral theologians as in the thought of Aquinas, or that of important subsequent scholastics such as Francisco Suárez (see Schneewind 1998: 82). In this recasting, the entirety of law is dependent upon the conscience of the individuals who consent to it through agreement with one another (Wight 2005: 53). Yet, despite this worldly alteration to the scholastic view, both Grotius and Pufendorf continued to set up their theses on property within the problematisation of the economy in terms of the relationship between divine and worldly forms of order. Like Aquinas, they presented their ideas as *revealing* an already existing, essential and absolute order determined by God.

For example, Grotius's key interventions on the nature of private property, first in *De Indis,* published in 1603, then in the more influential pamphlet *Mare Liberum,* published in 1609, sought to apply the natural law approach to questions of international trade, specifically the controversies surrounding rights over the newly significant shipping lines between the various European powers and the East. His overall argument was that no one could claim monopoly over those lines because no one can claim dominion over the seas – as per the title of the pamphlet, they are 'free seas'. Most of *Mare Liberum* is devoted to applying this argument specifically to the Portuguese, who did claim rights over the shipping lanes at the time, but what interests us here is again how the mechanics of Grotius's argument manipulated the Thomistic relationship between the divine and the earthly in a particular way with regard to property and economic activity in general.

Dealing with property first, it was very much defined by its existence as a tangible thing in Grotius's work. Following Aristotle and Aquinas, Grotius thought of property as arising naturally from human engagement with the material world – it was a reflection of the ongoing need to provision for life. In result, he thought that property can only arise from occupation – *i.e.* use (Grotius 1916: 27) – and that ownership lasts no longer than the occupation of the thing in question lasts (Grotius 1916: 30). This served Grotius's specific argument about the freedom of the seas, since, if private property is limited by the ability to occupy, then 'the sea can in no way become the private property of any one, because nature not only allows but enjoins its common use' (Grotius 1916). In result, no state has the right to block shipping lanes by claiming ownership over them, the underlying rationale being that, by having occupation, or use, as a pre-requisite for property, the legitimacy of claims to property are circumscribed by the prior nature of the thing in question. Along with this defence of property came a defence of trade, which Grotius saw emerging naturally from the facts of geography:

> Nature had given all things to all men. But since men were prevented from using many things which were desirable in every day life because they lived so far apart, and because ... everything was not found everywhere, it was necessary to transport things from one place to another ... hence commerce was born out of necessity for the commodities of life.
>
> (Grotius 1916: 60–62)

Grotius concludes from this that 'the universal basis of all contracts, namely exchange, is derived from nature' (Grotius 1916).

These arguments should be read within the political context of the period. Grotius was a servant of the Dutch state and the impetus for his addressing these themes was the desire to provide a defence for Dutch trading interests against those of Spain and Portugal. Holland was a rapidly rising power at the time and the expression of its interests as 'universal' or 'natural' can be understood simply as hegemonic rhetoric (Wilson 2009). Read as a node in the development of thought on the nature of the economy, however, the way in which he frames the argument is important. Grotius's is a much more commercial articulation of the natural law applied to economic matters. What is 'natural', in Grotius's account is driven more directly by concerns for use and economic productivity, rather than the pursuit of godliness as in Aquinas. But, whilst Grotius makes no use of scripture in the justification of his argument – preferring Roman and Greek literature amongst others – *Mare Liberum* is notably begun with a classically Thomistic declaration that the laws of nature are the product of divine will, produced by means of natural reason and are thus universal in scope (Armitage 2004: xiv). This amounts to no more than an unjustified statement, but what it evinces is a particular way of translating the truth claims of Thomistic thinking into a commercial setting.

Later, Samuel Pufendorf would generalise some aspects of Grotius's thought on the natural law in commercial society, applying them to property and contract as a whole but with a more directly scriptural tone. In his book *On The Law of Nature and of Nations*, property is again understood substantively as emerging naturally from human interaction with the material world: 'for since it pleased God to bestow life on man, He is also understood to have granted him the use of those things without which His gifts cannot be preserved' (Pufendorf 1994: 174). From here, the notion of contract is built up: to claim dominion over a thing is to bar someone else the right to that thing, which constitutes a tacit or express agreement (Pufendorf 1994: 178). Since property is essential to the provisioning of needs, the ensuing contract is just, although a rather weighty proviso is attached: 'and so the law of nature is understood to approve all agreements men have introduced concerning things, provided they do not involve a contradiction or disturb society' (Pufendorf 1994).

In Pufendorf's most significant work, *Elements of Universal Jurisprudence*, published in 1660, the idea of contract is, for the first time, explicitly wedded to issues that we would recognise as 'formally' economic. Over a hundred years before Smith's analogous thesis in *The Wealth of Nations*, Pufendorf appears to straddle the divide between price formation set by custom and market-based price formation set by exchange. Whilst he considers the former to be the most usual, as related through law or custom, we read on to find a relatively well-developed notion of price formation based on production costs ('labors and expenses'), credit opportunities ('deferred profit') and preference formation ('a special feeling') (Pufendorf 1994: 48). In a striking precursor to subjective value theory, he marks out such price formation as moral in that price is derived from the value that people attach to physical goods (Pufendorf 1994: 192), in contrast to Grotius's emphasis on the virtues of use and productivity. But despite this, Pufendorf states the limits upon the price mechanism without compunction as a matter of fact. Some things are simply beyond the commercial space, and so not amenable to price, including 'the higher regions of the air, the ether, the celestial bodies, and the vast ocean' (Pufendorf 1994: 192). Some things are socially circumscribed via the law, others are just too tricky to price, and most importantly, 'there is no price upon the head of a free man, because to be free and to be subject to commercial exchange implies a contradiction; for as soon as someone is put up for sale he ceases to be free' (Pufendorf 1994).

Pufendorf can happily live with such limitations upon contract and property because his justification is still set within the Thomistic conception of the virtue of orderly conduct within society. The linchpin of his account is not contract, but agreement, and the whole point of Pufendorf's work is still to show how humans, despite their corrupt actions, can live in society together with the basic aim of increasing their sociability (Tully 1991: xvi). Or as Pufendorf puts it, 'the Creator would not have given reason to men ... unless he had wished to destine them to cultivate society' (Pufendorf 1994: 80–81). In turn, exchange and the price mechanism exist to enable people to live such a cultivated life, in deference, if not servitude, towards God (Pufendorf 1994: 48). What we have here, then, is a quite different act of translation to that of Grotius. Where Grotius used the theological foundationalism of natural law forcefully, yet adjacently, to his defence of free trade, Pufendorf allows it to weave directly into his account of commerce, but in a more *ad hoc* way.

Property and commercial order

The accounts of private property put forward by Grotius and Pufendorf each represent translations of the Thomistic problematisation of property into more recognisably commercial settings. Each bears a slightly different relationship to Aquinas: the degree of fidelity to the Godly purpose of property, the different ways of emphasising the orderly characteristics of property and different degrees of attachment to the commercial aspects of property ownership according to the different degrees of development of European economic relations. But it is in John Locke's 1689 work that this process of translation becomes most clear, as presented in 'Of Property', the much-discussed chapter of the *Two Treatises of Government*.

Many have read this chapter within the context of Locke's more general call to emancipation from spiritual authority over the people, or in terms of a liberal struggle against authority and power in general (Lloyd Thomas 1995: 93). Others emphasise that Locke was politically involved, with a strong personal and party interest in providing justification for parliamentary rule over monarchic (Gough 1966: xvii). But once again, it is the mechanics of Locke's argument which interest us here. Whilst Locke's understanding of property is set within a more modern concept of the political, the question of how to justify private ownership was still set within the same problematisation of the economy in terms of a contradiction between common ownership according to natural law and private property according to earthly law.

In contrast to Grotius and Pufendorf, Locke's translation is oriented towards a political theoretic aim of finding a suitable route between the poles of tyranny and anarchy, liberty and authority. The *Treatises* are opened with a Hobbesian concern that 'general freedom is but general bondage' (Locke 1967: 119–120), but where, for Hobbes, such a prospect demanded the dominating power of the leviathan, for Locke, parliament, through the institution of property, could perform the same function (Locke 1967). To this extent, Locke's account of private property, whilst economic in implication, was only so within the context of his answer to the political problem of power. To the natural law tradition however, Locke owed his universalistic outlook. Even though he was in essence defending a specific form of political order, he placed, in line with the natural law tradition, a consistently strong emphasis on people's innate sense of reason as enough to derive acceptable rules for every possible human eventuality (Buckle 1991: 125). In terms of the relationship of his argument on property to the natural law, whilst the mechanics of his argument are different to those found in Grotius and Pufendorf, the ultimate framework of seeking to relate property to an absolute scheme of meaning remains.

Nevertheless, as James Tully has shown, the critical difference was that, where previous natural lawyers had derived their justification of property entirely in terms of abstract agreement, Locke added a new functional criterion to the justification of private property specifically: property could only be justified within the context of what it was used *for*, rather than on the condition of use in general, as in Grotius and Pufendorf (Tully 1980: 99). And in Locke's account, the primary function of property was the preservation of humanity. This subtle modification allows space for Locke's famed emphasis on productivity through labour as a critical component of his justification of a system of private property outside the notion of agreement. Locke argues that consent (i.e. agreement) is unnecessary since the natural world has already been given to humanity by God, and so no extra agreement is necessary in order to lay claim to things (Locke 1966: 16). Instead, Locke's central defence is that, since we own our body and its capacity for labour, we own the physical product of that work:

> Whatsoever, then, he removes out of the state that nature hath provided and left it in, he hath mixed his labour with, and joined to it something that is his own, and thereby makes it his property.
>
> (Locke 1966: 15)

This 'mixing metaphor' has been the source of much consternation in political theory, but in Locke's formulation, it is only so to the extent that it helps fulfil a social function as described above. As such, tight limits are placed upon the validity of this labour theory of acquisition by two provisos. The first suggests that 'enough and good' be left over for others to appropriate the fruits of their own labour (Locke 1966: 18). Like Pufendorf, Locke believes the material world to exist for the purposes of the improvement of humanity in common (Locke 1966). Furthermore, the ultimate human duty is to respect God through preservation of both the self *and* the community (see Mansfield 1979: 28). The other proviso is, again, derived from Locke's belief in the purpose of self-preservation: we must not waste. As he explains,

> 'God has given us all things richly' ... But how far has he given it us? To enjoy. As much as any one can make use of to any advantage of life before it spoils ... whatever is beyond this is more than his share, and belongs to others.
>
> (Locke 1966: 17)

The tension between Locke's labour theory of acquisition and the provisos has given birth to a variety of interpretations, each one laying claim to what Locke 'really meant' by it (see Sreenivasan 1995 for a selection). I do not intend to survey these perspectives here. Instead, I want only to note that they are almost identical to those found in Pufendorf. The difference is only the context within which these provisos are expressed: Pufendorf relates them as direct features of the natural law, whereas Locke expresses them in terms of their ability to make private property work as a social system. Perhaps because of how directly the provisos echoed Pufendorf, they seem to work seamlessly within the substantive conception of the economy bequeathed by the natural law tradition in which the nature of property is circumscribed by the nature of the particular property in question. In terms of the subsistence economy that he draws his examples from in 'Of Property', Locke seems to rather be stating the obvious: where people only labour and acquire for their subsistence needs, population, economy and the use of material resources will be in balance. By its very nature, a subsistence economy implies not labouring for more than one needs to subsist, making wastage unlikely in the first place. But the medieval way of life had been shattered well before Locke's time by changes in demography, technology and economic system (see Bean 1963; Blanchard 1970; Harvey 1991). By this period, commercial society was a nascent reality, and so Locke conducts a second defence of property specific to this newer world, auguring a new mode of problematisation.

The transition from subsistence economy to commercial society is presented as a fall from grace in the *Two Treatises*. In place of the innate value of things in the subsistence economy ascribed by God and validated through the human impulse toward self-preservation, price in commercial society is, for Locke, based more or less on avarice alone: 'the desire of having more than man needed had altered the intrinsic value of things' (Locke 1966: 20). Locke's published and unpublished work is littered with disparaging remarks about the tendency towards covetousness and advice to limit the extent of self-interest as a mechanism for ordering human affairs, but nevertheless, even though private property in commercial society may result in substantial inequality, moral wrong or other, Locke argues that we have consented to such a property system since it was initially based on labour and human productivity, even if only in the distant, even hypothetical, past (Locke 1966: 26–27).

In this new vision of order, Locke has to find other theoretical props to fulfil his two provisos. Where they were incorporated into Pufendorf's account in an *ad hoc* way, Locke, for the first time, uses a specifically utilitarian justification. He argues that the appropriation of land increases productivity such that 'he who appropriates land to himself by this labour does not lessen but increase the common stock of mankind' (Locke 1966: 20). This was the ideology of 'improvement' (see also Wood 2002: 106) that Polanyi had documented as against 'habitation', as discussed in Chapter Two. The implication was that, whilst a mature system of private property may well result in hardship for some, the 'enough and good' proviso may still be honoured through increased productivity.

This was an extremely distinctive point of translation of the Thomistic problematisation of property into a commercial context. In the first half of 'Of Property', Locke is a classical natural lawyer through and through. Like Grotius, he sees private property as a result of the human need to subsist and like Pufendorf, this need is embedded within a religious discourse of communal service to God. This context appears to shape the provisos that Locke attaches to appropriation. However, within the context of commercial society, Locke functionally replaces this purpose with a more directly utilitarian justification for private property, a move made possible by the emphasis on the role of any system of property in sustaining social order. The provisos may still apply, but their basis is radically altered. Instead of residing within the natural law context of subsistence and self-provisioning, commercial society demands that they are met through commercial productivity.

Locke's complicated argument thus gathered economic themes together in a new way, perching between the mode of problematisation bequeathed by the natural law tradition and the reality of commercial society that surrounded him at the time. From this new combination, the two main arguments for capitalism that Polanyi recognised grew. Firstly, even though today Locke's prelapsarian/ postlapsarian argument strikes one as a rather cumbersome way to generate a moral argument for private property, it was necessary so that he could apply the universalistic outlook of the natural law tradition specifically to the context of commercial society. Secondly, and in service of this prior theoretical aim, he built the productivity associated with capitalist development into his theory of justice in private property ownership. This was the last time in which the juridical foundation of property would be explored in such depth within the natural law mode of economic problematisation.

Locke abstracted

Locke's influence on subsequent legal and political thought was prodigious and was felt throughout all significant political theory in the eighteenth century. As Harold Laski put it, 'English political thought, in the seventy years before the French Revolution, did little more than work out the implications of Locke's philosophy' (Laski 1962: 161). John Trenchard and Thomas Gordon's *Cato's Letters* (1723) adopted wholesale Lockean principles of government and property which, combined with a republican philosophy, were used to lay the intellectual foundations of the American Declaration of Independence. In terms of the development of thought on property, what is striking is how readily the complexities and the moral and religious context of Locke's argument would be left behind, leaving only a caricatured, 'disembedded' conception of property in absolute terms. The work of the English lawyer William Blackstone is most instructive in demonstrating this.

In 1765, Blackstone published the *Commentaries on the Laws of England* and whilst it is generally recognised that there was little originality in the hefty book, its virtue was in providing a complete and systematic Lockean approach to the English common law, which, until then had been fragmented and poorly understood. At the heart of the *Commentaries* is a much more intense and caricatured individualism, where the sole aim of state and society is to protect the absolute rights of the individual (Blackstone 1959: 30). This is reflected in his account of property rights:

> There is nothing which so generally strikes the imagination, and engages the affections of mankind, as the right of property; of that sole and despotic dominion which one man claims and exercises over the external things of the world, in the total exclusion of the right of any other individual in the universe.
>
> (Blackstone 1959: 131)

Throughout the book, the perfect, despotic property relation is treated as the ideal in each case and the more like despotic dominion a property right looks, the more powerful the right is (*e.g.* Blackstone 1959: 243).

Gone is the complexity of Locke's account, where private property is recounted as a by-product of humanity's fall, replaced by private property as the paradigmatic case and foundation for justice claims. As such, Blackstone managed to provide an authoritative justification for the *status quo* of private property in English law by combining a thorough knowledge of the inheritance of the

English common law with the power of a selective reading of Locke. Indeed, it is the power of this amalgamation – rationalistic, Lockean philosophy on one hand, the inherited wisdom of common law on the other – that made Blackstone's work so persuasive in England, whilst also making it seem approachable abroad. In result the book had a significant impact upon the course of the American Revolution as well as laying the foundations for legal orders elsewhere. Thomas Jefferson and Abraham Lincoln were advocates for it, and colonisers of all walks of life regularly used the *Commentaries* as a means to resolve minor disputes (Jones 1973: liii). Indeed Blackstone had intended the *Commentaries* to be applicable elsewhere precisely because Britain was an active coloniser at the time (Hall et al. 2005).

The emergence and diffusion of Blackstone's pristine and abstract account of private property as despotic dominion out of the more messy, politically and theologically located account of property found in the work of Locke and his forebears is important because it illustrates how idealised precepts become distilled out of the more nuanced and varied history of ideas that precede them. All lawyers worth their salt recognise property as a bundle of contingent, differential and variously limited claims to goods, as Blackstone himself did: whilst Blackstone is often credited with providing the first full and absolute account of private property in law, the remainder of the chapter in *Commentaries* is devoted to explaining how the various English categories of private property – estate, title, deed, tenure etc. – place legal limitations upon how far this absolute right can be claimed. But by the same token, this mode of exposition set up despotic dominion as the natural right, leaving the limitations embedded in the weaker common law. Dominion is placed at a lexically prior point in the analysis to possible limitations upon it, in much the same way that *laissez-faire* economic thought presents the market as the natural fibre of society upon which political power intervenes and disrupts. The contingency of dominion itself is effectively discounted.

Over the next century, the framework of jurisprudential thinking on economic matters was to change immensely, with the concept of property being subordinated to that of contract, which in turn foregrounded the idea of individual self-interest instead of the more loose and societal notion of agreement found in the work of the natural lawyers. In many ways, the ideas of contractual justice were already there in Blackstone, even in Locke and Pufendorf before, but simply obscured by a different linguistic frame. Blackstone employs a conception of the sovereign individual, from which flows his conception of despotic dominion – the extension of individualism into the material world – since the idea of absolute rights in a thing implies that the thing should be subject only to the will of the owner. In result, contractual relationships can be the only just way to organise people's property. However, the concept of property still had much substantive content to it. As we have seen, property was essentially a material thing in the natural law tradition, with restrictions upon use imposed by the qualities that any particular thing has. In Locke, the provisos generalise this notion in relation to land, implying that use is restricted by the need to ensure the reproduction of society and advancement of humanity in general. In Blackstone, although the provisos are absent, the English common law places similar limitations upon use. Contracts, as far as they related to property, were thus also circumscribed in particular ways.

By the nineteenth century, however, a much purer notion of contract rooted in individualist philosophy was to emerge. By this time, the aspiration to reduce social life to a set of the simplest possible rules had become an accepted method of approach to legal understandings of economic interaction (Swain 2015: 202). As Gordley notes, by this time 'contract was defined in terms of the will of the parties ... the will of the contracting parties or of the owner was then used as a first principle to explain as many legal rules as possible' (Gordley 1998: 67). The process was gradual, but by the latter half of the century, the most influential and widely read legal theorists were calling for as abstract an expression of contract as possible as the foundation of all law.

For example, in 1867, the prominent and widely respected English lawyer Stephen Leake advised his reader that, where contract had been previously dealt with in relation to specific matters such as land conveyance, sale of goods insurance etc., his thesis would find originality in 'treating the law of contracts in its general and abstract form' (Leake 1867: v). Similarly, Christopher Langdell's popular *A Summary of the Law of Contracts* built an entire conception of American jurisprudence upon a tautological exposition of a contract, where the principle is two people agreeing 'upon the basis of their willingness to agree' (Langdell 1880: 1–10). Other examples abound, not only from Anglophone countries, but from continental Europe, including France and Germany (Gordley 1991: 161). This gets us ahead of ourselves, however. Whilst Blackstone's caricature of Locke's account of property marks the end of process of translation of an understanding of the economy in a legal sense, it took place at exactly the time in the history of ideas when a whole new problematisation of property was emerging that, whilst clearly echoing the structure of the natural law problematisation, was sat squarely within the new philosophical contradictions of Enlightenment thought.

4 Justice, price and power

Property and justice in Enlightenment thought

In 1740, just over fifty years after Locke's *Two Treatises on Government*, Hume published the *Treatise on Human Nature*. In terms of translating matters of political economy out of a theological context, Hume is pivotal in so far as he was the first major political theorist to explicitly reject the role of religion in structuring political affairs. Book III of the *Treatise*, where Hume's most significant treatment of the relationship between justice and property occurs, opens with a rejection of the natural lawyers' attempts to grasp issues of justice through recourse to divine or 'natural' universals. Nevertheless, in terms of the final outcome of Hume's resounding advocation of the principles of justice and property, there is little that is truly novel when compared to Locke. Both seek to defend private property and Hume readily falls back on the benefits of material prosperity as justification in the same way as Locke. What is new is the framing and emphasis. As to the former, by retaining parts of Locke's overall argumentative framework, Hume effectively reproduces the universalism and abstraction of the natural law account, but translated into the context of an individualist ontology of self-interest. As to the latter, what emerges is a much more complete and assured argument for the co-constitution of property and justice. Such is the quality and cohesiveness of Hume's writing that, by the assumptions that he employs, his argument is extremely persuasive, representing the first time that a philosophy of the individual, only implicit in Locke, would be used explicitly to justify property rights.

The essential shape of Hume's argument is identical to Locke's in that it arises from a comparison between a state of nature and commercial society, but the terms upon which each is understood is radically altered. For Locke, we saw how the state of nature is imbued with an inherent justice, where each labours in proportion to his or her needs, free from interference. For Hume (who dismisses state-of-nature arguments in fact, but entertains them as useful argumentative devices anyway), this is quite literally the realm of beasts. Whether 'slim in needs, as a sheep, or voracious as a lion', the point is that, in such a state, 'advantages hold in proportion to wants' (Hume 1888: 485). For humanity, the idea of such harmony is a fiction. In contrast, he states an economic vision of human nature:

> Of all the animals, with which this globe is peopled, there is none towards whom nature seems, at first sight, to have exercis'd more cruelty than towards man, in the numberless wants and necessities, with which she has loaded him, and in the slender means, which she affords to the relieving these necessities.
>
> (Hume 1888: 484)

For Locke, entering commercial society is an inevitable fall from grace, legitimated by the God-given propensity toward industriousness and mitigated by the fruits of commercial society. For Hume, whilst no less inevitable and no less artificial, the justice and utility aspects of commercial society are mutually reinforcing. As he remarks, 'by the conjunction of forces, our power is augmented; by the partition of employments, our ability increases; and by mutual succour we are less expos'd to fortune and accidents' (Hume 1888: 485). He accepts much more readily the ameliorating effects of commercial society and because the utility of this system of property is so great, the concomitant system of justice is of absolute necessity:

> [Once people] have become sensible of the infinite advantages that result from [society] ... they must seek a remedy. ... this can be done after no other manner, than by a convention enter'd into by all the members of the society to bestow stability on the possession of those external goods, and leave every one in the peaceable enjoyment of what he may acquire by his fortune and industry.
>
> (Hume 1888: 489)

Whilst, following Hobbes rather than Locke, property and justice are matters of human agreement rather than natural law, property is still pitched as a matter of justice abstractly defined:

> After this convention, concerning abstinence from the possessions of others, is enter'd into, and every one has acquired a stability in his possessions, there immediately arise the ideas of justice and injustice; as also those of *property*, *right* and *obligation* ... 'Tis very preposterous, therefore, to imagine, that we can have any idea of property, without fully comprehending the nature of justice, and shewing its origin in the artifice and contrivance of men. The origin of justice explains that of property.
>
> (Hume 1888: 490–491)

In terms of the content of Hume's defence of property, much of the arguments covered in Chapter Three of this book remain. The natural law concern with legal principles upon which to derive social order is still in evidence. Nevertheless, in contrast to Locke's argument that private property is one possible way to order society in such a way conducive to society and the 'preservation of mankind', by rooting his argument in an ontology of self-interest, rather than divine order, Hume's achievement is in his bold argument that a system of private property is the *only* possible solution. Whilst this system may well be artificial in a sense, it is an inevitable product of human nature living in society.

Hume poses this argument within the context of a new contradictory account of human nature central to Enlightenment moral philosophy: the opposition of self-interest and benevolence as the two fundamental motivating sources of human behaviour. In Hume's universe, proximity is the measure of benevolence, and so of morality also: ' ... our strongest attention is confin'd to ourselves; our next is extended to our relations and acquaintance; and 'tis only the weakest which reaches to strangers and indifferent persons' (Hume 1888: 488). Since society, particularly commercial society, implies a vast majority of people that we do not know and therefore do not personally care for, benevolence cannot be a useful principle for social organisation. This leads Hume to conclude that social justice must be based on self-interest, which in turn produces his justification for private property. The key advance that Hume makes is thus to build his defence of property rights from the same rational, universal postulates about human nature as inform his juridical outlook in general. Self-interest may well replace the natural law as the foundation of his argument, but the universality of the mode of argumentation remains. Indeed, by constructing a notion of property and ownership from intuitive moral assumptions in this way, all substantive identity of factors of the economy – Grotius's maritime particularities, Pufendorf's limitations on price, the Lockean emphasis on the function of property – are all irrelevant.

This new mode of argumentation freed Hume from the contradiction that framed the thought of all the natural lawyers on the economy: how to justify the holding of private property in the context of the biblical or natural conception of property as owned by God. Yet, with this new form of universalism came a new contradiction, one which would prove just as durable in framing later thought on the relationship between property and justice: If property was the material expression of an abstract, if artificial, form of justice, surely that justice was put under threat by an uneven distribution of property? In later work, Hume was to admit this problem within the confines of a thought experiment: in *An Enquiry Concerning the Principles of Morals*, first published in 1777, he imagines a class of rational, but subservient, beings, coexisting with humans. The latter have absolute command whilst the former are only servile and obedient. In this condition, 'the restraints of justice and property being totally *useless*, would never have place in so unequal society' (Hume 1902: 191). Hume regards this as self-evidently the relation between humans and other animals, and goes on to chastise Europeans for maintaining such logic in relation to 'Indians', and men towards women (Hume 1902). But what about in relation to property in general? If property is unevenly spread, do people then have different amounts of justice?

If Hume's thought experiment just about touches on this problem, Jean-Jacques Rousseau's contemporary treatment of the issue drew out the contradiction to its fullest extent by generalising an opposition between freedom and power in relation to property. Like many of the scholars that have been discussed in this book so far, Rousseau conceived his theory within the confines of a state-of-nature argument. Like Hume, the state of nature is hypothetical for Rousseau (Rousseau 1984: 78), but unlike Hume, it is a meaningful image of the truly free individual. In *A Discourse on Inequality*, he explains:

> As long as men applied themselves only to work that one person could accomplish alone and to activities which did not require the collaboration of several hands, they lived as free, healthy, good and happy as the could be.
> (Rousseau 1984: 116)

However, upon entering society and the division of labour, all that changed:

> [F]rom the moment that one man needed the help of another, and it was realized that it would be useful for one man to have provisions enough for two, equality disappeared; property was introduced, work became necessary and the vast forests were transformed into pleasant fields which had to be watered with the sweat of men, and in which slavery and misery were soon seen to germinate with the crops.
> (Rousseau 1984)

The similarity to Locke's analytical framework is evident. Even though the religious aspect is not explicit, Rousseau still sees humanity's entrance into society and tacit legitimation of inequality as a fall from grace – indeed the essay was commissioned in part as an attempt to explain evil in a non-theological way (Masters and Kelly 1994: xi). However, where Locke regards the ensuing system of private property as unfortunate but just, and Hume regards it as justice itself, Rousseau stresses the injustice of inequality emotively as 'the fatal enlightenment of civilized man' (Rousseau 1984: 115). The basic idea that ownership of material things confers a certain type of freedom upon the holder is never in dispute. However, Rousseau emphasises that the institutionalisation of ownership, i.e. property, was only for the benefit of those who *had* substantial property:

> The poor, having nothing to lose but their freedom ... The rich, on the contrary, being vulnerable, so to speak, in every part of their possessions, it was much easier to injure them; and it was necessary in consequence for them to take more precautions for their own protection.
> (Rousseau 1984: 123–124)

So, to summarise, property does indeed confer one civic freedom, but that freedom can only accrue in relation to how much property one actually has.

Rousseau's next major work, *A Discourse on Political Economy*, which was penned for inclusion within Diderot and d'Alembert's *Encyclopédie*, developed this line of argument. An archetypal Enlightenment project, the *Encyclopédie* sought to challenge all vestiges of the old order, and in this respect, Rousseau does his part, providing several pages of critique of the idea of paternalism as a social principle. Instead, he recognises property as the foundation of civil society, an essential ingredient of individual freedom and the only reason to obey law without arbitrary power. However, Rousseau's tirade against power does not end with the monarchy. Rather, he suggests that the freedom that property offers is only one side of the coin. On the other is a different type of power relation, where the alienation that owning property entails must necessarily be enforced. To convey the sharpness with which Rousseau apprehends the limits of this new problematisation of property, it is worth quoting the text at length:

> Look into the motives which have induced men, once united by their common needs in a general society, to unite themselves still more intimately by means of civil societies: you will find no other motive than that of assuring the property, life and liberty of each member by the protection of all. But can men be forced to defend the liberty of any one among them, without trespassing on that of others? And how can they provide for the public needs, without alienating the individual property of those who are forced to contribute to them? With whatever sophistry all this may be covered over, it is certain that if any constraint can be laid on my will, I am no longer free, and that I am no longer master of my own property, if any one else can lay a hand on it.
>
> (Rousseau 1755)

For Rousseau, if we are to understand freedom as the ability to will something, then freedom is the power to exert that will over another and prevent them from exerting their own will. And this means that, if one has property, one has civil freedom and power, but at the expense of the civil freedom and power of another, since having property necessarily entails alienating someone else from it (Singer 2000).

Rousseau's approach to this new problematisation of property in terms of freedom and power was profoundly influential. It is this logic that paved the way for Marx's emphasis on property as a form of coercive power. Similarly, Max Weber argued that freedom in commercial society was entirely dependent upon the distribution of property, and that the less egalitarian that distribution is, the more people are able to coerce one another within the framework of contract law (Weber 1979: 232). For present purposes, however, a comparison of Hume and Rousseau's thoughts is useful because the two scholars neatly present us with antipodean points on the continuum of Enlightenment thought on this new problematisation of the economy.

Hume and Rousseau, whilst for a time enamoured with one another, fell out spectacularly as documented at the time by Hume in a pamphlet entitled *A Concise and Genuine Account of the Dispute between Mr Hume and*

Mr Rousseau, and more recently (and rather less partially) in *Rousseau's Dog: A Tale of Two Philosophers* by David Edmonds and John Eidinow (2007). Although this dispute was a thoroughly personal and ugly one, the mutual suspicion which fostered it spoke loudly of the different intellectual worlds that each of them inhabited. Hume was an establishment man whose work was as measured and temperate as his personality, whilst Rousseau was a radical outsider, whose work and lifestyle were strictly critical and anti-establishment. In virtually all respects, they were complete opposites, and in regards to commercial society, they reached opposed conclusions on its value to humanity. The new foundation of the justice of property in terms of self-interest offered up a new continuum of positions that one could take which they staked out in the strongest possible ways.

But despite the difference of their interpretations, the mode of problematisation of the economy remains similar: both share an understanding of commercial society, and the property relations upon which it is based, as a kind of complete form. This understanding is not reached through identification and comparison of specific, actual practices of property ownership, or of actual contract law. There is no contingency in their accounts, no room for variation or difference. Rather, they understand the problem in complete and abstract terms, with a system of property emerging as the material expression of a more abstract system of order rooted in contract. In an echo of Locke's formulation, and despite their secular expressions, the situation of their theses within a contrast between prelapsarian and postlapsarian human conditions lends a further universalising dynamic to the analysis. Whether beneficial or detrimental to the human condition, the economy as a nexus of property relations, appears to them as an objectively real system of order.

Price and power

Adam Smith's deep personal and intellectual affiliation with David Hume is well known. We are now also better understanding the influence that Rousseau had upon Smith. In the rare occasions when Smith does address Rousseau in published work, it seems merely to be raised in order to be dismissed. One example of this is his short dismissal of Rousseau's lionisation of the 'savage' state of humanity in the aforementioned *Discourse on Inequality* (Smith 1980: 250–251). On this fundamental issue, Smith situates himself squarely with Hume. Nevertheless, as recently explored by Dennis Rasmussen (2008) and Istvan Hont (2015) the situation was more complex: Smith did spend a great deal of time wrestling with Rousseau's challenge to commercial society, and the influence of that process can be traced both in his unpublished work explicitly, and in published books implicitly. This intellectual position, sitting somewhere between the two poles of Hume and Rousseau, results in a certain form of ambivalence which, whilst retaining much of Hume's account of justice in property, expresses a distinctly Rousseauian concern for the potential for power to frustrate that system.

In result, Smith's position on property is more nuanced in *The Wealth of Nations*. He takes on much of Hume's account initially. Whilst the first duty of the sovereign is to protect from outside attack, the second is 'that of protecting, as far as possible, every member of the society from the injustice or oppression of every other member of it' (Smith 1891: 560). Smith again sees justice as co-constitutive of property, since property is the main reason that people are likely to do active harm to one another. The passions of envy, resentment and malice may exist in any human, but it is only with the ownership of external possessions that this can be transformed into significant harm:

> The affluence of the rich incites the indignation of the poor, who are often both driven by want and prompted by envy to invade his possessions … The acquisition of valuable and extensive property, therefore, necessarily requires the establishment of civil government.
> (Smith 1891: 561)

Yet for Hume, justice and property are rather an all-or-nothing affair: a state of nature with no property, no justice and no civil power or a society with property, justice and civil power. Indeed, since he rejects the former as a fiction and constructs his vision of justice directly from his moral philosophy, civil society can only ever be an absolute. Smith, in a more historicist tone, sees the growth of property rights as more of a continuum, where, the more extensive property becomes, the more power must be exerted by government to protect it:

> Civil government supposes a certain subordination. But as the necessity of civil government grows up with the acquisition of valuable property, so the principal causes which naturally introduce subordination gradually grow up with the growth of that valuable property.
> (Smith 1891: 561)

We therefore begin to see the same opposition between freedom and power that is latent in the discussion of private property in Rousseau's account. One way to make this opposition clear is to analytically separate two meanings of property. On the one hand and in line with Hume, property is an extension of our will into the material world. Therefore, property is freedom of action. On the other, and drawing on Rousseau, property is an institution of power which subordinates all by enforcing non-interference with the property of others, regardless of how much they have. Where Hume establishes private property as a guarantor of individual freedom, Smith acknowledges that it must coexist with structures able to defend each from all, which are essentially power relations in that they rely upon subordination.

The tensions in this mode of problematisation also lurk in Smith's description of the price mechanism. For Smith, price serves a positive political and social function in co-ordinating the activities of people in a way that supplants the sovereign authority posited in earlier accounts (see Tribe 2015: 71). His ultimate concern is to show how people might live sociably with one another, and the price mechanism fulfils the role of providing a social fabric without the enforcement of hierarchy or obligation (Tribe 2015: 42). But, this is only the case in so far as the mechanism operates on 'natural' prices, which depend on the specific uses to which money is put. As Smith explains,

> When the price of any commodity is neither more nor less than what is sufficient to pay the rent of the land, the wages of the labour, and the profits of the stock employed in raising, preparing, and bringing it to market, according to their natural rates, the commodity is then sold for what may be called its natural price.
>
> (Smith 1891: 37)

As Matthew Watson has argued, for free exchange to take place within Smith's vision, the terms of the exchange must be struck on the basis of the intrinsic value of the product – what Smith calls its natural price – rather than the distribution of social power amongst the parties to the exchange (Watson 2007: 274). Normally, market prices will tend towards natural prices and, where some disturbance occurs, the forces of supply and demand will eventually remove the distortion (Smith 1891: 58) but, the possibility of systematic distortion is always there.

As so often highlighted in selective readings of Smith, he remarks that 'people of the same trade seldom meet together, even for merriment and diversion, but the conversation ends in a conspiracy against the public, or in some contrivance to raise prices', but less regularly cited is his extension of this idea to monopoly power:

> The price of monopoly is, upon every occasion, the highest which can be got. The natural price of the price of free competition, on the contrary, is the lowest which can be taken ... The one is upon every occasion the highest which can be squeezed out of the buyers ... the other is the lowest which the sellers can commonly afford to take, and at the same time continue their business.
>
> (Smith 1891: 62–63)

Some unevenness in the spread of power is a necessary feature of existence in a world in which there is anything other than competition between large numbers of exact equals. At one end of the spectrum, as soon as two people decide to co-operate rather than to compete (which is the whole point of the division of labour), they form a social unit within which the guiding principle is no longer competition. Through economies of scale, the garnering of expertise and knowledge, skill, trust *etc.*, such a social unit will inevitably have some power to set price. By this account, the power that a trade union or government exerts in the economy is similar to that exerted by a firm. Such co-operative blocs, whether market based, like firms, or based in social endeavour, like unions, will always exist in any but the most basic economy. Therefore, power must always be evident to some degree. At the very least, Smith's account seems to imply that we have some moral compunction to make sure that power is not too unevenly distributed amongst market participants. The freedom that Smith's market implies is thus at least partly contingent upon equitable social arrangements.

As such, Smith's system of private property and price emerges from the moral need to manage power within the context of a society of essentially free individuals. He takes the basis of Hume's defence of private property as the basis of legitimacy in the price mechanism, but combines it with an awareness of Rousseau's idea that private property is a means to power, and thus has to be controlled by ensuring that price must operate on something approaching the natural price of commodities. Smith's understanding of price thus emerges from the problematisation of the economy in terms of freedom and power, but the absolutist conclusions of either the Rousseauian or Humean response to that form of problematisation are eschewed. Rather than seeking to solve the problem in a theoretical sense, Smith is happy to declare that practical, contingent actions should be taken to address it. This 'middle ground' approach was distinctive to Smith. As Hont remarks, Smith's vision of commercial society sat between extreme visions of human nature as at base benevolent or antagonistic, and of societies based purely on self-interest or benevolence (2015: 9). Methodologically, Smith did not entertain the universalist and absolutist mindset of the natural law approach that still characterised, in different ways, the political economy of both Hume and Rousseau. He was instead a historicist and a particularist, more interested in deriving cautious conclusions from empirical evidence than in deducing conclusions from abstract theory (Hont 2015: 106).

The bifurcation of political economy

As we have seen, historical articulations of the nature of the economy have gone hand in hand with articulations of the nature of justice, and have often been framed within a desire for the conditions for order to emerge. Within that broad gambit, the recurrent form of problematisation is the relationship between the abstract and the real and the desire to provide theoretical reconciliation between the two. In the theological context, the problem is the relationship between the biblical injunction that property is given to humanity in common by God, and the utility of private property. This is expressed in pure form by Aquinas, and the natural lawyers after him all set about finding ever more ingenious ways to solve the problem, consistently emphasising themes of order and productivity in order to do so. Locke is pivotal because he used the argumentative device of the Fall of Man in order to re-articulate that order in specifically commercial terms, opposing property in common and property held by individuals directly.

Although the Enlightenment scholars re-founded their understanding of property on a humanistic philosophy of the individual, that opposition of individual and community was maintained in Hume and Rousseau's work through their reliance on the metaphor of the Fall. Moreover, this opposition effectively allowed the translation of the theological paradox into humanistic terms. The neatness, the clarity and the universality of Hume's account came at the cost of paradox, illustrated by the contrast with his opposite, Rousseau. Smith's unique intellectual position between these two scholars produced a complex synthesis which was marked by a sense of the theoretical paradoxes produced by the new world of contractual relationships between free individuals, both in terms of property and price. Most importantly, these potential paradoxes meant that the economic sphere had to be mediated and regulated by some force external to it, above all a sense of fairness and justice, as laid out plainly in Smith's *The Theory of Moral Sentiments* (Smith 1976).

It is striking how far this complex context of moral problematisation fell away in later theses on the nature of the economy. In the century after the publication of *The Wealth of Nations,* the seeds of the Industrial Revolution in England grew into the vast oaks of global capitalism, and from here on, explicitly moral justification for systems of property and contract become difficult to find. Concepts of property and contractual relationships between people had grown up alongside a commercial conception of society, but by this point the sheer utility of a system of private property in terms of wealth creation had perhaps come to be prized over its ability to deliver social order. From here on, more baldly utilitarian justifications, which featured in Locke, Hume and Smith in subtle and hedged forms only, took hold.

Jeremy Bentham, for example, was dismissive of the idea of property as any sort of right at all and he admitted, to a degree, Rousseau's point that property is not necessarily any good for those with none (Bentham 1978: 51). Nevertheless, he found justification purely in the abundance and industry that private property garnered (Bentham 1978: 52). Ricardo's early nineteenth-century theories of specialisation and comparative advantage were informed by a utilitarian logic also (*e.g.* Ricardo 1963: 67). By this time, political economy was coming to be seen as a set of principles which could be elaborated in service of improvement. Beyond Ricardo's effort, James Mill's *Elements of Political Economy* (Mill 1963) led the way in England, followed by John Stuart Mill's *Principles of Political Economy*. Mill the elder opened his book with the same utilitarian defence of market-trading in much the same way as Ricardo (1963: 1), as did his son who, although in a more circumspect tone, justified private property with reference to the utility that wealth delivers (Mill 1915: 199).

It was the marginalists, Stanley Jevons, Carl Menger and Léon Walras who were then to formalise the concept of utility, laying the foundations for the mathematical mode of economic analysis that has dominated the discipline ever since. In much the same way that Blackstone departed from the natural law tradition by distilling the abstract essence of the natural law approach to property, the tension, moral ambivalences, and sense of social costs evinced in the Enlightenment debate over the nature of the economy were gradually forgotten, replaced by technicality. Private property and contractual justice was assumed and economics thus allowed to happily grow into a science of wealth maximisation.

No doubt it was in part the extent to which the moral content of earlier economic thought had been suppressed that produced Marx's fiery opposition to the liberal economic view in the mid-nineteenth century: the completeness and assuredness of economic liberalism had to be matched by an equally complete and assured rejection of it. In contrast to the more fluid political economic debate during the eighteenth century over the virtues of commercial society and the relative costs and benefits of private property, trade, markets and the contractual organisation of society in general, Marx sought to re-describe political economy from first principles: production instead of exchange, capital instead of market, surplus value extraction instead of profit. This form of critique owed much in form to Rousseau's inversion of Hume's theory of property and contract in that both sought to re-describe relations of freedom in terms of power, but where Rousseau's vision is unstable, emotive and contingent, Marx's is absolute: his work betrays a search for something so certain and concrete as to resist critique. We have seen how the idea of a fall from grace was pivotal to changing justificatory schemas for economic activity in the work of Locke and Hume, and in this context it is worth reflecting briefly on the eschatological content of Marx's own work.

Marx's early work was written in the context of a German intellectual scene which was preoccupied with the relation between God and humanity, often expressed in the idea that, in contrast to times past, now God is man. In elaborations of this idea by Hegel and Feuerbach, religion amounted to a form of alienation which concealed this more fundamental truth and one which divided one's self (Hegel 1807: 251). Marx turned this theory on its head by taking it out of the theistic realm and into the material conditions of existence by travelling down the path, common to his contemporaries, of transferring alienation to the philosophical level, then to the political and finally to the economic (see Marx 1963a, 1963b, 1963c). Just as Hegel believed that religion, in its highest form, could allow us to reach the state of absolute knowledge, Marx believed that mankind's relationship with labour held the key to life without contradiction (Tucker 1961: 24–25). In later work, and through his collaboration with Engels, this notion of alienation would be applied to the conditions of the working class and in particular the mechanisation of work-life (*e.g.* Marx 1973: 43–44). By the time of writing *Capital*, Marx continued to humanise the concept, relating it specifically to the way in which workers experience their place within the capitalist economy. In one of the more passionate chapters of volume one, Marx talks of the worker as enslaved, dominated by and subjugated to the dehumanising power of capital (1995: 384). The meaning of alienation is ultimately intact, but it is made completely specific to how the workers around him at the time might have experienced it. Labour is objectified, machinery dominates the worker and a true understanding of his or her productive process is veiled (Marx 1995: 390–1).

The relationship between Marx's early and late work has been pored over many times, but the desire to find some ultimate scheme of meaning reverberates throughout, whether through the attainment of species-being in 'On the Jewish Question', or in the sense of the destruction of capitalism due to the declining rate of profit in *Grundrisse* and *Capital*. This quintessentially modernist desire to *prove* these things was arguably Marx's greatest failing. Intellectually, it would provoke decades of unenlightening debate about the precise conditions under which his logic could be said to hold or not hold, or over the precise meaning of this or that term. Politically, it provided a rhetoric of certainty which would be manipulated to destructive effect by authoritarians around the world.

The complete, ontological, and ultimately eschatological, nature of Marx's opposition meant that no compromise could be reached between his position and that of the liberal political economy emerging at the same time. As such, the nineteenth century can be thought of as a period in which the tensions emerging from the problematisation of the economy in the Enlightenment period came to harden into opposed positions, each of which had its own inner account of truth and reality of the nature of the economy. Where this content is at least explicit in Marx's work, it had become buried beneath the utilitarian dogma of its economic liberal opposite. It would be a full two centuries after the publication of *Wealth of Nations* before any fundamentally new modes of problematisation of the economy in the terms described in this chapter, this time couched explicitly in terms of the opposition of market and state.

5 Transcendence and the disembedding of economic ideas

Price and order in neoliberal thought

Illustrating the way in which the history of ideas often unfolds through oscillations of thesis and anti-thesis, Marx's rejection of liberal economics provoked an equally complete rejection of his own system by the economist Eugen Böhm von Bawerk and by other contemporaries in the late nineteenth century Austrian school of economic thought. In turn, Bawerk would inspire Ludwig von Mises, who was the most intellectually significant founder of the Mont Pelerin Society (MPS), the progenitor of neoliberal thought. A variety of work on the history of neoliberalism has recently emerged, all of which places emphasis on the MPS as a 'thought collective' (Mirowski and Plehwe 2009) or 'epistemic community' (Habermas 2006: 79) which exerted a powerful and singularly important effect upon the development of political economic thought, both scholarly and popular, over the course of the twentieth century (Burgin 2012; Mirowski and Plehwe 2009; Peck 2012). By all accounts, the formation of neoliberal ideas in the collaboration and contest between Mises, Hayek, Walter Lippman, Karl Popper and other members of the MPS exerted an unusually great impact upon the course of world affairs, translating their philosophy into practical policy at a variety of key historical junctures.

It is important, therefore to put the MPS, and neoliberalism more generally, into the context of the story of problematisation of the economy that we have observed so far – to recognise that the MPS and the neoliberal ideas which they promoted did not arrive out of thin air, or 'like some revelation in Hayek's bathtub at Mont Pelerin's Hotel du Parc' (Peck 2012: 39). As Peck and all other recent scholars of the MPS agree, the group's philosophy was always messy and hybridised from the very beginning, and in its most original early theoretical innovations, the MPS was consciously reviving and transforming the explicitly moral content of economic thought which had lain dormant in nineteenth century utilitarianism as it was applied to economic questions.

Smith's dualism between competition and monopoly, and its philosophical root in the dualism between freedom and power, assumed a pivotal role. In tune with classical liberal thought in general, the scholars of the MPS were fundamentally concerned with establishing the maximal conditions of freedom and minimising the ability of one to coerce another. What was different was how intensely and directly the MPS mapped this binary opposition of power and freedom on to the dualism of market and state, or in their vernacular, competition and planning. This extreme rendering was already evident in the work of Walter Lippmann, whose colloquiums in the 1930s were an important precursor to the MPS. Burgin gives us a strong sense of this new intensity in the following:

> Lippmann established a stark and dispiriting binary: those who wrote on contemporary economics were either committed to freedom or to totalitarian collectivism, and he perceived the vast majority of his contemporaries to be advocates of the latter. The 'premises of authoritarian collectivism have become the working beliefs, the self-evident assumptions, the unquestioned axioms ... of nearly every effort which lays claim to being enlightened, humane, and progressive', he asserted with astonishing sweep. Those who considered themselves liberals, progressives, or radicals were 'almost all collectivists in their conception of the economy, authoritarians in their conception of the state, totalitarians in their conception of society'. This polar understanding of economic policy, and its corresponding insinuation that gradual changes in the economy led inevitably toward a dictatorial state, became the defining trope of free-market polemics in the decade that followed.
>
> (2012: 60)

The first point of the MPS 'statement of aims' drafted in 1947 begins by declaring that 'individual freedom can be preserved only in a society in which an effective competitive market is the main agency for the direction of economic activity' (cited in Plehwe 2009: 22–23), and most of the following nine points effectively extend on this theme either directly or by warning of the perils of state-directed totalitarianism. In the foundational text of economic philosophy of the late Austrian School, *Human Action* (published in English in 1949 with an earlier German version in 1940), Mises expressed an equally resolute tone:

> Liberty and freedom are the conditions of man within a contractual society. Social cooperation under a system of private ownership of the means of production means that within the range of the market the individual is not bound to obey and to serve an overlord ... There is no kind of freedom and liberty other than the kind which the market economy brings about.
>
> (Mises 1949: 280)

For Mises, anything else must be an imposition of arbitrary power upon the individual.

With a force that only ideological fervour can deliver, Mises went on to argue that every conceivable freedom is based upon economic freedom, since, in any lesser condition, the authority, whoever it may be comprised of, has license to impose its will upon the individual in any way and at any time it chooses. Of course, Mises had a specific target in mind when thinking about power and authority in the economy: the communist state. His discussion rings out with an impassioned denouncement of the communist system as an unjust exercise of power over the individual. But by virtue of the abstract way in which he phrased the argument, all government activity was to be understood as morally suspect:

> The state, the social apparatus of coercion and compulsion, is by necessity a hegemonic bond. If government were in a position to expand its power ad libertum, it could abolish the market economy and substitute for it all round totalitarian socialism. In order to prevent this, it is necessary to curb the power of government. This is the meaning of all the struggles which men have fought for liberty.
>
> (Mises 1949: 281)

In Hayek's much more widely known polemic, *The Road to Serfdom*, published in the same year as Polanyi's *The Great Transformation*, the feel is exactly the same (Hayek 1994).

This group of authors was on a quest to emancipate people from the horrors of totalitarian rule and, in the process, to reiterate the sovereign right of the individual to self-determination. Thus, Hume's account of property as justice came back around, but embedded within a well-developed and sophisticated account of market economics and the price mechanism. As for Smith, the Austrian school was presented with the same terms of problematisation: a conceptual tension between monopoly and competition, which the Austrians extended to include the fabric of the market in its entirety. Mises suggested that, by engaging in the division of labour and specialisation, an individual or group of individuals inevitably tends towards monopoly in some sense. At the most basic level, a firm might have a monopoly over its premises and sales and the services that one lawyer provides will differ, however imperceptibly, from those that another delivers. In this sense, they have a monopoly (Mises 1949: 277). Again like Smith, Mises recognises that this results in a theoretical gap between monopoly price and competition price (Mises 1949). However, the key point is that, for Mises, *both* types of price are legitimate and just since both emerge from the process of competition itself (Mises 1949: 283).

Mises's justification for this viewpoint is labyrinthine, but his approach is captured in his notion of economics as a 'catallactic' science, by which he meant that all market outcomes can be understood in terms of the individual choices that go to make them up (Mises 1949: xiv). The type of economy that catallactic science posited was later coined 'catallaxy' by Hayek (Hayek 1978: 308), and fact that the object was defined after the methodology is significant: the methodology of catallactics manufactured the epistemological security necessary to make the ontological assumptions implied about the nature of economy-as-market suggested by the notion of catallaxy, which is the very essence of formalism, to use Polanyi's term.

The most significant thing about catallaxy – and this will become apparent in the following chapters – is that it establishes the market as *epistemologically pre-existent* to whatever power groupings may emerge as a result of competition, co-operation and specialisation. The essentials of this argument are repeated across the Mont Pelerin Society's work, for example by Hayek in *Individualism and Economic Order* (Hayek 1948). Murray Rothbard also re-affirmed this idea in his effort to revise Mises's thoughts on monopoly. He describes a Smithian continuum from competition to monopoly, but alters the appraisal of what constitutes the just exercise of power. For Rothbard, if a monopoly, cartel, firm or other has been produced on the market, then its size and power are automatically legitimate, even if it involved collusion. Monopoly price is just as just as any other price, therefore (Rothbard 2004: 657).

This particular response to Smith's problematisation of price, and the Enlightenment problematisation of the economy in general, travelled unchanged into Chicago School economics, principally via Milton Friedman. For Friedman, 'competition is an ideal type, like a Euclidean line or point. ... there is no such thing as "pure competition". Every producer has some effect, however tiny, on the price of the produce he produces' (Friedman 2002: 120). Again, he goes through many different aspects of monopoly power in the economy, but, to cut a long story short (see Van Horn 2009 for the fuller story), Rothbard's conclusion remains: such powers are legitimate since they were produced by the market mechanism itself and can, in theory, be dissolved by it legally. Yet the basic conception of the market is the same as Smith's in that, by engaging in the division of labour, specialising and generally being competitive, we distort the market in some way, with the maximum distortion being conditions of monopoly.

The Austrian and Chicago schools cannot claim to have solved the problem, since it is a conceptual paradox associated with the mode of problematisation. Rather, the change is in their appraisal of it with reference to power and freedom. In Smith's account, the distinction between natural and market prices implied power as an intrinsic part of the price mechanism and it can be inferred that we have a moral compunction to ensure that market prices approach natural prices in order for Smith's invisible hand to really work as a social system. In the work of the Austrian and Chicago School, freedom became a pre-price mechanism concept. Instead of accepting that any social system will inevitably require navigating between the poles of freedom and power towards a well-ordered society, they foundationalised the notion of freedom to such a degree that power could only ever be understood as the sum of individual freedoms expressed on the market. The problem of market power, which is essential to the competition-monopoly dualism, was thus conceptually transcended.

To reiterate, I do not want to downplay the various complexities, tensions and different positions which were at play in the MPS. Angus Burgin and Jamie Peck in particular have done a great deal to demonstrate that the MPS and the ensuing neoliberal project was always fractious, with many competing visions as to the appropriate aims for their new economic philosophy. The stripped down, hyper-market liberal accounts of Lippmann and Mises were only one voice amongst other, more moderated, ones which admitted various degrees of role for state and political authority generally. Even Hayek's version of the Mont Pelerin creed in *The Road to Serfdom* admitted a larger role for state – '"planning for competition" rather than "planning for freedom"' (Burgin 2012: 92). Similarly, the Friedman of the early 1950s saw himself, along with other MPS members, as a critic of *laissez-faire* rather than a supporter, precisely on account of the possible threat of individuals coming together to monopolise and thus to exert power over others unjustly (Burgin 2012: 181).

But, it was indeed the stripped down, simplistic, pro-market vision which reverberated longer and had the greater impact upon the development of economic thought. Friedman's 'soft', ordoliberal views hardened significantly over the 1950s (Burgin 2012: 171), and along with his colleagues at the University of Chicago, that harder position would provide the foundation for a range of decisive and powerful interventions into global political economy, from the restructuring of the Chilean economy (see Klein 2007; Valdés 1995), through to the transformation of many more countries through interventions on the appropriate role of international economic institutions such as the World Bank and the IMF. Beyond this, Chicago School scholars' views on the virtues of selling public assets, the construction of markets to provide public services, and above all the perils of regulation which challenges the authority of markets to decide economic outcomes, all became orthodoxy in the West over the course of the twentieth century.

Not discounting Friedman's own extraordinary personality, intelligence and energy, which undoubtedly served a critical role in propagating the stripped-down version of neoliberalism, the Cold War context added an additional oppositional form to economic thought. Few would argue that the Soviet bloc constituted anything but a system of domination. For many of those in the grip of the Soviet, there was a sense that nothing less than human freedom in principle and in practice was at stake in this ideological battle. In turn, questions of property, markets and price were driven to extremes with only two possible alternatives: a 'free' market economy or a full, centrally planned socialism. The extreme mode of argumentation was already in evidence in the work of Lippmann and Mises, but the real and palpable opposition of communism and capitalism provided a strong, real-world foundation for the kind of absolutist, oppositional mode of thought that the Chicago School exhibited.

Given this, where the MPS had seen itself as an explicitly philosophical enterprise, and one which had often faltered in converting its insights into practicable policy advice, the Chicago School economic thought of Friedman and his contemporaries regarded the moral case as having already been decided upon. In the same way that the moral ambiguities of Enlightenment thought on the nature of the economy and the price mechanism receded over the nineteenth century, the ambiguities and tensions of the early neoliberal pioneers was also gradually marginalised, to be replaced by a much purer emphasis on the virtues of markets against that of states. For Polanyi, it was the nineteenth-century utilitarians who peddled the disembedded market myth in that they saw life purely in economistic terms. In contrast, the economism of the Mont Pelerin/Chicago School was not one of ignorance, but wilful denial of all the tensions in the market mechanism that emerged from the Enlightenment problematisation of the nature of property and contract and, in Smith's case, price. Theirs was every bit a market *philosophy*, but one that denied the existence of the underlying contradictions of power and freedom at root – the same technique that Isaiah Berlin berated contemporary Marxists for indulging in.

The disembedding of economic ideas

In Chapter Two, we identified the underlying characteristics of Polanyi's critique of economism in terms of its critique of certain types of knowledge claims in general. This, I argued, allows us to move beyond the more simplistic denunciations of *laissez-faire* economic ideas which have been so often highlighted as a weakness in his thought. In response, I have now presented a more substantial history of economic ideas which concentrates on the problematisation of economy in terms of logical contradiction and possible transcendence. I have highlighted how 'the economy' has often been conceptualised within the confines of a central contradiction, whether between biblical and earthly conceptions of property, between property and freedom or property and power, or between competition and monopoly. In turn, I have mapped out the various ways in which those engaging with each form of problematisation have attempted to resolve or transcend it. In some cases – Pufendorf, Smith, early MPS thought, for example – such resolutions are pragmatic and hedged. In other cases – Grotius, Hume, Rousseau, late MPS/Chicago School thought – they are foundationalist and essentialising.

From this analysis, two important lessons emerge. The first concerns the *longue durée* of ideas about the economy as a sphere of human engagement distinct from the political and social. At the three critical periods – the culmination of the natural law tradition in Locke, the Enlightenment debate between Hume and Rousseau and in the early activities of the MPS, there are immediately striking moral ambivalences in play. At each point, a powerful new mode of abstraction comes into being which specifies the economy as a distinct sphere, yet its arrival is marred by a sense of loss or doubt. For Locke, this doubt is wrapped up in the contrast between prelapsarian and postlapsarian justifications for private property. Similarly, to greater and lesser degrees, Hume, Rousseau and Smith all recognised both the virtue and the vice inherent in the artificial world of contractual relationships between property owners and market participants. And, at least until the 1950s, the members of the MPS held a variety of opinions on the problem of power in the market economy. But in all three cases, whilst the new mode of abstraction would retain its centrality in shaping later thought, the moral ambivalence would be forgotten. Locke's theoretical fix of justice-through-property-after-the-fall would emerge as Blackstone's despotic dominion and Smith's substantive concerns about justice and fairness would be stripped away as economics began to be codified by the political economists of the nineteenth century. In this sense, each set of economic ideas became disembedded from the moral context in which they were posited.

This same dynamic is central to understanding the influence of the neoliberal thought collective on economic thought since. The MPS view on price and markets in general was driven not by brute economism or a concern for economic efficiency in the formal sense, but rather by a subtle and philosophical weaving together of narratives about political and social ends, building a powerful sense of the kind of society that could be achieved through the complete application of the price mechanism. Price was still a moral concept for Mises and Hayek, but the intensely moral and political positions that characterised early MPS thought were not to prove its most important legacy. Instead, through the work of Friedman and others, a very simple, pure faith in the ability of price mechanisms to solve human problems took root. Will Davies has characterised this change as a kind of moral crisis of neoliberalism:

> The seeds of the market's moral crisis are sown, once prices lose any relationship to an intrinsic notion of fairness. Budget airlines that advertise at one price, and then sell at another share a similar disdain for the moral authority of the price system as teenage looters for whom theft is simply more efficient than shopping. Visible, institutionalised prices become just one more empirical phenomenon within the shifting sands of capitalist evolution, rather than legitimate arbiters of worth, as Hayek had once hoped.
>
> (Davies 2014: 106)

All of this tells us that, over the long term, the history of economic ideas appears to abhor ambiguity. Simple, clean, abstract ideas win out over important but insoluble moral conundrums as the decades go by. Perhaps this is to be expected. As knowledge is handed down from person to person, from teacher to student, text to textbook, it becomes handy to have a distilled essence to pass on. It is perhaps also inherent in the transition from idea to policy practice as well. Locke's theory of property was certainly a reflection of the political battles of his day, but it was Blackstone who translated that thought into a programme of practicable governance, facilitating its transition into something performative in the world of law and policy. Similarly, while Smith's intellectual influence was prodigious, it was the codified, foundationalised version of market economics that emerged in the nineteenth century which really produced a system of government rooted in the *laissez-faire* idea. The same dynamic was once again at work in the neoliberal tradition. On the path from philosophical debate to 'actually existing neoliberalism' (Chandler 2014) a more pristine faith in the market emerged, and one which could be expressed and understood in simple terms as a practical heuristic for policy-making.

The second important lesson from these chapters is that ideas about the economy as a realm of potential order – 'visions of perfectibility' – have always been essential to this project of construction. As we will explore in the following chapters, recent conceptions of the market exhibit a variety of theoretically complex articulations of the potential for order to emerge from competitive, price-responsive engagement between people and firms in markets. But the idea of economic order in general can be traced right back to the Thomistic concern with the attainment of cosmic order on earth. The perfection of God was gradually supplanted by the perfection of a humanist, but no less abstract, conception of property and contract over the course of Enlightenment, but the related lesson is that this move came at the cost of a new form of paradox. The continuum of thought between Hume, Smith and Rousseau illustrated that the new liberal vision of anchoring theories of economic engagement in the freedom of the individual and the freedom to forge contracts independent of external authority begat a necessary paradox in relation to the possibility of power and domination to frustrate that very vision.

This paradox between freedom and power is of course at the centre of classical liberalism. From its inception, the idea of freedom as non-interference produced the obvious problem that life is scarcely possible without some form of interference on the part of others. Since Berlin's distinction between positive and negative forms of liberty, liberal political philosophers have done a lot to get over this paradox. More sensitive accounts of positive freedoms – freedom *to*, rather than freedom *from* – have provided the basis for a variety of interventions seeking to resuscitate an Aristotelian concern for human flourishing. And some of this approach has drifted into areas of economic scholarship. For example, Amartya Sen's Nobel Prize-winning argument (1999) that economic development could be understood in terms of positive claims to freedom of opportunity, and the concomitant requirement that states act to protect those freedoms, has influenced practicing development economists in important ways. Nevertheless, to the extent that the price mechanism remains at the heart of the way in which the economy is conceptualised as a sphere distinct from the political – which is to say to a great extent – the liberal paradox of freedom and power remains.

Given the centrality of the paradox, it is no surprise that the problematisation of price in terms of the paradox of monopoly and competition was the primary impetus behind the re-moralisation of accounts of the market in the neoliberal tradition. This was *the* central problem to be solved whilst the economy was still understood in moral terms. But where Smith was happy to simply appeal to our better sense of judgment in order to decide on whether economic outcomes are just, neoliberal thinkers sought to solve the problem of power within the parameters of the market model itself. Like Smith and Rousseau, Mises, Rothbard, Hayek and Friedman all accepted the basic tension between competition and monopoly and the fact that any actor in a price mechanism always has an effect on price. However, by assuming 'the market' as ontologically prior to the agents that populate it these authors arrived at the conclusion that any price is just, because it is produced by that market and can, in theory, be legally dissolved by it. By ontologising the market in this way, they effectively transcended the terms of the problem, conceptually closing the open contradiction of Enlightenment thought on contract.

Marketised social protection

It is this mode of political economy – as the resolution of contradiction through transcendence – that will become apparent in the following chapters. Whilst it is too much to draw a straight line from the utterances of the members of the Mont Pelerin Society to the various theories and policy regimes examined, it is in most cases clear that the same underlying conceptual shift was at work. The rationalism and essentialism that Polanyi had observed in late eighteenth/early nineteenth century political economy was being replayed, but in a different way. What we will see over the course of the following three chapters is that, in the time since Polanyi wrote *TGT*, a new political economic paradigm emerged where the aim was not merely to cope with the type of contradictions that Polanyi highlighted between habitation and improvement but, drawing on the neoliberal phrasing of the power-freedom problem, to erase or transcend the source of tensions altogether. In this new world, the interests of capital would dovetail perfectly with those of labour, the market would deliver social goods, the interests of the individual would be transparently realised through the institutional makeup of the economy. This was not so much 'markets *versus* social protection', as in Polanyi's thesis, but a perfected combination of the two: 'marketised social protection'. The history of thought on the economy as a distinct sphere is marked by a manifest desire for conceptual unity through abstraction, and this new world of marketised social protection was no different in that respect. What was new was specifically the way in which the new vision of perfectibility sought to transcend the opposition of habitation and improvement altogether.

Over the following pages, we observe three distinct economic policy areas in which such regimes of marketised social protection have taken form. Roughly conforming to Polanyi's three 'fictitious commodities', these areas are finance, the environment and welfare provision. In terms of finance, I chart out how economic policy discourse became increasingly underscored by the idea that market actors themselves could act as transmission belts for the types of structural risk that the financial system was itself producing. By defining the nature of the market in a particular way – as consisting of a given set of assets and a given set of investors – the theories that provided the intellectual justification for deregulation – particularly variants of financial portfolio theory and the infamous 'efficient markets hypothesis' – implied that markets could ensure structural economic stability of their own accord, resolving the tension between economic improvement through finance and the social habitation functions of the financial system as a matrix of human engagement.

In Chapter Seven, I move on to discuss regimes of marketised social protection of the environment through an analysis of the evolution of thought on carbon trading mechanisms, unpicking the economics of externalities as it evolved from Arthur Pigou's classic formulation through to that of Ronald Coase. Where Pigou had seen political authority as necessary in order to control environmental externalities (Pigou 1932), Coase made the revolutionary step of suggesting that, provided that property rights were complete in scope, externalities would never arise (Coase 1960). Instead, they would automatically be internalised through the price mechanism. In this case, then, the vision was of an infinite market connecting *all* potential assets and actors – the condition for resolving externalities and the thinking behind the popularity of carbon trading regimes as a way of combating global warming. I demonstrate the unrealism of this assumption by looking at how carbon trading regimes – specifically the European Union's Emissions Trading System and the Kyoto Clean Development Mechanism – have played out.

In Chapter Eight, I move on to discuss regimes of marketised welfare provision. Drawing on literature on the responsibilisation of individuals as a key motif of contemporary capitalism (O'Malley 1996; Langley 2007), I look at how welfare policy in the UK became increasingly underscored by the desire to make people personally accountable for their own long-term financial welfare whilst simultaneously attempting to deliver efficiency in the provision of that welfare via consumer choice. Although I suggest that the trend is evident in many areas of state provision, I look specifically at policies designed to encourage individuals to build up an asset base as a way to finance their own welfare needs – known as 'asset-based welfare' (Sherraden 1991) – as a partial alternative to state welfare provision. In this case, I argue that the economistic fallacy is the image of the individual as a rational capital accountant, capable of and willing to manage his or her long-term welfare interests as a balanced financial portfolio.

The primary emphasis is on understanding the history of these economic ideas with respect to the contradiction/transcendence couplet, and not on deciding on their success in empirical terms. But, in anticipation of the final chapter, we will also explore some of the fallacies inherent in the arguments for marketed systems of social protection which allowed policymakers to overlook the ongoing tension between habitation and improvement: financiers sought to *escape* the conditions of competition through innovation rather than to compute the risks *within* them. Carbon trading mechanism participants equally sought to *avoid* and *subvert* environmental property rights, rather than to passively allocate them in an 'economically rational' way. And the idea of asset-based welfare ignored the deep connections between personal finance and consumption practices which stood in tension, rather than in hand, with welfare provision. In all cases it becomes readily apparent that the Polanyian problematiques of habitation and improvement never went away, but merely appeared in new forms. Ordering economic thought in terms of politically popular visions of marketised perfection only served to deepen and widen the sense of an unbridgeable gap between what is and what 'ought' to be. To the varied fortunes of these new policy paradigms I now turn.

Part III
Marketised social protection

6 Money and finance

Monetary politics and economism

In Chapter Sixteen of *TGT*, Polanyi highlighted the way in which, by the twentieth century, money had come to play a dual role in the international economy, serving both improvement and habitation functions. Over the course of the nineteenth century, a stable form of international commodity money became essential to facilitate burgeoning global trade, hence the Gold Standard was established, which fixed the value of the currencies of participating nations to an arbitrary weight of gold. The effect of this, in theory, was to make the movement of money between subscribing nations an automatic by-product of payment for goods. If a country had a trade deficit for whatever reason, gold would leave that country, which would in turn depress domestic prices, boosting the competitiveness of exports and increased exports would in turn lead to a gold inflow, restoring balance. The opposite logic would operate in a country with a surplus. The Gold Standard also established the norm of 'sound money' – an even balance of payments account and low inflation – at the centre of all member states' actions (Polanyi 2001: 202–208). Initially, finitude of gold ensured lower inflation, but even as token money was increasingly utilised to stave off the worst deflationary effects of the system (a result of the same amount of gold being stretched across greater transactions as global trade grew), the 'rules of the game' still barred, or at least discouraged, states from directly manipulating the value of currency whether in order to adjust deficits or to offset economic cycles.

In theory once again, movement in domestic prices should not have mattered anyway. As per David Hume's quantity theory of money, upon which the Gold Standard was based, if the amount of money in an economy were to halve instantaneously, then all prices would also halve instantaneously resulting in no actual change in the relative fortunes of domestic economic actors. But Polanyi raised the obvious point that, in the real world, people and firms are not ambivalent about inflation and deflation because their livelihoods often depend upon the value of money on a day-to-day basis. Changes in that value affect different actors in the economy in different ways and, if the changes are big enough, can ruin the economy as a whole, destroying productive organisation instead of facilitating it. Naturally these possibilities are of interest to states and their creditors, but as Barry Eichengreen has argued, this was also a time in which voting franchises were expanding across Europe, meaning that populations had become more able to demand that governments act to maintain domestic monetary and economic stability (Eichengreen 2008: 2). Either way, Polanyi argues that nationalised central banking developed in order to manage the supply of credit so as to ensure a relatively stable economic environment for business in what amounted essentially to the mass socialisation of enterprise risk (Polanyi 2001: 201–202), the generally accepted perception being that, without such structural protection provided by political authority, price fluctuations would be large and continuous, making private enterprise too risky (Polanyi 2001).

Central banks, particularly the Bank of England, manipulated the money supply by sterilising capital flows, discouraging convertibility and, in some cases, even by trading gold on the open market (Knafo 2005) – all measures which contravened the logic of the Gold Standard. As such, governments found ways to slow, direct and manage changes in the price of money in order to enable the domestic economy to function. In times of growth and productivity, when trade was strong and predictable, central banks were able to do this effectively, but after the 1929 crash, this was no longer possible. With trade no longer forthcoming, countries tumbled out of the mechanism, forced to prioritise the domestic demands on money over their long-standing commitments to the gold peg. In turn, this laid the foundations for new ideologies of nationalism and 'self-sufficiency' (Polanyi 2001: 226). As Polanyi put it, 'the failure of the international system let loose the energies of history – the tracks were laid down by the tendencies inherent in a market society' (2001: 256).

For Polanyi, it was not necessarily the actual pressures exerted by the Gold Standard system, but rather the perceived need to remain 'on gold', driven by a conception of the relations between states' economies in terms of a perfectly functioning market. This idealised view of the exchange rate system perpetuated the conflict between states' obligations to the international market for money and to domestic societies without offering the conceptual resources necessary to address it. Within the liberal view, the only available explanation for actions contravening the logic of the Gold Standard system was the immoral and deviant desire for power. In one particularly memorable passage, Polanyi sarcastically dissects this view:

> The liberal argument ... asserted that sometime in the early 1880s imperialist passions began to stir in the Western countries, and destroyed the fruitful work of economic thinkers by their emotional appeal to tribal prejudice. ... After the Great War [World War I] the forces of Enlightenment had another chance of restoring the reign of reason but an unexpected outburst of imperialism ... upset the wagon of progress. The 'crafty animal',

the politician, had defeated the brain centers of the race – Geneva, Wall Street and the City of London.

(Polanyi 2001: 221)

As I noted in Chapter One, it was striking how readily the era which Polanyi discusses was recalled in the wake of 2008. The idea that the sub-prime mortgage crisis was the 'worst financial crisis since the Great Depression' was iterated repeatedly in the press (*e.g.* Jagger 2007; Louis, 2007), but also by influential economists (Shiller 2008), in documentary films (Open University/BBC, 2009), and by the IMF (Stewart 2008). And as countries around the world once again found themselves increasingly sensitive to the changing financial landscape, it was equally striking how the dots were joined between economic crisis and protectionist response. China's control over its currency's exchange rate (keeping the value of the yuan low in order to boost exports) became viewed increasingly as a dangerous example of 'beggar-thy-neighbour' protectionism, echoing the experience of the 1930s (*e.g.* Evans-Pritchard 2008; Krugman 2010; Navarro 2008). In 2009, the US signed in a stimulus package including a provision that barred federal funding for certain projects unless supplies were sourced in the US (US Congress 2009). This move was widely paralleled with the post-Great Depression 'Buy America' Act (Righter 2009), with Chinese Minister for Foreign Affairs Qin Yang arguing at the time that 'it is unreasonable to politicise the yuan exchange rate issue or engage in trade protectionism against China under the guise of the exchange rate issue' (Changzheng 2010). The debate has rumbled on, with Trump making accusations of Chinese currency manipulation throughout his electoral campaign and during his presidency so far, and with China rebuffing those accusations by turn.

Moreover, the eurozone crisis proved to be a virtual re-enactment of Polanyi's analysis of the 1930s. Mechanically, the eurozone is similar to the Gold Standard in that it fixes the exchange rates of currencies belonging to states with very different particular characteristics, including relatively higher and lower levels of productivity and wealth, different export/import characteristics as well as more nebulous differences in political climate and cultural particularities. And as we might expect, this arrangement provoked exactly the same kinds of problems as under the Gold Standard. Disparities between national participants in the eurozone mechanism were masked for some time by the proliferation of cheap credit, currency derivatives and a variety of off-balance sheet accounting techniques applied to national finances. But the massive contraction in global credit provoked by the sub-prime mortgage crisis removed that mask, with the results that a series of calls for fiscal 'readjustment' amongst debtor states were made, all in the name of maintaining the integrity and value of the euro, regardless of the harmful effects of the resulting austerity drive upon peoples' livelihoods in those nations (see Blyth 2013).

I have discussed the parallels between Polanyi's account of the Gold Standard and the politics of the eurozone crisis elsewhere (Holmes 2014a), but suffice to say, when the conditions that Polanyi described of the Gold Standard have been reproduced, the political tensions arising have borne a distinct resemblance. Just as in Polanyi's case, this dynamic made ideologies of nationalism, xenophobia and insularity more politically legitimate, with a sharp rise in euroscepticism taking place across the union (Chang 2012: 299; Medrano 2012; Serricchio et al. 2013: 56–58; Schimmelfennig 2014) and with increased visibility of nationalist, racist and fascist parties as major political forces. Even beyond this 'rise of the far right', it often proved more appealing for commentators to frame the crisis, and recovery efforts, in terms of the conflict of national interests – most often those of Greece and Germany – than in terms of the structural failures of the monetary system itself.

Yet it would be wrong to skip over the differences between then and now: in terms of monetary international political economy in general, things have come a long way since the Gold Standard. True, whilst the post-war Bretton Woods system was supposed to allow a forum for negotiation over currency pegs, it was never very successful in this role. In result, the same conflict between national and international demands on monetary policy (see Triffin 1960 for the classic statement of the problem) – this time in the US – led to its demise in 1971. But since then, the international monetary system has drifted further and further away from a norm of fixed exchange rates to one of floating rates. The advantage of such a norm *vis-à-vis* the monetary tensions that Polanyi identified is that it at least softens the contradiction that he saw between the international and domestic roles of money into a tension. The less fixed a currency's value is, the greater degree of autonomy a state has to trade off between monetary policy in the interest of supporting the international value of the currency for trade purposes and policy geared towards serving the needs of the domestic economy. This is so particularly since the 2008 financial crisis, when monetary intervention in defence of domestic financial systems has become a normal central bank activity. As we have seen, the Gold Standard de-legitimated monetary policy geared towards domestic economic goals, despite such goals being widely pursued, which produced the cognitive dissonance that undermined the economics of the system. Floating exchange rates at least make the trade-off explicit.

But what is not included in this sketch is the growing dominance of the private financial sector on states' perceptions of their policy options and interests. Across state after state, the lifting of exchange controls from the 1970s onwards, the changes to lending criteria and the expansion of access to financial markets to a broader spectrum of the population beyond traditional banks have come together to enable the rise of the gargantuan global financial industry that we know today. The nominal value of transactions undertaken in the private circuits of financial money now dwarf public accounts and the technologies of creation, trading and valuation of money in all its forms have shifted further and further towards the control of private financial market actors (Ryan-Collins et al. 2016). Foreign exchange markets push currency values up and down in a way not possible before, the ratio between central-bank-created money and private-bank-created money has grown vertiginously, securitisation has newly monetised whole asset classes and under the banner of financial innovation, entirely new forms of money have been created apace (Pryke and Allen 2000).

This situation seems quite normal now, but we shouldn't forget quite how dramatic the key turning points were. One such point was the crisis of the Exchange Rate Mechanism (ERM) – a precursor to European monetary union – in 1992, where the UK government 'did battle' with private financial speculators over the price of the pound. In contrast to the overt political management that went before, the government acted in this case as just another market speculator with its own opinion about the proper price of the currency. In the face of the combined clout of the world's major currency speculators, the Bank of England's reserves were woefully inadequate and so the pound was forced out of the mechanism, signalling a key victory for financial markets over state. In the following year, France was only spared the same fate by the European Central Bank, which widened the currency margin from 2.25% to 15% to prevent the franc from falling out of the mechanism as the pound had (Sidiropoulos et al. 2005: 379). The Asian financial crisis in 1997 followed a similar pattern in that the governments of the region (Thailand initially, then Indonesia and South Korea amongst others, and eventually Russia), in the face of the overwhelming resources of the global investment class, were unable to support their currencies through the use of reserves. Along with more-or-less constant pressure from bond markets on government's self-perception of their ability to engage in borrowing and spending, and an increasing fear of capital flight if non-finance friendly policies were pursued, these developments again marked a fundamental change in the way in which finance and economy were organised.

How was it that a class of global investors was allowed to accrue so much power by states? How did recurrent crises not lead to demands for curtailment of that power? These questions were thrown into sharp relief by the global financial crisis in 2008. How, given centuries of evidence for the risks posed to the economy by the unfettered activities of financial professionals, did the deregulation of finance become a norm of economic policy? The discipline of economics and its almost exclusive theoretical focus on neoclassical free market models came in for much flak. Queen Elizabeth's famous interrogation of economists at the London School of Economics in 2008 summed up the sentiment. Paraphrasing, she asked, why did none of these supposed experts notice the coming of the crisis? Economics students across the world began to challenge the authority of their own discipline, with organised walk-outs of economics modules at Harvard and publicly broadcasted challenges to the curriculum in the UK (Concerned Students of Economics 10 2011). Even the Bank of England took pause to consider whether economics, as a discipline, was churning out the right sort of minds to understand the economy, co-organising a conference entitled 'Are economics graduates fit for purpose?' in 2012 (see Coyle 2012a). Popular films like *Inside Job* cited the existence of a 'revolving door' between regulatory and regulated roles, promoting much justified suspicion concerning the capacity of governments to effectively regulate the financial industry on behalf of the broader economy and society.

The question remains though: *why* did deregulation of the financial industry become an accepted norm of economic policy? Capitalism depends on a degree of social legitimacy in order to function (Watson 2009a: 2) and so the important question is how the deregulatory norm became a saleable policy idea. In this chapter, I want to suggest that at least part of the answer to that question comes in the way in which economic theory presented a vision of financial order which would reconcile the tension between improvement and habitation through the operation of the price mechanism. In this vision, the risk-offsetting functions previously delivered by the state could now be delivered by financial market actors in a system of marketised social protection. No longer was the state required to act counter-cyclically, to stabilise price movements or to otherwise intervene in the operation of financial markets in order to protect productive organisation. Operating at precisely the same intersection that Polanyi saw as crucial to the dynamics of the Gold Standard – between money as a means of payment to facilitate productive organisation, and money as a market-traded commodity – investors were instead seen as capable of taking on the burdens of providing economic stability in the context of free credit markets. As such, it offered a mode of reasoning in which the tension between improvement and habitation could be transcended conceptually, if not in practice.

Financial market efficiency

Crucial to this new vision was a particular presentation of the idea of 'the market' as something independent of the activity of financial investors. Although couched in technical terms, this was essentially an outgrowth of the Misesian notion of the market as a tissue of human relations, epistemologically pre-existent to whatever human actions took place upon it. This idea was applied to finance through the development of portfolio theory over the middle of the twentieth century, first under the pen of Harry Markowitz, who was a student of Friedman at the University of Chicago and one of a number of economists at that time who were attempting to provide the mathematical tools necessary to achieve the goal of profitable investment given a world of perfect markets. The novelty in Markowitz's account was the idea that the characteristics of any particular currency, stock or bond or other asset were irrelevant to the rational investor. Rather, said investor should be interested only in the relationship between assets – their relative, not absolute, properties – in particular their degrees of correlation with one another in terms of the level of risk. The principle of diversification – avoiding investing in overly correlated assets – has been around as long as the concept of investment itself, but what Markowitz presented was the idea that an individual investor might be able to fully *know* how much risk she was taking at any one time, provided she knew the degree of correlation between assets (Markowitz 1952: 77).

This theory placed large informational demands upon the investor, in that she has to be able to compute all the various correlations between potential assets. At the time at which Markowitz put the theory forward, this put portfolio selection theory beyond all but the most established institutional investors capable of undergoing the required calculations. Given that problem, the next important step was the construction of a variable capable of expressing the risk/return properties of an asset in relation to that of the market as a whole, since that variable would make it simpler to decide how risky particular investments were in relation to one another. This step was taken by means of the development of the concept of 'beta', which, within portfolio theory, refers to the aggregate risk/return profile of an asset in relation to the market in its entirety. For example, say I invested in a fund which held all of the stocks available on Standard & Poor's index of 500 large-cap American stocks (S&P 500) with its investments in each company automatically held in proportion to weight on the index, my fund would be said to offer me pure beta exposure since my fortunes would rise and fall in direct correlation with the market as a whole.

In the Capital Assets Pricing Model (CAPM), developed over the course of the 1960s and 1970s by a further slew of Nobel Prize-winning economists, beta would be expressed as a coefficient that reflects the volatility of assets, where the beta of the whole market is 1.0. The further the beta coefficient deviates from 1.0, the less correlated it is with the market as a whole (Black et al. 1972; Sharpe 1992). According to CAPM-based portfolio theory, pure beta is the best possible type of exposure. As William Sharpe explains, 'the optimal combination of risky securities must include *all* securities; moreover, the proportion of each security must equal its proportionate value in the market as a whole' (Sharpe 1970: 82). This is because the market is assumed to be informationally efficient. Sharpe again: '[it] deals with a world in which there is complete agreement about future prospects' (Sharpe 1970: 80). So, prices reflect available information on fundamental values and investors respond to price triggers rationally by holding the most diversified portfolio possible, *i.e.* holding the entire market.

This conceptualisation of 'the market' was extremely significant for the investment industry because it offered a simple, transferable and scalable algorithm which could be adopted by any investor so as to hold an 'optimal' portfolio. And despite theoretical challenges by behavioural economists over the past two decades, it still forms the core rationale for most institutional investor strategies (*i.e.* pension funds, mutual funds, endowment funds *etc.*). But it also contains an extremely significant public policy implication: if financial markets are efficient, then the possibility of systemic distortion of prices – *i.e.* the departure of financial market valuations from 'fundamental' values – is impossible. In such a world, financial crisis is not possible.

If the concept of beta manufactured a mathematical proxy of 'the market' then the development of its other, 'alpha', constructed a particular image of the savvy investor acting upon that market. Alpha is the inverse of beta, referring to returns that cannot be explained by the movements of the market as a whole (Sharpe 1992, 2007: 100). When it comes to an investment decision, seeking alpha requires one to somehow weight one's investments towards particular assets over others in the same market. For example, if I were to invest in only five companies from the S&P 500 instead of in a fund tracking the entire index, and those companies did particularly well compared to the rest, then my investment would have earned an alpha return: I put the same amount of money at risk, but earned a better return from it. In order to earn alpha, one effectively has to 'beat the market' either through good timing or stock picking. So, in contrast to beta, alpha is supposedly all about the skill of the investor, depicting them as a discrete actor who *acts upon* the market. It is not only that portfolio theory assumes the existence of a market, but also that it depends upon a specific definition of the market as consisting of *a given set of investors and a given set of assets*. The market is not only there, but it is essentially static and knowable.

This assumption is, of course, just that: an assumption. In the real world, the scope of the market lies purely in how people choose to define it. For example, a manager investing in a stock market index with a wide range of stocks like the S&P 500 might calculate beta values on the basis of that index only, but at the same time, the manager is excluding the risk/return characteristics of stocks on other markets, for example the Nikkei 225 or the FTSE 100. If the S&P performs better than the others, have you then earned alpha in the global marketplace? At the other end of the spectrum, if you were to invest only in one type of stocks, say hi-tech, at a time when those stocks were generally outperforming other industries, say the late 1990s, would that not be better characterised as beta exposure? Clearly the beta benchmark hinges on what we call 'the market' in any one instance, what metrics we use to compare assets, who the investors are and what they are investing in.

Despite these conundrums, this new understanding of the market had important effects on the global investment industry. As we will see below, the growing visibility of the concept of alpha in investment practice was manifested in the concomitant rise of a new class of sophisticated, independent investors who sold themselves on their ability to deliver alpha returns. In contrast to traditional fund management which, they argued, sought merely to ride on the wave of economic growth and extract normal returns from investment, these new investors sold themselves on the basis that it is possible not just to ride the wave, but seek out eddies and irregularities in order to earn a better return on it. Good for them, we might say. But this portfolio theoretic idea was to become situated within a more general view of the functioning of financial markets which would produce an all-embracing vision of the economy which sat at precisely the same conceptual juncture as the Gold Standard – between the role of finance in the service of improvement and of habitation – reproducing the cognitive dissonance that underpinned that system but in a different way.

To see this, we have to consider the central theoretical weakness in CAPM theory: the assumption of informational efficiency in the marketplace. If markets *are* informationally efficient, then opportunities for alpha should not exist, since it implies the deviation of prices from fundamental values. Since information flows around the economy instantaneously, any pricing irregularity resulting in alpha must be eroded into beta equally instantaneously by competitive forces acting through the price mechanism. In theory, therefore, alpha should not exist. This tension is a reflection of what Matthew Watson calls the 'contradictory microfoundations of financialisation' (2009b). On the one hand, conditions of financialisation demand that firms attempt to drive their stock price into greater increases than the market average in order to generate capital gains, but, 'fund managers' basic theoretical training … revolves around the logical demonstration that an individual stock cannot systematically out-perform the market average' (2009b: 255).

Whilst working at the University of Chicago under the mentorship of Merton Miller, Eugene Fama proposed the now famed 'efficient markets hypothesis' (EMH), which offered a way to effectively synthesise the contradiction between alpha and beta by taking a more nuanced view of the flow of information around financial markets. Where CAPM assumed perfect information flow, for Fama, financial markets might exhibit varying degrees of informational efficiency, each with different implications for how financial markets allocate capital (Fama 1970). Individuals across the investing population may not necessarily behave optimally, precisely because information on the performance of assets is often restricted (Fama 1970: 383). Sometimes information about firms and assets is public, some private, sometimes the past performance of an asset is a good guide to how it will perform in the future, sometimes not. Moreover, financial markets are always constrained to some extent by geography, language, culture, technology and the measuring of costs against benefits incurred by investors in gathering as much information as possible in order to make the 'correct' investment decision. The entire pool of investable assets across the world is obviously much too large and too complex to be fully informationally efficient in the sense assumed in CAPM.

When reading the actual papers in which Fama developed it, the hypothesis appears as little more than a methodology for establishing the characteristics of different financial markets: the degree of informational efficiency was not an assumption, but rather something that could be tested empirically. But it also had an important normative dimension for public policy: if markets could exhibit different degrees of efficiency, and if such efficiency was an intrinsically good thing, then it was something which could be sought by policymakers. And given that, the alpha-seeking investor suddenly acquired potential structural significance. Even if particular investors are acting in a less-than-optimal way, perhaps exhibiting a bias towards stocks in their home country or in particular markets with which they are more familiar, the investor, on her quest for alpha, can rectify the resulting sub-optimal allocation of capital. So the argument runs, having a large amount of alpha-seeking investors investing all over the marketplace is like having a small army of experts dedicated to finding price discrepancies wherever they may be, thus enforcing efficiency in the discovery of prices that reflect fundamental values, what Marieke de Goede calls a 'market perfecting enterprise' (de Goede 2005: 143).

In this narrative, if a stock, currency or instrument is undervalued or overvalued by a sub-optimal, beta-led investing population, the investor can go long or short on the asset as she sees fit and signal the correct price to the rest of the market, earning a return in the process. One practitioner presents the commonly argued case that, if every investor became passive in the sense that they only sought beta exposure, markets would become 'ludicrously inefficient', since no one would be attempting to correct prices, instead simply following the herd and making do with beta returns (Jaeger 2003: xiii). Investors would thus appear to act as a structurally helpful counterbalance to the 'irrational exuberances' of the rest of the market. Generalising this, to the extent that markets were unhindered, financial markets could not help but manage the risks expressed across the entire market effectively, reducing the need for the types of overt state-led regulation of finance which served to control fluctuations in financial prices before.

In 2008, the idea that financial market investors would be naturally driven to manage economy-wide risk on behalf of governments suddenly seemed bizarre. Many, were quick to pile on, arguing that belief in EMH was the key driver behind the crisis because it had legitimated a climate of over-lax regulation and limited governmental oversight. In a public enquiry on the crisis, Alan Greenspan declared that he had 'found a flaw' in his philosophy of deregulation (cited in Andrews 2008). Paul Volker declared faith in rational expectations and market efficiency as the cause (2011). Even hardened Chicago School economist and lawyer Richard Posner argued that deregulation had gone too far (2009). It is easy enough to take such positions in retrospect, but it isn't enough to just say that it was an incorrect view, as if it was the wrong answer to a civil service entrance exam question. The question still remains: *why* was market efficiency such a persuasive policy idea in the first place? How did it come to be so dominant in the public policy image of what finance was and how financial markets related to the rest of the economy?

My answer to this question is that this type of economic theory sold as a policy idea because it offered a vision of the economy in which the contradiction between habitation and improvement could be transcended, implying that no difficult political choices had to be made between the interests of financiers and those of the rest of society or between financial industry-propelled improvement and the stability of the economy for everyone else. It was a new vision of perfectibility in regards of money, but where the Gold Standard vision depended on denying the role of finance in supporting habitation, the market efficiency view implied that habitation and improvement could be secured together. To see this all in action in a more empirical sense, we can observe how these ideas developed through the lens of the hedge fund industry over the second half of the twentieth century and into the twenty-first.

Hedge funds and financial innovation

Hedge funds were in many ways the archetype for the new era of private sector finance from the 1980s onwards. Using nothing more than intelligence, guile and a solid internet connection, these 'new market wizards' (Schwager 2001), could wring stratospheric sums of cash out of financial markets for personal gain, tearing up the cosy and predictable relationships between banks and stockbrokers that had existed before. But the hedge fund model can be traced all the way back to Alfred Winslow Jones, who is generally recognised to have set up the first such fund in 1949 (Ineichen 2003; Lindgren 2007). Jones sought to eliminate market-wide risk from his portfolio by selling short shares that were participating in the same market environment as his long portfolio as well as using the same technique to exploit price differences for similar goods in different marketplaces. Having faith in his abilities, he also borrowed significant sums in order to amplify his bets. These characteristics – short selling, arbitrage and leverage – are the distinctive markings of the hedge fund investment model, all geared towards outsmarting the lumbering beta-led investor population in the search for alpha returns.

Over the 1980s and 1990s, hedge funds came to be seen as the very expression of the power of the private financial industry over state management of the economy. They were, for example, instrumental in many of the key battles between market and state actors over the power to determine the value of money discussed above. George Soros received much critical opprobrium for using his *Quantum* hedge fund to bet against the value of the pound during the ERM crisis. Such was Soros's fund's reputation that, after having made the bet, many other hedge fund managers expressed their greater belief in his power to determine the value of the pound than that of the UK government, turning the possibility of being forced out of the ERM into a certainty. Hedge funds appeared to have made massive profits by using a similar strategy against the Thai baht in 1997, propelling the Asian financial crisis and deepening their infamy, although provoking little in the way of a regulatory response (Harmes 2002: 157).

In the wake of the sub-prime mortgage crisis, the sector again drew flak for much the same reasons: profiting at the expense of general decline. Short-selling strategies had proven to be useful in exploiting the dynamics of the crisis (Mackintosh 2008; Credit Suisse/Tremont 2008) but this time, regulators across the globe were surprisingly quick to pounce. The US Securities and Exchange Commission (SEC) banned short sales in over 900 financial companies, the Financial Services Authority (FSA) in the UK enacted a similar ban on its financial stocks and respective regulatory organisations from all major trading bases around the world went on to follow suit (*Financial Times* 2008: 32). Nevertheless, the focus on short selling in the SEC and FSA rulings only really functioned to defend the values of stocks at the height of the crisis, and certainly did not present any serious challenge to the viability of the hedge fund sector. Moreover, these headline-worthy events masked the true penetration of the hedge funds into the workings of Western capitalism. For one thing, the number of hedge funds and their assets under management had increased greatly since the 1980s. In 1990, there were under 1,000 funds managing $25 billion in assets, but by 2004, there were more than 8,000 managing almost $1000 billion globally (Hardie and MacKenzie 2007: 60) with best estimates of assets under management by 2008 hovering around the $2.5–2.7 trillion mark (Hedge Fund Intelligence 2008; International Financial Services London 2008).

More importantly, the hedge fund model had, over the previous two decades, become increasingly integrated into the wider ecology of finance both in terms of a profusion of hedge fund-related institutional forms and as a specific type of investment ethos. In particular, vast sums of money were being increasingly diverted from the traditionally risk averse pension fund sector, which had previously restricted itself more or less to pure beta strategies, into the racy world of alpha-led hedge fund investment. Greenwich Associates found that the mean allocation of pension assets from pension funds to hedge funds rose from 1% in 2001 to 5% in 2004 and was up as far as 20% for endowment funds (Ezrati 2006: 122). Reliable survey data suggested that, in 2000, the institutional share of hedge fund capital flows was around 2% compared to 98% for individuals. As of 2008, those figures had changed dramatically, with institutional investors' share rising to 55% share (International Financial Services London 2008).

To attract more pension fund money, hedge funds were starting to be indexed in the same way as ordinary stocks and shares by companies like the FTSE group, Standard and Poor's and Wilshire, with hedge funds making conscious efforts to make their portfolios more accessible to the wider investment community (Fung and Hsieh 2006: 1). 'Funds of hedge funds' started to appear, which take investments and invest them in a variety of hedge funds and synthetic derivatives were developed in order to replicate hedge fund long/short strategies (Gieve 2006: 448; Jacobs and Levy 2007). And although a significant proportion of hedge funds are discrete institutions, built around one investor who fronts at least half of the capital themselves, many more function as departments within established financial institutions. For example, at the break of the credit crunch, Barclays, Goldman Sachs, UBS and HSBC all appeared in the top ten largest funds (or funds of funds) with JP Morgan topping the list (International Financial Services London 2008: Table 1). All of this meant that, by 2008 hedge fund or hedge fund-like investment vehicles were central to the functioning of the global investment system.

Some of this activity was based in the 'real' economy, where hedge funds were increasingly to be found providing alternative means of finance to traditional bank-based company loans. As Philip Coggan of *The Economist* noted,

> [H]edge funds are virtually setting up an alternative financial system, replacing banks as providers of liquidity to markets and insurers of last resort for risks such as hurricanes, and replacing pension and mutual funds as the most significant investors in many companies.
>
> (Coggan 2008: 1–2)

Some hedge funds sought instead to generate value by behaving more like private equity firms, buying up ailing businesses and finding ways to boost their share price. More importantly, they were propelling the growth of financial derivatives. Greenwich Associates found that, during the year April 2006/April 2007, hedge funds were responsible for nearly 30% of all US fixed-income trading, 55% of activity in all US investment-grade derivatives, a whopping 80% for high-yield derivatives and an equally staggering 85% of volume in distressed debt securities (Karmin 2007). Whole new classes of products were being rolled out in order to meet the needs of these new investment vehicles. Financial innovation is as old as capitalism itself, but the speed at which convertible bonds, credit default swaps, managed futures, options of all sorts, as well as collateralisation, tranching and securitisation in general blossomed over the 1990s and 2000s was quite remarkable.

How were we to make sense of this explosion of innovation and the wider transformation of the financial sector? There was only one option in the increasingly pervasive language of portfolio financial theory: the sector had become immensely more skilled at managing risk. If fund managers were rational towards risk, and if they had the newly developed theoretical tools in order to rationally manage risks in their investment practices, why else would they want to trade more? Within the context of EMH thinking, increased investment activity was a veritable boon for market-provided structural risk management. The increased centrality of alpha-type investment practices must have been bringing stronger forms of efficiency closer than ever before. Again, this view seems bizarre now. Both before and after the financial crisis, academic research (as opposed to the mountains of puff literature produced from within the industry itself) consistently showed that hedge fund returns could largely be explained in terms of taking on extra systemic risk rather than in terms of the exploitation of alpha opportunities (Fung and Hsieh 1997, 2001; Fung et al. 2008; Foster and Peyton Young 2008a, 2008b). Herding effects were found to be rampant in the industry, indicating that, far from acting as an army of price discrepancy busters, hedge funds were, often acting as a group, ramping up asset prices and extracting rentier incomes in the process (Boyson et al. 2006: 29–30; Till 2004).

The EMH view was, nevertheless, readily taken on by policymakers right up to the crisis in 2008. Engelen et al. (2010: 35) collected some typical quotes from 2007 including chairman of the US Federal Reserve, Ben Bernanke: 'in some respects financial innovation makes risk management easier' because it can be 'sliced and diced, moved off the balance sheet and hedged by derivative instruments'; the Bank of England: 'in recent years, there has been much greater scope to pool and transfer risks, potentially offering substantial welfare benefits for borrowers and lenders'; and most unfortunately, Adrian Blundell-Wignall of the Organisation for Economic Cooperation and Development (OECD): 'sub-prime lending is a new innovation ... the big benefit is that people who previously could not dream of owning a home share in the benefits of the financial innovation'. Regulators applied the same logic to hedge funds verbatim. In one report, the US Federal Reserve assumed that capital markets deliver welfare in proportion to their efficiency and thus warded against regulation of hedge funds on the basis that such regulation 'would likely diminish the beneficial effect of hedge funds on market liquidity and price discovery' (Kambhu et al. 2007: 14). The FSA echoed these sentiments precisely, arguing that hedge funds 'significantly enhanc[e] liquidity and market efficiency' (Financial Services Authority 2005: 5). In the immediate wake of the sub-prime crisis, it was even suggested that hedge funds be liberated from government restrictions in order to pick up these distressed assets in order to stabilise stock markets (Shrimpton 2008), appealing to the idea that hedge funds could mitigate the effects of the crisis, rather than exacerbate them. Reports in the aftermath continued to absent hedge funds from any significant blame (Lysandrou 2012).

Concluding comments

It is easy to smirk at the ridiculousness of the views of professional economists and regulators in the run up to the crisis, but to smirk is to see regulators simply as captured or duped by the ideology of financial professionals. We need instead to reflect on how that ideology worked and why it could be persuasive at all. By the argument presented in this book, the answer to this question is that it worked because it offered a way to transcend the key problematique of capitalism that Polanyi identified between habitation and improvement. The EMH view suggested that there was not only no tension between the interests of financiers in making profit and the stability of the economic system as a whole, but that in fact the latter was dependent on the former. The EMH view did not merely sweep the structural risks associated with financial innovation under the analytical carpet. Rather, it turned them on their heads: increased trading was proportional to increased risk management. As you will recall, risk is, according to Polanyi, the key property of a market in productive organisation that necessitated a system of central banking provision and state oversight. Thus, if the structural role of sophisticated investors like hedge funds came to be understood as one of reducing uncertainty *as well as* providing more liquidity, then they appeared as both force for economic improvement and structurally protective price stabiliser. Crisis could not occur within a market by this description.

Ultimately, to make sense, this view depended on the Misesian understanding of the market. By the time Sharpe, Scholes, Merton, Black and Fama took up their pens, the idea of an already existing market was firmly embedded in the intellectual tradition of economics and particularly amongst the Chicago/Harvard/Stanford circles in which they moved (see Mehrling 2005). Within this framework, it did not make sense to speak of market size, or of the notion that inflation in the size of a market might also inflate the risks associated with it, since 'the market' is already omni-present and infinite in scope. This then mutated into the notion that financial markets can be described as consisting of a given set of investors and a given set of assets. Within that world view, the power of competition to stabilise prices made perfect sense.

But this view had no way to conceptualise actual economic growth and transformation – *i.e.* improvement – in the financial sector. The explosion of financial innovation over the 1990s and 2000s was a reflection not of a sudden increase in the abilities of financiers to manage risk but rather of the ordinary capitalist practice of finding new ways to generate profit. And this translated into the drive not to compute and hedge against a given set of risks, but rather to create entirely new classes of risk. The development of fixed income options out of Treasury Bonds in the 1980s, of credit default swaps out of corporate debt in the 1990s, and of collateralised mortgage obligations out of plain old mortgage debt in the 2000s all followed the same pattern (Bookstaber 2007). Rather than engaging in an existing, given, competitive marketplace, financiers sought effectively to evade those conditions of competition by creating altogether new markets. Indeed, to innovate within the context of a system of private property rights and patent law was simply to establish a temporary monopoly over something as reward for the effort expended in the act of innovation itself. The difference here was the lack of patent law, contributing to the rapid growth of financial innovation in general over recent decades. Lacking such a structural/legal mechanism of resistance, actors in the marketplace were free to innovate their way out of one market in the constant search for a new one in which to secure profits. Provision of finance is a part of the ordinary business of capitalist growth and the liquidity provided by new shadow banking mechanisms offered by hedge funds and hedge fund-like business models were no different. But all common sense suggests that the extension of finance to a wider range of borrowers must come with additional risk. Similarly, the rapid profusion of derivatives propelled by hedge funds should have been recognised for what it was: an expansion of the volume and number of classes of risk available to be taken in the name of speculating for profit.

There were various lines of causation leading up to the 2008 financial crisis, but amongst them, the practices of financial innovation stand out. The creation of new markets constructed new equivalences between different people and different types of assets, which were then recycled through layers and layers of derivatives contracts of one type or another. The growth of financial capital apparently depended upon this intensive co-mingling of fates, but ultimately the complexity revealed its chaotic nature: the speed at which a set of defaults in the backwaters of the US mortgage market turned into a global recession vividly recalled 'the hazards of planetary interdependence' (Polanyi 2001: 190) that Polanyi saw as the necessary other to the unchecked growth of international capital market integration.

The 1929 crash, the Great Depression and the failure of the Gold Standard system comprehensively demonstrated that there is a conflict between the social demands put on the financial system as a machine for driving improvement and as a means for delivering habitation and the experience of financial crisis since 2008 has powerfully re-illustrated that conflict. The difference is that, where the *laissez-faire* economics of the Gold Standard denied the habitation supporting functions of the financial system, the EMH view internalised the entire problematique within its description of a properly functioning financial system. It was this combination of opposites – habitation within improvement, society through economy, state risk management via market actors – that generated the conceptual space and political legitimacy for the vast growth of the financial services sector across the world. It sold because it offered the hope of a 'win-win' situation without any of the traditional political trade-offs between economic stability and economic freedom, or between the powerful investment classes and the rest. But on the other hand, this mode of thought led to a profound conceptual ignorance of the way in which actors like hedge funds creatively competed against one another to generate risk. Although the following chapters deal with utterly different policy areas, this same pattern – where an underlying economistic fallacy rooted in the idea of transcending the opposition of habitation and improvement – conjoins the various cases discussed.

7 Nature and climate change

Polanyian ecological politics

Polanyi's insights on the relationship between environment and economy look no less relevant today than those regarding money and finance. As we saw in Chapter Two, he did not dispute the benefits of material growth produced by the forces of exponential economic improvement – a 'boundless increase of wealth' (2001: 88) – occurring since the Industrial Revolution. The problem was rather a world view which saw *only* this improvement. In Polanyi's stylised history, nature comes increasingly to be thought of as the commodity 'land' in a process starting with the English enclosures and ending with British colonialism. During the Tudor period, the privatisation of farmland via enclosure, whilst spurring increased productivity, also sped up the degradation of soil. Then, with the growth of industrial capitalism in the nineteenth century, the birth of the modern town and city demanded exponentially increasing amounts of food and raw material supplies, which entailed further economic rationalisation of the English countryside. Finally, economic growth would require the extension of production to overseas and colonial territories in order to sate demand (Polanyi 2001: 188).

All of this led to much economic growth, but as he remarks,

> The economic function is but one of many vital functions of land. It invests man's life with stability; it is the site of his habitation; it is a condition of his physical safety; it is the landscape and the seasons. We might as well imagine his being born without hands and feet as carrying on his life without land.
>
> (Polanyi 2001: 187)

Land, or nature, is simply the material world in which human life is lived: an inescapable, banal condition of being. Today, advances in ecological and biological science lend credence to this view: living things, including humans, are all reciprocally dependent upon one another for the reproduction of the environment upon which they depend. Although the length of the modern food chain and the industrialisation of agriculture serves to obscure this web of relationships, we are still obviously dependent upon the soil in order to grow plants to eat, plants are dependent upon insects and animals in order to procreate and everything is dependent upon the macro-ecological cycle of carbon through the flora and fauna of the planet in order to regulate the climate and the chemical makeup of the atmosphere and oceans (Clapp and Dauvergne 2005; IPCC 2014).

In treating nature as a material resource and subjecting it to logics of efficiency and growth, the inflation in the size of the economy had detrimental effects on the environment as a site of habitation. Polanyi lists the possible victims of unchecked growth including, somewhat presciently, 'the climate of the country which might suffer from the denudation of forests, from erosions and dust bowls' (Polanyi 2001: 193). Given that the habitation functions of the environment do not respond directly to the supply and demand mechanism, Polanyi argues that it was natural for confidence to turn to 'such forces outside the market system, which are capable of ensuring common interests jeopardised by that system' (Polanyi 2001) – *i.e.* legislation. Speaking of the nineteenth century he notes that the colonial territories did not have the political and legal infrastructure required to tame the exploitative actions of incoming colonialists, leading to mass land-grabbing and unchecked cultivation, whilst in Europe, legislative mechanisms were developed enough to prevent the worst excesses of the growth of the economy upon nature: common law across Europe acted to slow down the effects of urbanisation by providing allotments, preventing population movements from occurring too fast and preventing too many cases of the over-grazing that had led to the ruin of the soil in early-modern Spain (Polanyi 2001: 191). As such, in England at least, economic improvement was partially hindered by political authority acting in the name of habitation.

The continued exponential growth of human industry has driven our sense of the tension between habitation and improvement up to the global level (Gray 2002), epitomised by the centrality of climate change to contemporary debate on the relationship between human activity and the rest of the environment. The sorts of localised environmental degradation that Polanyi talks about in *TGT* have been replaced by the sense of a generalised contradiction between global economic growth, which is largely based on the burning of fossil fuels, and the resultant emission of greenhouse gases into the atmosphere, and the viability of the planet as a habitat for humans, which is dependent upon the emission of those greenhouse gases being massively curbed. Quite apart from the sheer difference in scale, this globality presents unique problems that rule out the types of political responses that Polanyi details. Globality means that the colonial expansion method is out: there are no other climates, other oceans, or other land masses that we can move on to. As Kenneth Boulding argued, the earth is like a spaceship in that it is a closed system in respect to physical materials (Boulding 1966), and so we have to a) live on the resources available on the planet and b) live with whatever environmental damages occur as a result of production. Barring techno-futurist fantasies of uploading human consciousness to 'the cloud' and thus dispensing with the need for a habitable planet altogether, we cannot respond to environmental degradation as the nineteenth-century colonialists did – by finding virgin territories upon which to build value. Garrett Hardin captured the predicament neatly enough, by noting that, when environmental problems are global, 'there is no "away" to throw to' (Hardin 1993: 201).

The globality of the problem also presents unique difficulties for the legislative options that Polanyi details in domestic contexts. Without a global state-like authority to counteract or inhibit competition, any concerted, universal action to constrain and control the self-interested action of firms and individuals seems difficult. Whilst states understand themselves as locked in global economic competition, a traditional regulatory approach to climate change is fully exposed to the pantheon of game theoretic problems associated with the anarchistic view of international politics: free-riding, collective inaction and the tragedy of the commons (Copeland and Taylor 2005; Hardin 1968; McLean 2008; Silva and Zhu 2009). Conceived in this way, climate change appears something like a 'prisoners' dilemma' (Dreshner 1961; Poundstone 1992). Assuming that preventing climate change via the mitigation of carbon emissions costs money, then the benefits from defecting (*i.e.* not mitigating emissions) will always exceed the benefits from cooperating (*i.e.* mitigating). If everyone defects, then a particular individual has no interest in co-operating, and even if everyone else co-operates it is still in a particular person's interest to defect and act as a free rider on the effort of others (McLean 2008: 185). By this rationale, the two methods of dealing with environmental degradation familiar to capitalist society – expansion to new territory or inhibition of productive activity by law – are rendered inoperable. The conditions for a double movement of the type that Polanyi envisaged simply do not exist when states conceive of themselves as players in a game of global economic competition for growth.

Obviously there is nothing physically stopping states from refusing to consider themselves as part of that game, but the odds are stacked against any such refusal by the degree to which economic growth is embedded in the fabric of political practice. Governments are turned in and out on the basis of whether they have delivered it and for good reason: we live in a world where livelihood has become dependent on it. As Serge Latouche notes, 'The need to accumulate means that growth is an "iron corset". Jobs, retirement pensions and increased public spending (education, law and order, justice, culture, transport, health, etc.) all presuppose a constant rise in Gross Domestic Product' (2009: 16). To this extent we appear stuck in an intractable tension between the simultaneous need for improvement and the need for habitation.

This chapter examines international environmental policy interventions rooted in the notion of transcending this contradiction between habitation and improvement. In the previous section we saw how twentieth-century financial theory sought to erase the Polanyian contradiction between financial growth and financial stability by arguing that financial capital was compelled, by its nature, to self-regulate in the interests of economic stability. The CAPM and EMH suggested that free financial capital simultaneously boosted material welfare for a wide social constituency, provided the optimum level of finance for production and also made the process of price discovery efficient, overcoming the tension that Polanyi identified. In this chapter, I examine a set of policy responses to climate change – principally the various mechanisms of international carbon trading that have been established in recent decades – that were similar in that they were also based on economic theory which sought to erase the tension between improvement and habitation by theoretical *fiat*, whilst also responding to the despondency of game theoretic approaches to climate change.

As in Chapter Six, policy developments concerning environmental degradation and pollution mitigation were prefigured by changes in the way that economists thought about the material world over the twentieth century. Just as portfolio theory had melded economic growth and structural protection into a theoretical unity, social cost economics made a transition from traditional Polanyian double movement dynamics towards a synthesis of the desire for growth and the protection of the environment as a site for habitation, reflecting a quite different form of economistic fallacy to the biological essentialism that underscored Polanyi's version.

Externality and social cost

The most basic way of preventing a given form of pollution is to ban it. Thinking in terms of air quality for example, the UK Clean Air Act of 1956 simply made it illegal for factories to have polluting chimney stacks in residential areas (UK Parliament 1956). Similarly, legislation controlling dangerous substances (radioactive material, chemical waste *etc.*) or enforcing certain environmental standards (car engines, production processes *etc.*) are other cases of straightforward, Polanyian protection of the habitation functions of nature, where political authority is used in opposition to economic development. However, over the course of the twentieth century, the idea of simple legislative prevention gradually fell out of favour in academic economic circles. At the root of the discipline of economics is the idea that human progress depends upon growth – improvement – and by this rationale, inhibiting growth for the purpose of mitigating environmental harm can be unwise because, as well as mitigating the harm, such action may also prevent all the benefits and efficiencies that would come with whatever is causing the harm. In the most general terms, the question for economists therefore came to be: how to remedy the harm caused by particular forms of economic growth whilst minimising the restraint put upon that growth in the first place? The conceptual device economists have used in order to capture the 'harm caused' element of the equation is that of externality.

Arthur Pigou first formalised the notion of externality in his 1920 volume, *The Economics of Welfare* (Pigou 1932). Pigou defined an externality as a divergence between the net private and net social product, which occurs when

> One person A, in the course of rendering some service, for which payment is made to a second person B, incidentally also renders services or disservices to other persons of such a sort that payment cannot be exacted from the benefited parties or compensation enforced on behalf of the injured parties.
>
> (Pigou 1932: II.II.4)

Pigou defines marginal net *private* product as that which accrues to the person or firm investing the initial resources from which the profit opportunity is derived, whereas marginal *social* product refers to the total marginal product (whether positive or negative) 'due to the marginal increment of resources in any given use or place, no matter to whom any part of this product may accrue' (Pigou 1932: II.II.5). The important thing about this distinction is that it makes conceptual space for the idea that net private product – a term we could easily substitute for less formal terms like 'profit' – might diverge from the best interests of society as a whole.

In Pigou's example, a capitalist may increase her own marginal product by investing resources in a factory. However, the smoke emitted by that factory will 'inflict an uncharged loss upon the community, in injury to buildings and vegetables, expenses for washing clothes and cleaning rooms, expenses for the provision of extra artificial light, and in many other ways' (Pigou 1932: II.IX.11). In other words, when the interests of improvement may be served, the habitation functions of the environment may be damaged. Elsewhere, he uses the example of sparks emitted by a new train line that cause fire damage to neighbouring crops. In this case, the total social product is lowered due to the damage, even though the train company is making good profits. So, whilst the interests of the private capitalist have been served by their respective investments, an externality – a cost borne by parties external to the trade – has been enacted, which requires remedy. From here, Pigou suggests the state as the appropriate remedy:

> It is plain that divergences between private and social net product of the kinds we have so far been considering cannot ... be mitigated by a modification of the contractual relation between any two contracting parties, because the divergence arises out of a service or disservice rendered to persons other than the contracting parties. It is, however, possible for the State, if it so chooses, to remove the divergence in any field by 'Extraordinary encouragements' or 'extraordinary restraints' upon investments in that field.
>
> (Pigou 1932: II.IX.16)

Such 'encouragements' refer to bounties granted for the mitigation of such externalities by the contracting parties whilst 'restraints' refer to taxes or liabilities. These 'Pigovian taxes' are a theoretical step forward from straightforward prohibitive regulation. Rather than simply preventing an activity, they enable the activity to continue whilst compensating those who lose out from it.

In the 1960s, Ronald Coase was to make a departure from Pigou's logic by doing away with the distinction between private and social product. Instead of positing a theoretical community upon which externalities are foisted, he suggested that, actually, we are comparing between harms which are different, but of the same basic type: 'The real question that has to be decided is: should A be allowed to harm B, or should B be allowed to harm A?' (Coase 1960: 2). In one example, Coase notes that, if a farmer's stray cattle trample another farmer's field of corn, 'an increase in the supply of meat can only be obtained at the expense of a decrease in the supply of crops', meaning that 'the nature of the choice is clear: meat or crops' (Coase 1960: 2). Expanding on Pigou's train example, Coase argues that, if train companies really were made liable for all the damage that they inflicted upon nearby crops, two possibilities would be present. Firstly, since crop-owning farmers know that they will receive full compensation for damaged crops, they are likely to continue to use track-side land, even though such a state of affairs will lead to more destruction of crops and a lower output. Indeed, since profits are effectively insured by the train company, more track-side land is likely to be sought for crops, lowering the total product further (Coase 1960: 32–33) – a moral hazard. Secondly, knowing such a state of affairs to exist, the train company is much less likely to install a line or choose to run extra trains in the first place, which also lowers output (Coase 1960).

Given these effects, Coase concludes that the total product will only actually be maximised if *no* liability is enforced upon the train company. Although liability (which could be in the form of taxes, as per Pigou, as much as legal claims for redress) might be just in that it constitutes recompense for injury in the specific instance, it may prevent the actors involved from realising their highest *potential* product. In order to demonstrate that a higher total social product obtains where no liability is enforced upon the train company, Coase assumes that the farmer will respond to the decreasing marginal utility of the track-side land by ploughing elsewhere. So, just as grain can be substituted for by meat, so the farmer's track-side crops can be substituted for by crops planted elsewhere. Finally, Coase adds a value into his equation that represents the product derived from the farmer ploughing elsewhere, turning what would otherwise have been a negative value into a positive one for total social product. The farmer might equally give up farming to become a train driver, or, better still, invest the proceeds of his land sale into shares in the train company.

Coase's upending of Pigou's logic is key to understanding the theoretical appeal of market-based approaches to environmental protection today for two reasons. Firstly, there is no distinct social interest for Coase, but merely the sum of private interests. As such, any aspects of the environment that are expressed as habitation functions are conceptualised instead as just another scarce resource that can be valued like any other. Secondly, where Pigou allocates costs and benefits on the basis of a static snapshot of the economy, Coase thinks in terms of opportunity cost, thus approaching the problem 'by comparing the value of the product yielded by factors in alternative uses or by alternative arrangements' (Coase 1960: 40). In order to do this, he assumes a market economy in which substitution is facilitated by the full transferability of property rights (Coase 1960: 44). Whereas, for Pigou, property is a concept that is attuned by the nature of the thing in question (*i.e.* private versus social goods), these details are unimportant in Coase's analysis. This is a distinctive type of economistic fallacy, since it amounts to the particular assumption that the market *already exists* as a medium between *all potential assets and actors*.

Where Pigou's model made for a more conservative approach, favouring the rights of existing producers at the expense of new ones, Coase reworks the conceptual scheme to favour innovation and transformation, since, if the market has selected for such investment, then substitution will automatically occur and the total net product will be raised, compensating for any externalities. As amongst the Chicago economists and in portfolio theory, the market is understood as pre-existent to the actors that comprise it. To be clear, Coase recognises that there may well be substantial costs attached to substituting factors of production for one another in this way: his equally influential theory of transaction costs is a formalised recognition of this. But even so, the very fact that he recast a problem of externalities as a problem of transaction costs constituted a radically different approach to framing the market, since the goal then becomes one of reducing transaction costs to make substituting factors of production easier and thus enabling economic growth rather than hindering it.

Coase's analysis is presented in ideal theoretic terms, where the conclusions flow logically from the assumptions. However, in order to generate a strategy for market-based management of the environment, the policy priority is obvious. If efficient, maximal outcomes follow once clearly defined and easily transferable property rights are assumed, then it is the task of policymakers to create those property rights and to make them easily transferable. Thus, in the same way that the efficient markets hypothesis converted the Markowitzian model of financial behaviour into an ideal to be pursued through policy, Coase's theory of cost was thus converted by later authors into a legislative agenda. Richard Posner was ultimately the most influential of these apostles, but in terms of natural resources and the environment specifically, Kenneth Arrow's dressing of Coase's insights in the garb of equilibrium theory in the late 1960s was critical. Arrow argued that, where externalities are present, Pareto optimality (a state in which it is impossible to make any one individual better off without making at least one individual worse off) can be restored by bringing those externalities within the remit of the price system, where they are no longer externalities because they are properly priced and can thus be bargained upon (Arrow 1969), which suggested the idea of market creation as a way to solve externalities (Medema 1994: 91).

Also in the 1960s, J.H. Dales was the first to take Coase's logic and transform it into an argument for pollution trading. Like Coase, Dales aimed to think not in terms of polluters and polluted, but in terms of the combined fate of the two – 'a society-wide problem' as he puts it (Dales 1968: 101). 'Every line of action involves costs and benefits and sensible behaviour depends upon nothing more than adopting the line of action that yields the greatest profit, *i.e.* the greatest excess of benefit over costs' (Dales 1968a: 35). In much the same way as Coase, Dales conceptualised the habitation functions of nature as just another scarce resource. Given this scarcity, Dales argued that private property rights are the only means to avoid a tragedy of the commons:

> [U]nrestricted property rights [*i.e.* commons] are bound to lead to all sorts of social, political and economic friction, especially as population pressure increases, because, in the nature of the case, individuals have no legal rights with respect to the property when its government owner follows a policy of 'anything goes'.
>
> (Dales 1968a: 67)

Referring to common water sources, he says that

> [T]he existence of a natural pricing system depends crucially on the institution of ownership. What is not owned cannot be priced since prices are payments for property rights or rights to the use of an asset. In the course of allocating property rights to assets among different owners, the price system in fact transforms most potential 'technological externalities' into 'pecuniary externalities', a synonym for prices ... We can now reformulate the problem and blame its complexity not on nature and the laws of fluids, but on man and his failure to devise property rights to the use of natural water systems.
>
> (Dales 1968b: 792)

This, in a nutshell, is the underlying marketised environmental protection argument – *the market must be complete if it is to resolve externalities*. The argument runs that only once property rights have been fully assigned can externalities become internalised. In other words, it is only once the reach of the market mechanism is extended to include everyone and everything affected by the trade, that that mechanism can efficiently deliver on the preferences of all parties. In the case of the environment, the habitation functions that it serves must therefore be fully commodified and treated as a scarce resource. Only once this is done can a system of marketised environmental management work properly. This idealism thus presents a visionary and theoretically complete solution to the problem of externalities, but one that depends upon its own complete realisation for success.

Political consensus on pollution trading

Dales's Coasean approach was the last stage in the theoretical development of emissions trading as a policy idea. The baton was then taken up by authors such as Alan Kneese and Charles Schultze (Kneese and Schultze 1978), Robert Hahn and Gordon Hester (Hahn and Hester 1989) and Thomas Tietenberg (Tietenberg 1985) who all applied his theory to various types of pollutants and provided the specific policy advice necessary for implementation. There is now a vast academic literature on such 'cap-and-trade' environmental policies and no end of commentary from politicians, policymakers and journalists: debate over what the appropriate level of the cap is, how emissions rights should be allocated, what a fair distribution should look like, what actuarial standards should apply, what mechanisms of enforcement should be used *etc.* is endless. However, virtually all of this commentary agrees on the *principle* of capping emissions and distributing the remaining pollution 'budget' via a market mechanism.

Whilst there had been a few small-scale attempts to set up localised emissions markets during the 1970s and 1980s, the important policy development was sulphur dioxide trading, which was legislated for in the Clean Air Act Amendments in the US in 1990. The local success of the resulting sulphur trading schemes was enough to establish emissions trading as the preferred mechanism for dealing with atmospheric pollution in general, so much so that it was explicitly mandated in the 1997 Kyoto Protocol as a mechanism through which countries were allowed to reduce their quoted emissions (Zapfel and Vainio 2002). During the following few years, several countries, including Denmark and the UK, experimented with carbon markets of one sort or another, whilst BP and Shell claimed (largely nominal) successes through their own internal schemes (Braun 2009).

In the case of climate change, the principle of pollution trading sat well with the actuarial tone of policy advice emanating from the principal scientific authority on climate change, the Intergovernmental Panel on Climate Change (IPCC). Over the course of its first twenty-five years of existence, the IPCC had forged a wide-ranging international consensus around a cap-based policy goal, which was, in theory, backed up by a scientifically derived imperative: the rise in global temperature should be limited to no more than two degrees Celsius above that which existed prior to the Industrial Revolution. The EU embraced this priority early on (Council of the European Union 2005: 41; Tveitdal et al. 2009) and it has been the defining motif of all recent major climate conferences, including the London G8 summit in 2008 and every annual UN climate change conference since then. The most recent of these, held in Paris in 2015, led to an agreement by all 195 participating countries that temperatures should be kept 'well below' (UNFCCC 2015: Art 2.a) the two-degree threshold, reflecting the more probabilistic climate scenario tables produced in the most recent IPCC report (IPCC 2014). In turn, using the forecasts and models provided by the IPCC, most international climate policy now thinks in terms of a carbon budget, i.e. a total quantity of carbon dioxide that can be emitted whilst staying below the threshold.

In line with Coase's thinking, a system of carbon emissions trading came to be viewed as the best overall system for allocating that budget. As a result, large markets in permits to emit pollution into the atmosphere were developed. Of the various schemes now in existence around the world, the European Union's Emissions Trading Scheme (ETS) is by far the largest, with the majority of all emission trades conducted under its banner. Established in 2005, the ETS was conceived as the principal mechanism through which the EU would be able to meet its Kyoto commitment to limit its atmospheric carbon emissions (Braun 2009: 477). Trades on the mechanism generate European Allowances (EUAs), which can be bought and sold on the European Climate Exchange. The first phase of ETS implementation, which ran from 2005 to 2007, was essentially a self-contained testing period, in preparation for Phase II, which ran in line with the Kyoto 'commitment period' from 2008 to 2012. Phase III stipulated a cap on carbon emissions which is to be reduced year by year, calculated to meet internationally agreed targets on reduction by 2030, with the desire to further integrate the ETS with other smaller carbon trading systems elsewhere in the world (European Commission 2015: 98).

Central to the popularity of the ETS was the way in which it worked with two developmental policy projects: the Clean Development Mechanism (CDM) and Joint Implementation (JI), which were both granted legislative existence in the Kyoto Protocol climate treaty. These projects furnished countries detailed in Annex I of the treaty (UNFCCC 1998) with the ability to meet their own commitments for mitigating carbon by funding 'clean development' projects in other countries instead of by reducing their own domestic emissions. Since Kyoto specified that a full 50% of abatement costs had to be achieved in the emissions trading sector under the protocol, 'reductions' achieved through the creation of CDM or JI credits translated directly into substantial cost savings for Annex I nations. JI projects allow Emission Reduction Units (ERUs) to be traded between countries with different binding emissions targets and were mainly intended for projects in the so-called transition economies, including Russia, Ukraine, Bulgaria and Romania, who had significantly less onerous targets than Annex I countries. The CDM enabled Certified Emission Reduction units (CERs) to be created in countries in so-called developing nations – e.g. China, Brazil, India and the African nations – who did not themselves have binding targets to be met. Credits from both systems could then be traded on the EU ETS and count fully towards the funding country's emission reduction target. This growth/development-centric method of meeting climate change obligations proved popular amongst wealthy states keen to bolster their developmental credentials whilst avoiding the costs of mitigating atmospheric carbon at the same time. The EU made it clear that the transference of credits from developing to developed countries should form a substantial part of both parties' attempts to meet their Kyoto obligations (European Commission 2009: 4) and the process became central to the way member states thought about meeting carbon reduction obligations (Robinson and O'Brien 2007).

The most striking thing about the growth of carbon trading as a tool of policy is the way in which it commanded political consensus. In Chapter Six, we saw that, whilst the murky world of hedge funds and financial innovation was argued to be a self-managing mechanism for economic stabilisation by some economists, the image of the new financial wizards amongst wider political circles and the public had never been particularly good. In contrast, carbon trading co-opted a broad political spectrum – from left-leaning environmentalists on the one hand through to right-leaning business advocates on the other. This consensus was evinced first in the development of the US sulphur dioxide emissions market discussed above. In the US, sulphur dioxide emissions were known to be causing damage to people and the environment, but various states stood to lose out economically from regulation, which was enough to prevent concerted action. Sulphur trading proved to be a route around this impasse, marrying the aim of reducing sulphur pollution with a market mechanism that, as well as being ideologically appealing, promised the minimum economic cost (MacKenzie 2007).

As the debate about global warming took off in the 1990s, a consensus emerged around carbon trading and, in much the same way, the EU ETS scheme was selected for by surrounding political norms. In the early years of the millennium, the Kyoto framework seemed to be under threat with the US withdrawal in 2001 and the failure of the Hague conference in the same year, leading to a sense of desperation amongst the EU institutions, keen to find any way of meeting their Kyoto obligations (Zapfel and Vainio 2002). Thus, the pressures of competitive, anarchistic international relations appeared to be making their inescapable logics felt. Added to this, a taxation approach had failed in the 1990s due to heavy lobbying from business quarters and also to the stipulation in the EU treaty that, whereas environmental policy measures require only qualified majority voting, any taxation policy requires unanimity (Braun 2009: 273). Given that the EU is hardly renowned for success in unanimous voting procedures, emissions trading became seen as the only viable policy option.

This institutional condition goes some way toward explaining the success of the emissions trading approach in the EU, but the degree of consensus was still striking, including not only national governments and the various organs of the EU itself, but also a swathe of environmentally minded NGOs on one hand and hard-nosed business interests on the other (Egenhofer 2007: 454). Huge volumes of econometric analysis on carbon trading also began to be produced year in, year out, on the fine detail of carbon trading regimes. Authoritative voices on climate change, for example the UK's *Stern Review of 2006*, combined stark warnings about the threat of climate change with an enormous amount of faith in carbon markets to adequately address the problem. Influential economists seemed also to be convinced, including Richard

Sandor (architect of the Chicago climate exchange) who opined that '[t]he early evidence indicates that environmental sustainability can be compatible with maximisation of shareholder value' (Sandor et al. 2002: 1607). A system of marketised environmental protection seemed to be able to keep all stakeholders happy.

Like emissions trading in general, the CDM was also a consensus policy, appearing to offer a unique opportunity for reconciling the apparently opposed aims of developing poorer parts of the world in the manner of existing Western capitalist development, whilst cutting back on net carbon dioxide emissions. Key to this was the notion of sustainable development, which was first popularised in the UN's *Brundtland Report* in 1987 and has framed much development policy since (Bernstein 2001). The CDM appeared to harness the power of traditional neoliberal, market-based development rooted in the transfer of financial and technological resources and force it to work in favour of the environment via 'appealing multi-levelled, public/private, North/South structures of governance' (Bäckstrand and Lövbrand 2006: 70).

From the perspective of Annex I countries, the CDM had the obvious attraction that it enabled them to buy the right to emit more carbon dioxide than the Kyoto Protocol permitted whilst simultaneously serving developmental goals *and* reducing net global carbon emissions. The CDM was in this sense the ultimate realisation of sustainable development theory because it sought to serve the three 'circles' of sustainable development all at the same time: ecological, economic and social (Holmberg and Sandbrook 1992: 25). As Kerr et al. have noted, this vision of a game in which the results appeared to be positive-sum underscored the attraction of the CDM: 'played correctly, the CDM could provide a win-win situation for all parties involved: developing countries receive funds for undertaking sustainable development projects that benefit local communities, developed countries gain a cost-effective mechanism to reduce greenhouse gasses and the global population benefits from greenhouse gas reduction' (Kerr et al. 2006). The CDM promised a virtuous circle of enrichment for capital, society and the environment all at once.

Clearly, then, the initial success of the emissions trading policy paradigm and the CDM can be explained in terms of the constraints of the political and ideational landscapes in which they were adopted. Both dialled into popular policy themes whilst avoiding less popular ones. Both were creative in seeking to overcome the apparent contradiction between a growing global market based on the emission of carbon dioxide and the need to shrink those emissions in a fair way – *i.e.* between habitation and improvement. Both sought to achieve the worthy aim of environmental protection through acceptably marketised means. As in Chapter Six, however, if we pick apart exactly how these opposed goals were sought in practice, we see an underlying economistic fallacy at work which obscured the tension between economic growth and environmental habitation that Polanyi documented.

Emissions trading in practice

Despite the degree of consensus and all the time, money and expertise devoted to the ETS programme, it is difficult to be positive about its impact, and this is due precisely to the simplistic conception of market and price which underpinned the 'win-win' appeal of the system. In ETS thinking, the price of carbon can be set *a priori*, with business passively internalising the externalities of production and trading permits according to price signals only. But this was not the case on a number of counts. Firstly, lobbying against the imposition of carbon costs on industrial firms proved consistently strong (*The Economist* 2013) and it often proved far more profitable for corporations to bid for concessions, allowances and changes to the system than to actually pay for carbon production (Spash 2010: 176–177). Secondly, the implications of the fact that, by treating carbon as a commodity, it is drawn into the general orbit of price in the economy at large, were not recognised. These implications were demonstrated robustly when, during the global economic downturn after 2008, the price of carbon was decimated, making CERs virtually worthless and so completely undermining the system. It is still an open question as to whether the ETS can fully recover from the damage that this event caused.

Thirdly, since the remit of the ETS was limited to a certain set of countries, it inevitably set up an incentive for businesses to relocate carbon production elsewhere. In discussions around Kyoto, this was coined as the problem of 'carbon leakage' (Manne and Richels 1999) where it was noted that the effect of the implementation of climate policies in subscribing countries was often simply a hike in prices for energy-using companies domiciled there, making such business cheaper in non-Annex I countries (Sijm et al. 2004: 9). Since then, the problem of carbon leakage has been prominent in discussions about the future of the ETS, and the EU's approach to phase III of its implementation has been dominated by it. The response to the perils of carbon leakage was to over-allocate free emission allowances to firms and sectors where the risk of the off-shoring of carbon was deemed large (a list that accounts for a full quarter of net EU emissions and 77% of those attached to industrial processes [European Union 2009]). The hope was that such action would remove the incentive to re-locate to non-ETS countries, but of course this way of addressing the problem directly undermines the incentive to reduce emissions, which is the whole point of the system.

Given these issues, the only other response available has been the push to extend the system by interlinking it with other emissions markets, in theory reducing the size of the 'off-shore' to which carbon could be sequestered. In Article 25 of the original ETS *Directive*, the EU stated that agreements with external countries should be sought with a view to facilitating the mutual recognition of credits from other trading systems (European Union 2003), and this view was understood to have been reinforced by the Paris agreement in 2015 (UNFCCC 2015). Limited links by the EU ETS to non-EU carbon markets have been made, including those in Norway, Iceland and Lichtenstein, with links to new regional systems in California and Quebec in the pipeline. Barack Obama's aspirations to legislate meaningful cuts in the production of carbon in the United States provoked much discussion in carbon trading circles about the viability of a US-wide carbon trading system to be ultimately connected to the EU ETS (Jopson and Crooks 2014; Repetto 2013) and China has also been considering developing its own emissions trading scheme on the back of five regional carbon markets which opened up in 2013 (Jiang 2014; Shen 2014).

One cannot predict for sure how successful these efforts will be, but even absenting the issues of lobbying and the fragility of the price of carbon, they seem utopian. If we compare the ETS to Coase's model on which it is based, the theoretical nature of the problem becomes clear. The Coasean model depends on the system of property rights being coextensive with the extent of the externality in question, but given the inherently global nature of carbon dioxide emission, there is an obvious imbalance between that globally and the partial nature of the ETS: The market must be complete if it is to resolve externalities, but a complete market for carbon emissions is an unimaginable proposition given the ubiquity of those emissions in production processes and its global effects as a pollutant. Non-participation in emissions trading systems will always offer the double benefit of attracting polluting business and free-riding on the positive environmental effects of the efforts of participating countries (Copeland and Taylor 2005; Silva and Zhu 2009).

Even if we take ourselves out of this game theoretic understanding of states' interests, the ETS is barely nibbling upon an issue which is generic to industrial globalisation: the continual outsourcing of carbon production from wealthy nations to poorer ones. Angela Druckman and Tim Jackson identified this trend by analysing the UK's total carbon footprint from 1990 to 2004. Instead of picking a set of *producers* and tallying their emissions (as almost all emissions trading systems do), the authors added up the carbon involved in making all goods *consumed* within UK borders in 2004. Once accounted for in this way, they found that around 40% of such 'embedded CO2' was produced outside UK borders, a figure which rose by 9% since 1990 (Druckman and Jackson 2009: 2074). Although the UK might have mitigated its own carbon externality, it was simply being reproduced elsewhere by 'dirty' producers. It is difficult to conceive of an emissions trading system that could embrace the sheer complexity and interconnectedness of global trade, much less in the timeframes stipulated by the IPCC.

If carbon capital flight is the nefarious side of the relationship between the interior and the exterior of the carbon trading mechanism, the JI programme and CDM can be considered its legally sanctioned cousins. The future of both systems is as uncertain as that of the ETS in general now, but both were important in legitimating the growth of the ETS in the first place because each was so directly geared towards the ideal of sustainable development, fitting the win-win policy discourse. But CDM/JI projects can be considered as little more than institutionalised carbon off-shoring in that they amount to a way for

Annex I countries to pay for the outsourcing of emissions to non-Annex I countries. The difference is that CDM/JI projects have to demonstrate that they have reduced carbon emissions compared with what would otherwise have been – in the jargon, each individual project must prove 'additionality'. The additionality requirement means that a project proposal must demonstrate that it contributes to a *net reduction* of carbon emissions, otherwise carbon market value would be generated whilst emissions actually rise.

The problem is that this approach constructs a world in which it is relative reductions in emissions that count, rather than absolute ones. The additionality criterion – *i.e.* the baseline for 'what would otherwise have been' – is determined on a case-by-case basis by applicants demonstrating that there exists a cheaper option that was legal and feasible (CDM Executive Board 2004). As such, their baseline measurement is taken at the margin, rather than in respect of absolute emissions, and can therefore technically register carbon abatement whilst carbon emissions rise in absolute terms. To take an extreme example, a new, clean coal power station might add substantially to absolute carbon emissions, but if it can be demonstrated that a traditional dirty coal plant was an option, then the clean coal plant can be said to have 'reduced' emissions. A recent review of the JI programme reached damning conclusions to this effect. On the basis of detailed and wide-ranging statistical and qualitative analysis, the implementation of the additionality criterion was judged so poor – at least 80% of ERUs emerging from JI projects of low or questionable environmental integrity – that the programme seems likely to have actually incentivised far *higher* production of carbon dioxide than would have been the case if emissions reductions had been sought domestically (Kollmuss 2015).

Similar problems abounded in the CDM. Notoriously, a large proportion of CDM projects in the 2000s were based on the phasing out of trifluoromethane (HFC23) from industrial processes. These processes, which are heavily polluting by any measure, earned CER credits because 'what would otherwise have been' was an even higher level of pollution. Furthermore, since HFC23 is an extremely potent greenhouse gas, only very small amounts (relative to carbon) need to be mitigated in order to generate many CERs. As Donald Mackenzie noted, 'by decomposing a tonne of HFC-23 in China, one can – via the link between the CDM and ETS – earn allowances to emit 11,700 tonnes of CO2 in Europe' (MacKenzie 2007: 445). This quirk of carbon accounting made HFC23 a cheap option, but as the UNFCCC itself recognised, in aggregate, it is possible that the surfeit of emissions saving projects aimed at the industrial processes concerning HFC 23 led to a global *increase* in its production (UNFCCC 2006: 17).

This was something like William Stanley Jevons's paradox of coal but in reverse. Jevons argued that, whilst efficiency gains in the use of a resource might decrease the consumption of that resource momentarily, those efficiency gains lead to a reduction in price and thus incentivise more use of the resource, eventually leading to its exhaustion (Jevons 1865). In the case of HFC production, HFC was the cheapest option for carbon abatement, which paradoxically encouraged its production. In this respect it is telling that, during their heyday, CDM projects clung rigidly to the countries with the fastest development curve – countries that also had the fastest rate of increased emissions. At the peak of new project development in 2009, there were over 4,500 CDM projects in eighty countries, of which China accounted for a full 84%, with India and Brazil the nearest competitors with 4% and 3% market share respectively (Capoor and Ambrosi 2009: 34–35).

Recent recommendations to address these issues revolve around greater transparency, more accurate reporting, better pricing of different pollutants *etc.* (see European Commission 2017). But again the whole system seems like no more than a drop in the ocean of the general course of industrial development. The focus on additionally – 'what would otherwise have been' – sets a relativistic framework for thinking about emissions reduction which is completely out of step with the absolute nature of the problem: efficiency gains from the globalisation of production have always been continually swamped by increased resource use (Tisdell 2001). As the IPCC noted in their fourth assessment report, increased energy efficiency (or, in their words, decreased energy intensity) amounted to a 33% reduction in energy used between 1970 and 2004. However, this was offset nearly four and a half times over by a 77% increase due to global income growth and a 69% increase due to population growth (Pachauri and Reisinger 2007: 37). As they continued to note, the long-term trend of declining carbon dioxide emissions per unit of energy supplied actually reversed in 2000 and then maintained proportionality (ibid.). Whatever the virtues of CDM and JI in terms of economic development, in this context, it is difficult to see them as any more than rearranging the deckchairs in terms of addressing carbon abatement in general.

Concluding comments

The IPCC's latest synthesis report was critical of carbon trading as a policy tool. Whilst it retains tropes of 'sustainable development' and 'clean investment', the report lays a positive emphasis on the role of national and sub-national mitigation strategies, including governmental regulation and taxation, counterposing these strategies directly with the failures of emissions trading (IPCC 2014: 30). Moreover, the whole tone of thought on climate change has gradually shifted from a register emphasising solely mitigation, to one in which strategies of adaptation, response and resilience are just as, if not more, important. It may be that emissions trading comes to be seen simply as an extremely expensive failed policy experiment, or it may limp on as a part of the policy mix. Either way, the point is that it is a policy which speaks of the times in which it was hatched, sitting within the same paradigm of thought as characterised the development of financial economic theory: via the judicious use of price incentives, this policy paradigm sought to overcome the tension between habitation and improvement. In the context of game theoretic understandings of international politics and a political aversion to anti-market methods in general, the win-win mentality of the idea of carbon trading, especially when twinned with opportunities for sustainable development, sold well to policymakers.

By looking at the development of the concept of social cost in welfare economics, we have seen the theoretical roots of this consensus, stretching through Coase's theorem and its evolution through successive iterations of thought applying the model to environmental questions. Coase's model of social costs posited an idealised world in which the tension between social and individual costs of harm could be transcended by the application of a complete system of property rights, an idea which eventually realised itself in the attempt to price carbon and other emissions so as to force the 'externality' of emissions into the market mechanism. The problem was that the assumptions of Coase's model could not even remotely be reproduced in practice. The actual nature of greenhouse gas emissions – global diffuse, ubiquitous in human life – undermined any pretensions to the requirement of complete and well-defined property rights.

The related assumption of market participants as passive recipients of prices was similarly off the mark. In Chapter Six, we saw how, via its assumption of idealised market conditions, efficient markets thinking was conceptually blind to the ways in which financiers actively seek to escape the conditions of competition through financial innovation and market expansion. By thinking of firms as price-takers, carbon trading thinking also failed to recognise that firms, and people, are creative, and that there is no reason to think that participants are any more likely to obey the competitive regime than to subvert it, either by lobbying, playing on its accounting ambiguities, or avoiding its remit altogether. Together, these issues undermined, and will continue to undermine, efforts to control climate change through constructed market incentives of the sort offered under the ETS.

8 People and welfare provision

Welfare in the 20th century

As with land and money, Polanyi spends some time in *TGT* building up a stylised history of how the marketisation of labour changed the matrix of economic benefits and harms for workers as economies industrialised. For him, the critical event was the repeal of the Speenhamland Act in 1834, which had previously guaranteed a minimum income with aid from the parish authorities if an individual's wage fell below a certain level. Without this form of welfare, wages in England came to be determined primarily by the forces of supply and demand for the first time (2001: 174). Although this new system enabled far greater growth than ever before by allocating labour to where it was most productive, wages did not necessarily equate to adequate livelihood for workers. On top of the competitive pressure on employers to keep pay as low as possible in general, industrialisation was changing economy and society quicker than ever before, with innovation and mechanisation rendering the gainful employment opportunities of one year obsolete in the next. The same rapid change induced economic cycles, which in turn induced changes in the quantity of labour demanded at any one time, further raising the prospect of unemployment for the average labourer. Reliance on the labour market thus injected a new type of insecurity into livelihood.

Forty years odd after the repeal of Speenhamland, legislative steps to mitigate these pressures began to be introduced in England. Anti-combination laws were repealed, leading to the formal recognition of the trade unions in law (cf. Orth 1998) and a torrent of legislation was enacted in the interests of the English workers, including for example the prevention of the employment of the very young in mineshafts, enforced vaccinations, regulation of chimney sweeps and weavers, as well as laws of indirect benefit for the worker, such as enforced library provision, state inspection of gasworks and provision of rural drainage and irrigation works (Polanyi 2001: 152). At the same time, the Employer's Liability and Workmen's Compensation Acts were growing in scope, gradually providing greater legislative protection for workers in an increasing range of professions. The state was, for Polanyi, growing a new function, which was to take over some responsibility for the livelihood of workers beyond the vagaries of what the labour market could offer.

Over the course of the twentieth century, this responsibility can only be said to have grown substantially. Out of the ashes of the two world wars, the welfare state model emerged, with the Britain leading the way in developing direct provision of healthcare, large-scale social housing projects and a universal state pension mechanism. So often debate about welfare provision is conducted at the margin, with critics demanding marginally less spending on welfare and proponents demanding marginally more in this or that specific case but, if we zoom out a bit, we can absorb how fundamental the welfare state has grown to be in the UK: notwithstanding various peaks and troughs along the way, public spending has shown a broad trend increase up to today both in absolute real terms and as a percentage of economic output. In the latter terms, it rose from 15% in the pre-World War I period to a high of 45% in the early 1980s and whilst falling somewhat over the following decade, from 2000, it resumed its upwards trajectory until, in the wake of the financial crisis, it stood at 47% of GDP (Chantrill 2017a). Since the World War II, this measure has never fallen below 34% of GDP (Chantrill 2017a).

In the 1990s, however, a new narrative emerged which set debate over state provision of welfare in terms of a tension between habitation and improvement: state spending to support habitation came increasingly to be seen as in contradiction with the forces of economic globalisation that were driving productivity in the increasingly interconnected global economy. As we have already seen, the ERM crisis signalled the power of international investors over the British state to direct the value of sterling, but beyond that, the threat of investors leaving the country if they saw governments engaging in policies that they didn't care for – so-called 'capital flight' – became understood as a limiting factor on what levels of taxation and welfare spending governments were able to, or allowed to, engage in (Scharpf 1999; *The Economist* 1997). If government tried to raise corporation tax, then that corporation might simply move its plants abroad, taking jobs with them; if government borrowed to support employment or increase spending, they would be punished by bond markets; if they sought to raise tax from the populace instead, people would shift their earnings offshore. By this account, as Thomas Friedman memorably put it, globalisation appeared to amount to a golden straitjacket, where material enrichment necessarily came at the expense of political sovereignty over the economy (Friedman 1999: 87).

Like the prisoner's dilemma view of the politics of climate change, this description was never fact. But it doesn't really matter whether state spending does actually cause capital flight: as long as governments believe or can be persuaded that a threat of capital flight exists and that it constrains policy options, then they will behave as if their options have been so constrained (Hay 2002: 203). A Philip Cerny put it, traditional welfare state functions had been compromised to some extent, but rather than the operating capability of states simply having diminished, what changed was the way in which welfare provision and other forms of state spending came to be conceptualised in the public consciousness (Cerny 1994). It was the public *character* of public goods that was being undermined (Cerny 1994: 339). In result, privatisation and marketisation of state functions increasingly became a default policy position, in Britain especially, first in public utilities like gas, telephony and railways, then later in all manner of activities, from waste management to hospital building and the administration of benefits provision. Even the very mechanisms of government spending came to be privatised as government found ways to finance infrastructure spending through the private sector – the now notorious Private Finance Initiative contract model – rather than through standard public borrowing channels (Atkinson and Elliott 2007: 129).

But despite all this new anti-statism, in its Polanyian function of providing welfare in order to offset the risks of unemployment inherent in a labour market, the state remained stubbornly present. Public spending on social security specifically – the direct transfer of cash from the state to recipients for pension provision, incapacity and unemployment benefits, housing and family support – had followed the same upward curve as state spending in general over the post-war period, rising from 4% in 1948 to 10% in 1981, then continuing to hover between 9.8% and 12.2% until 2008 (Hood and Oakley 2014: 4). And as the British Social Attitudes survey found, public support for maintained or increased levels of public spending on health, education and social benefits was high for the duration of the 1990s and well into the 2000s (Taylor-Gooby and Taylor 2015). And despite the persistence of the welfare state, Britain's ability to attract capital did not appear to have been seriously damaged. This was a period in which the City of London was reaching the height of its power to net financial business from across the world. In general, the British economy was continuing to grow, as measured in GDP terms, in a relatively buoyant manner right up until the financial crisis in 2008. If there was a tension between spending on welfare and the ability of the economy to grow in the context of the globalising economy, it certainly wasn't a very clear or direct one.

Whatever the reality, the *sense* of a contradiction between the forces of economic improvement and the social expectation for habitation, became the problem that the British Labour government of the late 1990s and early 2000s wanted to solve in its approach to welfare provision. To this extent, it was a Polanyian problematique, but the terms of reference had changed. In Polanyi's example, Victorian economic thinkers simply denied the legitimacy of the provision of social security as an affront to the natural human incentives of hunger and pain which ought to be allowed to structure livelihood alone. In the late twentieth century, by which time welfare provision had become an entrenched part of the workings of the British economy, it was hardly possible for any government, let alone a Labour Party government, to argue for a return to the incentives of the workhouse. Instead, and in common with the previous two cases discussed, the government sought to transcend the putative globalisation/welfare spending contradiction, this time, by experimenting with the idea that individuals could be made personally accountable for their own welfare provision. If individuals could be sufficiently 'responsibilised' (Finlayson 2008, 2009; Langley 2007) in this way, then their welfare would be taken care of without their needing to draw on the resources of the state, obviating the discipline supposed to be bearing down on state spending by international financial forces. Thus, the need for habitation was not denied, but rolled into a new definition of what it could mean to be a rational economic agent in conditions of globalisation.

In the first case, we saw how portfolio theory depicted a world in which, given sufficiently complete application of the market mechanism, financial and social interests could not conflict. In the second case, we saw how a Coasean approach to the physical world guaranteed a proper distribution of environmental goods so long as property rights could be complete in scope. Both were undergirded by the desire to erase the source of contradiction between habitation and improvement by theoretical *fiat*. In the case of UK welfare provision, the desire to dissolve the contradictions posed by economic globalisation were set within a political semi-philosophy that made the dissolution of contradiction into a mantra for all policy: the 'third way.'

Marketised welfare provision

The right-leaning, market-focused approach to economic and social policy that had typified European governments from the 1970s looked, on the face of it, to be on the wane by the mid-1990s as electorate after electorate turned out conservative parties and turned in social democratic ones (Notermans 2000: 223). Yet this crop of social democratic parties by and large accepted the market-friendly, supply-side-economic world view of their predecessors. The British contingent, 'New' Labour, indicated this acceptance, breaking with the party's socialist past by writing the principle of common ownership out of the party constitution and by granting formal independence to the Bank of England. The latter would in theory free the Bank to pursue a monetarist agenda of maintaining low rates of inflation without the possibility of governments seeking to use the money supply to manage the economy in any way. With such changes of direction in mind, New Labour's approach to welfare provision and state services in general was often read as nothing more than a continuation of the established mantras of the Conservative Party and prevailing right-wing sentiment generally (Macaulay and Wilson 2008). But though there is truth in this proposition, it potentially misses out on the particularities that were evinced in New Labour's 'third way' philosophy and how that generated a particular attitude to the contradictions between market and state that characterised political economic discourse at the time.

Like Gerhard Schröder's 'neue mitte' and Bill Clinton's policy of 'triangulation', the third way ideology hinged on the idea that all that had been opposed in previous political philosophies of either the right or left, could either be forgotten or reconciled (Callinicos 2001; Mouffe 2000: 108). Early on in his political ascent, Tony Blair wrote in a pamphlet, excerpted in the culture section of the *Independent* newspaper, of how the third way would move politics beyond 'an old left preoccupied by state control, high taxation and producer interests, and a new right treating public investment, and often the very notions of "society" and collective endeavour, as evils to be undone' (2003: 28). The combination of opposites then reaches fever pitch:

> My vision for the 21st century is of a popular politics reconciling themes which in the past have wrongly been regarded as antagonistic – patriotism *and* internationalism; rights *and* responsibilities; the promotion of enterprise *and* the attack on poverty and discrimination.
> (Blair 2003)

Economically, this combination hinged on the transformation of the way in which the left delivered policy:

> The Third Way stands for a modernized social democracy, passionate in its commitment to social justice and the goals of the centre-left, but flexible, innovative and forward-looking in the means to achieve them.
> (Blair 2003: 28)

As Michael Freeden wrote of the third way during the same year,

> [T]he meaning of socialism has been retained by emphasising co-operation and mutual responsibility, but contained by combining it with a particular vocabulary of fairness towards individuals, greater productivity, consumer choice and, especially, identifying an economic *public* interest in which the market plays a key role.
> (Freeden 2003: 47)

For Anthony Giddens, this naturally implied a consumerist mindset: '[s]ocial democrats must now emphasize freedom of choice rather than the more traditional forms of state provision and egalitarianism' (Giddens 2002: 8). In contrast to the socialised redistribution implied in previous welfare arrangements, Blair, Freeden and Giddens all depicted a third way which drew on a different language that downplayed ideals of security and socialised risk-bearing and instead emphasised freedom, choice and individualism; in short, the language of consumerism and the market.

In the case of the British National Health Service (NHS), an emphasis on consumer choice in the use of state services gradually became more and more pronounced in New Labour policy, evinced in a growing focus on 'client involvement' and 'empowerment' as objectives of policy (Greener 2009: 318). This 'new public management' approach aimed to use consumer choice in order to sever the traditional link between patient and doctor and replace it with levels of management who speak on behalf of the patient to the doctor in terms of demands for efficiency and improved service (Dent 2006). Health-related parliamentary acts of 2007 and 2008 only served to accentuate the focus on choice and marketised forms of regulation whilst allowing secondary ideologies of empowerment and involvement to fade away somewhat (Vincent-Jones et al. 2009). Similarly, in terms of education policy, New Labour committed itself to an agenda that actively promoted market-style choice for parents and schoolchildren (Parsons and Welsh 2006; West and Pennell 2005) as well as for university students.

These policies dialled into discourses of individualism and consumerism that had become central to capitalist ideology in the West by this time, and no doubt, like the carbon trading discussed in Chapter Seven, that made the ideas easier to sell. However, such policies were strategies of governance more than morally driven positions: the purpose of this new marketised form of welfare was not to maximise choice for its own sake, but to use consumer forces as a tool to deliver efficiency in public service provision. For proponents, a framework of competition amongst public service providers and a system allowing individuals the maximum degree of choice between those providers could be thought of as a mechanism for regulating public service provision in the most efficient manner (*e.g.* Le Grand 2007). Consumer choice, as exercised by ordinary individuals, was to be the key to delivering the kinds of pressures required to deliver welfare in the light of ongoing forces exerted by globalisation upon the traditional welfare state as mentioned above. As such, individual recipients of services that the state had a hand in providing suddenly became enlisted as part of the efficiency delivery mechanism themselves.

And in order to facilitate this pressure on public services in the name of efficiency, the government recognised that it would have to produce 'confident consumers', capable of navigating the new array of choices available in their best interests (UK Department of Trade and Industry 1998). Only this pressure, it was argued, would lead to efficiency gains in the way welfare was delivered. Consequently, New Labour presided over the establishment of a number of league tables in order to provide metrics of comparison in public services. Perhaps the most notable examples are the university and school league tables, which have grown in scope since their introduction in 1992 to dominate the educational system. Metrics of comparison also came to be introduced for the NHS. On the front page of the NHS website, one could now obtain customer satisfaction scores as well as performance ratings on a scale of 'weak', 'fair', 'good' and 'excellent' for hospitals and for doctors. On top of this, companies such as Dr Foster emerged, specialising in procuring and disseminating similar metrics of performance.

Such metrics give the lie to the notion of this choice representing any genuine individual moral agency. After all, who would choose a weak hospital or an underperforming school? The choice is already prescribed by the metric: one will choose the best hospital, GP, school or university that one has access to, subject to one's constraints. And if access is scarce – places in the best schools and beds in the best hospitals are not unlimited – then metrics like these create the conditions of competition not only amongst providers, but also amongst consumers. This point is clearest in the case of education. League tables may well introduce an element of competition amongst universities and schools (leaving aside whether or not we think that is in itself desirable), but then they also encourage more competition amongst children and students themselves to secure places in those universities and schools. One consequence of this competition is the dramatic increase in extra private tuition, for those who can afford it, as children come under pressure to access selective institutions. Another is the rise of property prices and rents in areas close to more desirable schools.

This mixture of market and welfare, of consumer choice and efficient management mechanisms, transformed the discourse surrounding public services in the UK. Ever since, the British government has sought to actively foster the conditions for competition in public service provision by encouraging users of once publicly provided utilities like gas, electricity and telecoms to 'shop around' so as to enforce price discipline upon private sector providers, especially where consumers have failed to spontaneously live up to their newly assigned role in delivering efficiency in public services. Nowhere does Polanyi's pithy aphorism – '*laissez-faire* was planned' (2001: 147) – look more relevant than in the lengths that the British state has gone to in the attempt to marketise public services.

In terms of welfare specifically, New Labour engaged in a related but even more profound attempt to reconfigure the relationship between individual, market and state, an attempt which implied a transformation in the concept of welfare itself. If, so the argument went, people could be encouraged to build up sufficient stores of wealth on their own, they might be able to insure themselves against the risks of life and so never need to draw on the welfare systems offered by the state at all. This idea of 'asset-based welfare' initially became popular in the United States, where Michael Sherraden saw it as a new way to help low-income families in light of the perceived failure of the traditional methods of state welfare provision (Sherraden 1991). In the UK there was much research conducted amongst influential think tanks (including particularly in the UK the Institute for Public Policy Research, which was closely associated with New Labour generally) during the 1990s that suggested that having a financial asset base was key to personal development (*cf.* Dolphin and Prabhakar 2010; Paxton 2003; Regan 2001). The message of such research was that, by providing suitable incentives and giving people sufficient opportunities to build up assets, individuals could provide for their own welfare needs, effectively absenting government from responsibility (Finlayson 2009).

Pat O'Malley recognised this ideological trend early on as one of 'prudentialism', consisting of three elements:

> [T]he retraction of socialized risk-based techniques from managing the risks confronting the populace; their progressive replacement through the

extension of privatized risk-based techniques; and the articulation of this process with the strategic deployment of sovereign remedies and disciplinary interventions that facilitate, underline and enforce moves towards government through individual responsibility.

(O'Malley, 1996: 199)

In Paul Langley's words, this was 'the "responsibilisation of the self"', ... where risk management is forced back onto individuals and satisfied through the market' (Langley 2007: 75). And in order to achieve this goal, British and American governments recognised that they would need to assemble 'everyday investor identities' in the populace (Langley 2007: 69): they recognised that a nation of financially independent non-users of state services would not appear on its own, and so it tasked its financial regulator, the Financial Services Authority (FSA), with improving 'financial capability' amongst British citizens in general (Financial Services Authority 1998, 2004a, 2004b) and amongst the young in particular (Financial Services Authority 2004c). This policy shift was not presented primarily in terms of a victory for freedom of choice, but an emergent mechanism for the regulation of welfare provision in light of the perceived pressures of economic globalisation. Indeed, in his 2004 paper on the issue, chairman of the FSA, John Tiner, was explicit about the benefits of financial savvy in precisely these terms:

> Improving people's ability to make financial decisions is in everybody's interests. It saves people money, time and a lot of worry. And, in years to come, they will benefit from the informed decisions they make now and the freedom it gives them. It helps Government and taxpayers, because people are less likely to get into financial difficulties and fall back on state benefits. And the financial services industry will benefit from dealing with competent and confident consumers.
>
> (Financial Services Authority 2004a: 1)

The policies put forth played straight into the third way ideology by offering modest redistributive assistance from the state on condition of increasingly consumer-like behaviour on the part of recipients. For example, the Child Trust Fund (CTF), set up in 2002, was a scheme that provided every child with £250 deposited in a personal long-term savings account which could only be accessed upon turning 18 (UK Treasury 2003: 103). As Alan Finlayson argued (Finlayson 2008, 2009), policies like these were not significant in terms of the actual sums; rather their purpose was to 'kick start the savings habit' (Directgov UK 2010) in people who had not traditionally saved that much before – *i.e.* children and those with little money – enabling them to transfer their new 'savings skills' to other areas of their lives (Treasury 2008: 3).

Lack of access to bank accounts was also identified as a key problem (Cramer 2007: 11). To address this, Labour set up a 'Financial Inclusion Taskforce' with the headline aim of rolling out bank accounts to more people, extending lines of credit further and providing face-to-face advice (UK Financial Inclusion Taskforce 2006). Another example was New Labour's Key Worker Living policy, which consisted of two programmes. Firstly, Homebuy offered an equity loan of up to £50,000 to assist in climbing the first rung of the housing ladder. Secondly, the New Build scheme offered various shared ownership/ reduced rental schemes to encourage people to purchase mortgages (Battye et al. 2006). Both offers were conditional upon recipients fitting either into 'key worker', (*e.g.* nurses, teachers etc.) first-time buyer, or housing association tenant categories (Battye et al. 2006). Again, the total fiscal impact of the schemes was relatively small, but both aimed to foster market-based financial behaviour and the growth of a personal asset-base.

These policies were controversial from the start, with significant opposition within the British political system and disputes over the extent to which asset holding did in fact produce positive welfare outcomes at all (Prabhakar 2009). Most of the policies were abolished or drastically scaled back by the Conservative/Liberal Democrat coalition that replaced the Labour government in 2010. But asset-based welfare's moment in the sun was the perfect embodiment of the third way desire to fit opposed goals into a single policy vision. In the same way that carbon trading sought to overcome the tension between economic growth and environmental welfare and efficient markets thinking sought to overcome the tension between finance-led productivity and structural economic stability, the asset-based welfare ideal suggested that the tension between globalisation and the ongoing need for a social security system could be resolved if people could just be persuaded to adopt the right attitude to their personal finances. The responsibilised, financialised individual was to overcome the tension between habitation and improvement and between market and state by being entrepreneurial, risk-savvy, self-interested, prudent and responsible *vis-à-vis* society all at once.

Personal finances in practice

Like the other policies we have looked at so far in this book, asset-based welfare was rooted in a particular type of economistic fallacy. In the first case study, we saw how light-touch financial regulation was underpinned by the image of a static market consisting of a given set of investors and a given set of assets where risk is apportioned efficiently. In the case of carbon trading, we observed the idea of a complete market comprising all potential assets where externalities are internalised. Policies of asset-based welfare attempted instead to realise a particular form of economic rationality at the level of the individual. In each example discussed in the previous section, the assumption was that, with sufficient opportunity and advice, individuals will act rationally to maximise their welfare (understood as income) over the life cycle. For example, the Department for Work and Pensions (DWP) came to see long-term saving as a form of 'income smoothing', where individuals calculate their savings ratios by accounting for how much money will be worth to them in different periods of their life, especially retirement (UK Department for Work and Pensions 2009: 34). The Savings Gateway and Child Trust Fund policies effectively fulfilled a similar function, although they were not specifically geared towards retirement. Likewise, encouraging the take-up of mortgage debt tied in with the idea of the home as a financial asset used to fund future retirement (Watson 2008, 2009c). It was assumed, in each case, that the image of the prudential individual that Langley, Finlayson and others identified would realise so that each might manage her financial affairs over her lifetime. She would accumulate assets and go into debt at the appropriate stages, coming to the end of her life with a well-balanced account.

The idea of the economically rational individual who responds to price triggers based on self-interested reasoning – *homo economicus* in short – has long served as a straw man for critics of mainstream economics, but it can be rendered in many different ways. In the asset-based welfare policy view, it was specifically the ability to engage in 'rational capital accounting' (Lukes 2006: 80) that was emphasised. Yet, by relying on the acquisition of assets for the delivery of this type of policy, habitation and improvement were blurred. Just as for professional financiers in the EMH view, personal portfolio management of the type depicted in asset-based welfare policies presented individuals with the chance to manage risk, but also, simultaneously, to make money (Ismail et al. 2007). As Alan Finlayson observed, policies like the Child Trust Fund and Savings Gateway, whilst ostensibly about welfare, were also wrapped in the language of personal aspiration that was so central to New Labour policies in general (Finlayson 2009). This rephrasing served to abstract welfare provision from habitation sentiments and recast it as merely another form of personal consumption.

This amounted less to habitation via improvement, but habitation *as* improvement – the distinction between the two, evident in the traditional idea of welfare provision as social security, ebbed away. By this new account, it was *rational* for the individual to balance consumption and saving, to be entrepreneurial in adopting financial risk yet responsible in paying back debts. This new vision of *homo economicus* had clearly come a long way since Townsend's miserable depiction of the pauper driven by hunger and pain. But as Paul Langley noted, this new combination of appeals to the different images of the savvy investor and the self-interested accumulator made the type of subjectivity appealed to in these types of policy necessarily 'uncertain' (2007). How were individuals to balance their interests in short-term consumption against long-term self-provision of welfare through accumulation? Unfortunately, the evidence pointed to the fact that, whenever the lines between the two had been blurred in Britain, it was the improvement rationality that won out.

As many economists have long recognised, consumer debt has always had a role in sustaining patterns of present consumption *at the expense of* later consumption: 'buy now, pay later', as they say. Following E.P. Thompson, for example, Juliet Schor noted how Fordism was not only about selling cars and other expensive mass-produced goods, but also about selling the credit necessary to buy them:

> [A]utomobiles, radios, electric refrigerators, washing machines – even jewelry and foreign travel – were bought on the installment plan. [In the US] by the end of the 1920s, 60 percent of cars, radios and furniture were being purchased on 'time'. The ability to buy without actually having money helped foster a climate of instant gratification, expanding expectations, and, ultimately, materialism.
>
> (Schor 1993: 119; see also Martin 2002: 18)

Throughout the twentieth century, Western capitalism appeared to have become increasingly hooked on debt-financed consumption as a means of keeping the economy moving (Migone 2007), but crucially, governments were active enablers of this process. From the 1970s onwards, governments were increasingly abandoning Keynesian aggregate demand policies (public borrowing to finance investment), but at the same time, they were strengthening the ability of individuals to take on debt themselves in a system of what Colin Crouch pithily coined as 'privatised Keynesianism' (Crouch 2009: 390; see also Montgomerie 2006, 2013).

In the UK, the first significant piece of legislation to this effect was the 1974 Consumer Credit Act, which prevented the issuance of credit without a license and generally established a regulatory framework within which credit issuance could grow. This served to prohibit small-scale informal credit issuance – 'the slate' for example – and instead restricted lending to institutions capable of complying with a variety of legal and fiduciary obligations, transferring demand for credit upwards towards large financial institutions such as building societies and banks. Whereas informal relations of credit were usually embedded in small-scale, often personal relationships, putting ceilings on lending levels and preventing significant competition between providers, the newly emerging mass credit market pitted many lenders against each other in a much larger market system, paving the way for the explosion of the consumer finance industry over the following decades. The credit card industry also grew on the back of these changes, with general purpose and store-specific cards becoming available to all at almost zero cost (Blackburn 2006: 44).

A similar dynamic was at work in mortgage markets, where the 1986 Building Societies Act was significant on three counts: it curtailed the Building Societies Association's power to set industry-wide mortgage interest rates, meaning that lenders were now in competition with one another to offer lower rates; it removed restrictions on the ratio of mortgage to income, which had for decades been strictly limited to three and a half times salary, meaning that lenders could also compete to offer more leveraged deals requiring less up-front capital; and it started the process of offering building societies the chance to raise much more money in the wholesale money markets (Langley 2006: 288). The contemporaneous 1986 Financial Services Act, which deregulated other areas of personal finance and permitted centralised lenders to get in on the mortgage market (Scharpf 1999; Taylor-Gooby 2003), also intensified competition to lower interest rates, increasing the volume of and choice between forms of debt for individuals.

All of this new ability to engage in consumption on the back of debt sat easily with an increasingly materialist and consumerist culture in which 'positional goods' (Hirsch 1977) conferring status were increasingly prized (Warde 1994; Slater 1997). Consumption increasingly reflected self-identity, and so if debt facilitated greater consumption, then it facilitated greater expression of self-identity. But in the privatised Keynesian system, consumption came to have a social purpose too: borrowing on credit cards, stretching resources for a mortgage or taking out a loan to buy a car were now key drivers of aggregate demand and thus practically a civic duty. It is because of this state of affairs that we are now used to a running commentary on Christmas sales figures. When newscasters ask whether it will be a good Christmas on the high street, they are asking whether consumers are still willing to borrow enough to keep the wheels of productivity turning.

The problem was that the social responsibility of this privatised Keynesian citizen is directly at odds with that of the rational capital accountant at the centre of asset-based welfare policy. The former should maximise borrowing so as to maximise spending and thus maximise economic growth: she is *homo economicus* in impulsive consumer mode, feeding private sector productivity through her debt-based consumption. The latter should borrow strategically in order to develop her portfolio of assets upon which she can draw down on when necessary. She is instead the rational capital accountant navigating her way through the uncertainties of a world in which the state cannot be relied upon for subsistence. The statistics demonstrate that it is the former of these two figures which was overwhelmingly dominant during the period in which asset-based, welfare-type policies were being tested. Between 2000 and 2005, consumer credit lending rose by 65.8% and lending secured on dwellings rose by 94% whilst, during the same period, wages rose by a mere 24% (Atkinson and Elliott 2007: 63). Total outstanding mortgage debt in the UK increased from 50% of GDP to over 80% in the decade up to the global financial crisis whilst median mortgage payments as a percentage of income increased from just under 12% in 2002 to nearly 19% by 2008 (Turner 2009: 29–30).

If British citizens were becoming ever more leveraged in general, there was also a shift towards using mortgage finance to generate income. Some of this was via the development of buy-to-let mortgage lending (UK Pensions Commission 2004: 194) and, uniquely amongst their European neighbours, a rapidly increasing number of Britons were purchasing equity release mortgages in order to free up the value of their home for consumer spending (Toussaint and Elsinga 2009) including deals aimed specifically at the retired (Jones 2010: M3). As the Turner Report highlighted, over the course of the 2000s the combined value of products of this type actually overtook the value of mortgages for house purchase by the time of the financial crisis (Turner 2009: 31). Summarising these trends, Matthew Watson argued that

> There is now a deeply held sense within British society that activity on the housing market is not merely about providing oneself with somewhere to live. It is also about expecting to be able to cash in future capital gains, and expectations of that nature form an important part of contemporary house price valuations.
>
> (Watson 2008c: 287–288)

By recasting home equity as a source of income and thus drawing it within the realm of everyday consumption practices, it becomes an article of improvement and thus subjected to the laws of the market (this applies whether the home is being used for present or future consumption). This change became abundantly reflected in the price of housing, which had shot up dramatically (see Hay 2009).

All of this made for a less secure life for many in Britain. The stresses and strains of debt were already beginning to show during Labour's period in office, when cases of personal insolvency shot up in number from 24,549 in the year 1998 to 106,544 in 2008 (Insolvency Service 2010). During the same period, there was a clear increase in cases of home repossession that, whilst being boosted by the credit crunch, dated back to 2003 (Department for Communities and Local Government 2012). Throughout the 1990s and 2000s, levels of secured and unsecured personal debt continued to grow at a faster rate than the UK could generate earned income (Gifford 2009). Today, the UK economy remains marked by unprecedented levels of mortgage debt, and despite ever-more vocal critiques of the precarious nature of the UK housing market, the government remains preoccupied with attempting to increase those levels through latter-day versions of the Homebuy scheme (Montgomerie and Büdenbender 2014). And ten years out from the crisis, unsecured lending is as free as it ever was, with fears widespread that defaults on credit cards and car loans could form the basis of a financial crisis in the same way that defaults on sub-prime mortgages did in 2008.

The recent history of secured and unsecured debt thus reveals how wildly out of step the asset-based welfare idea was with the actual practices of personal finance that had come to characterise life in Britain by the turn of the century. Where they had the option, Britons tended to use debt to finance consumption. In some small part, this was because Britain was, and remains, a culturally consumerist nation, but it was also because wages alone had ceased to bring the rising standards of living that people had become accustomed to in the post-war period. On top of this, personal debt had become a mechanism for keeping aggregate demand up in light of reduced public borrowing and spending, injecting new money – every time credit is issued, money is created – into the economy to keep it turning. To expect that rational capital accountant subjectivity that underscored asset-based welfare ideas to emerge from all of this was utopian in the extreme.

Pensions in practice

Similar internal contradictions bedevilled the marketised social protection ideal as it was applied to pension provision. The traditional method by which individuals cater for their long-term financial welfare in the UK is through a pension, either from the state or from the private sector. In terms of the state pension – the epitome of Polanyian welfare provision – upon coming to government in 1997, New Labour promptly released a White Paper with the headline aim of reversing the 60:40 ratio of state to private pensions (Department of Social Security 1998), a move which, along with the commitment to honour Tory spending plans (Labour Party 1997) was a part of a more general attempt to demonstrate that their 'new' suffix was genuine by showing capacity for fiscal restraint (Hills 1998). Shortly afterwards, the government made the decision to index benefits to prices rather than to earnings (Langley 2006, 2007: 77) – a move which would drag the relative value of benefits down over time. The reasoning for this was partially related to the rise in the use of home equity as a viable alternative as discussed above, but it fitted in with a more general New Labour aim to cut back on the state's responsibility in long-term welfare provision.

On the private side, a bigger, qualitative shift occurred from a system predominantly made up of defined benefit schemes to one in which the emphasis is on defined contributions. A defined benefit scheme (DB) is one in which the benefits to be paid out to retirees are set in the rules of the fund, usually according to some combination of number of years' service and earnings level. In the past, the level of earnings would be taken as the retiree's final salary, although in more recent decades, the tendency has been more towards averaging some period of earnings (UK Office for National Statistics 2009: 3–6). In contrast, defined contribution schemes (DC) are more like a generic savings vehicle with some preferential tax treatment. In DC schemes, benefits received depend on how much you have contributed to the scheme and how well the funds have performed on the financial markets (UK Office for National Statistics 2009). The crucial difference between the two, therefore, is where the market risk lies. In a DB scheme, the risk and responsibility for provision is the burden of the employer, since they are contractually obliged to pay out benefits according to the rules. In a DC scheme, the risk is shouldered by the individual worker, so if the fund performs poorly, that will be reflected in lower future benefits.

The groundwork for this shift was again laid down by government policy, including the 1986 Social Security Act, which made membership of occupational (DB) schemes voluntary rather than compulsory, at the same time as financial markets were becoming more accessible to individual savers (UK Office for National Statistics 2009: 6–4). The effect of this action was to make DC schemes more attractive, particularly for employers who, in addition to shedding market risk, had much more control over their own level of contributions (UK Office for National Statistics 2008). But the real process of change only gathered pace during the 2000s. As the National Association of Pension Funds (NAPF) reported, in 1999, 78% of all pension funds were of defined benefit type, but by 2005 they accounted for only 49% (National Association of Pension Funds 2007: 11). By the time of the credit crunch, only 23% of DB schemes remained open to new members with many having closed their doors altogether (Timmins 2009: 3). By contrast, DC schemes became increasingly widespread. Having only been in existence since the 1980s, nearly half of all DC schemes were established since the year 2000 – an upswing that correlated in timing, if not in volume, with the decline of DB schemes (see National Association of Pension Funds 2007: 12; UK Office for National Statistics 2009: 6–5).

From the perspective of marketised welfare provision, this could have been a key opportunity for the emergence of the 'prudentialised' individual. Rather than having their risk handled for them, employees were now increasingly in charge of their own risk profiles. They would adopt the 'everyday investor identity' and rationally manage their own process of 'income smoothing'. Perhaps, with some luck, reliance on state pension provision would naturally wither, fulfilling New Labour's aspiration to reverse the ratio of private to state pensions too. In aggregate however, the British public did not live up to this ideal. Firstly, despite Labour's talk of keeping state pension costs down and shifting the ratio of pension provision towards the private sector, such 'hollowing out' never actually happened. Even when adjusted for inflation, government expenditure on pensions nearly doubled over the decade from 1997 to 2007 (Chantrill 2017b). By the time Labour got around to its second major overhaul of the system in 2007, talk of efficiency was forgotten, replaced by a moderately progressive emphasis on redistribution. The 2007 Pensions Act on state pensions not only reinstated the earnings link, but also reduced the number of qualifying years required, ended the practice of contracting out into the private sector and made the system more generous towards people engaged in full-time care of the young, elderly and disabled (UK Government 2007). Also, in the wake of the financial crisis, the Pension Protection Fund, set up in 2005, accepted sixty-three DB funds in the fallout from the banking crisis in 2008 (BBC 2009), ensuring a safety net for DB schemes struggling to make pay-outs.

Put bluntly, once pension services were liberalised and DC schemes became the most prevalent option, savings fell, leaving some people inadequately prepared for retirement, a trend which was accompanied by a steady fall in the number of people in private-sector pensions overall. The NAPF reported that, in the period between 2000 and 2005, membership of private-sector DB pension schemes fell by 600,000 people, whilst the uptake of private sector DC pensions only rose by 150,000 (National Association of Pension Funds 2007). Also, the government itself estimated that seven million people had inadequate savings for their retirement (UK Department for Work and Pensions 2006), whilst MORI found that a full 41% of surveyed adults in employment had no pension at all (Barker and Healey 2004). Partly, this was because many people were beginning to see housing as a better bet for the provision of long-term welfare than pension funds, which were generally assumed by respondents to be unable to provide a secure income in retirement (Barker and Healey 2004). But then other data suggested that many people were simply not interested enough to think properly about their pension provision, even when confronted with the facts (Pitt-Watson 2009). In this vein, Adair Turner's pension report found that there were 'inherent behavioural barriers to people making rational long-term savings decisions without encouragement' (UK Pensions Commission 2005: 3). For its part, the government agreed, castigating the general public for its 'financial myopia' and an inability to get to grips with the complexity of the pension system (UK Department for Work and Pensions 2006: 31).

One could argue that financial myopia is an entirely reasonable response to the evolution of pension provision in the UK. Given that the shift from state to private provision and from DB- to DC-style pensions both entail extra risk for the individual, it is unsurprising that increasing numbers of individuals have opted to shun that risk altogether. And now, with the stability of global finance in question since 2008, long-term savers might be seen as extremely sensible in opting not to allow their present income to be traded for uncertain future gains. At best, such swings might make the timing of retirement a lottery; at worst, it might make any long-term saving seem like a gamble in general.

How did the government respond to this marked reluctance to grasp the nettle of DC pensions? Although it started to beef up the state pension a bit and moved to protect existing DB schemes through the Pension Protection Fund, perhaps more important were moves to orchestrate the take-up of DC schemes. Initially, the National Pensions Saving Scheme (NPSS) was vaunted in 2005 by the Pensions Commission as a system that

> recognises the inherent inadequacy of a purely voluntary approach, but which stops short of full compulsion, relying instead on the automatic enrolment of employees, but with the right to opt-out, and with a modest level of compulsion on employers to make matching contributions.
>
> (UK Pensions Commission 2005: ix)

In turn, the NPSS was to purchase low-cost, bulk DC schemes from the private sector. Following the Commission's recommendations, Labour announced that all people would be automatically enrolled on NPSS schemes from 2012 onwards, with a 4% contribution from the employee, 3% from employer and 1% tax relief (UK Department for Work and Pensions 2006: 9). A very similar step was taken by the US government, which chose to oblige workers to save in 401(k) defined contribution pension plans (Starr 2007: 215).

A Polanyian irony again rears its head: a supposedly more marketised system of defined contribution pension plans actually required a significant amount of government intervention to put in place, in the face of individuals' unwillingness to adopt the 'everyday investor identity' (Langley 2007). The fact that enrolment was made automatic, but not obligatory, is also interesting. This type of strategy – dubbed 'choice editing' or 'nudging' (Thaler and Sunstein 2008) – is appealing to government because it acts to 'improve decisions' in the eyes of authority whilst apparently not interfering with particular individuals' free choice – one can still opt out or make a different choice. In reality however, choice editing is just another way to exert governance – to exact a form of behaviour from the populace. Nudging would not be deemed a useful strategy by government if it did not yield the result desired, and one can imagine that if it did not, then more traditional forms of obligation might be employed.

No doubt there were high ideals at work in the Pensions Commission and the DWP – the various reports and papers are full of benevolent sentiment and a genuine concern for the welfare of citizens. But as a system of marketised welfare protection, the NPSS was a heavily financialised solution which effectively sought to provide a huge boost to the financial sector by pumping savings back into the stock market, thus protecting those markets from the threat of disinterest on the part of everyday savers – a sort of aggregate demand booster for financial services. One can only speculate on the long-term impact of this policy, although, as Jan Toporowski has demonstrated, the last time government acted in this fashion – when it enforced the provision of DB schemes earlier in the twentieth century – it resulted in a long period of capital market inflation which can be traced right through to the explosion of pension fund-financed hedge funds in the 2000s (Toporowski 2003: 2).

Concluding comments

In this chapter, we have looked at the last of Polanyi's three fictitious commodities – labour – in order to re-think how the tensions of the double movement have been displayed in more recent welfare arrangements. Taking the UK as an example, I started by noting how the idea of marketised welfare protection was forged in the consensus politics of New Labour's 'third way'. Like the theoretical apparatus behind derivatives-based finance and carbon trading, I noted how marketised welfare provision was politically appealing because of the way in which it sought to meet the ends of habitation via the means of improvement. Although this trend was clearly manifest in policy relating to healthcare and education (where 'consumers' are encouraged to choose between 'providers' based upon rankings systems), it was most clearly evident in the approaches taken to long-term income security. In particular, the New Labour government was keen to encourage financial awareness/literacy as a means for people to take responsibility for their own financial needs as a potential antidote to relying on more traditional forms of state-sponsored welfare.

Drawing on Paul Langley's notion of 'uncertain investor subjects' (Langley 2007), however, we saw that such policies relied on a problematic view of the individual as a rational capital accountant. I emphasised that the problem with this policy stance was that it acted in the face of large, countervailing incentives which, as in other examples discussed in this book, acted to undercut these attempted regimes of marketised protection. In this example, I suggested that the economics of consumption at the macro- and micro-level strongly incentivised debt accrual and present consumption rather than long-term saving. In this sense, marketised social protection failed in regard to long-term welfare provision because the transcendence of the opposition between individuals as consumers under an ethic of improvement and individuals as people requiring habitation, never happened.

Part IV
Contradiction without transcendence

9 Habitation versus improvement today

The end of marketised social protection

For Frederic Jameson, fascism, communism and the New Deal – the same three ideologies which Polanyi grouped together as responses to the collapse of *laissez-faire* liberalism – were the intellectual settings for the 'last survivals' (1992: 304) of a modernist worldview in that each embodied a faith in technological progress, technocratic efficiency and the rationalisation of economy and society, without any of the epistemological uncertainty inherent in the postmodern mindset. Certainly, the totalising ideological visions of Nazi fascism and Third International communism are a thing of the past in mainstream capitalist discourse, and the unique combination of futurism, faith in government and desperation for order that gave legitimacy to mid-twentieth century welfare state expansion does not exist in the same way today. The simplistic visions of the *laissez-faire* economic thought that Polanyi denounced are also a thing of the past. The widening of the franchise over the course of the twentieth century has produced demands for governmental intervention in support of economic stability (Eichengreen 2008), the provision of social security and environmental protection. However partial, incomplete or ineffective governmental responses to these demands have been, they do exist. The ambition and scale of those properly modernist economic philosophies within which Polanyi's thought was set have all been tempered, replaced by a more fluid ideological terrain.

Nevertheless, I have argued that the 'high modernist' (Scott 1998: 4) mindset lived on, nested in more complex articulations of economic theory. The third-wayist approach to the provision of welfare, the sustainable development paradigm and the conceptual marrying of the desires of financiers with the needs of society were all examples of a way of thinking which suggested that the fundamental tensions thrown up by capitalist development over the course of the twentieth century could be resolved through careful, socially-minded application of the price mechanism. If *laissez-faire*, fascism, communism and the New Deal were indeed the last survivals of modernist economic ideology, then these programmes of marketised social protection were perhaps its ghostly apparitions, reflecting the same desire to find a coherent, conceptually unified way of understanding the economy, and a correspondingly hopeful vision of how it might be ordered and rationalised. In Polanyi's thesis, the Tudor statesmen and pamphleteers trying to understand the new phenomenon of poverty amongst plenty are depicted as *ignorant* of the underlying contradiction between habitation and improvement, clinging to pre-industrial and pre-modern ways of understanding and later, Townsend and Malthus are shown to have *denied* the contradiction with recourse to a simplistic biological essentialism. By contrast, the late twentieth-century ideal of marketised social protection accepted that the contradiction existed, then suggested it was possible to *transcend* it through policy design.

In this book, I have suggested that the problematisation of the economy in terms of contradiction and possible transcendence is a mode of thinking with deep roots in the Western tradition of political economic thought. In his reading of Foucault, William Connolly captures the transcendent mindset well:

> Foucault suggests that the retreat of the old dogmatism – where limitations in the finite world were to be transcended through a faith that linked humanity to the infinite – has been accompanied by the advance of a new dogmatism. The new dogmatism, ironically, endlessly renews the circle of finitude in its restless search for a mode of attunement or transcendence that might still the quest. The carriers of these tactics typically act as if they … are on the verge of perfecting a transcendental argument that will soon still the oscillation troubling them.
>
> (Connolly 2007: 56)

The transcendence offered by the idea of marketised social protection operated through economic theory 'attuned' to social ends. Through the construction of an idealised vision of financial markets as consisting of a given set of assets and a given set of investors, it was argued that market actors could not help but apportion risk efficiently around the market at the same time as increasing aggregate material welfare and ensuring economic stability. The vision of an infinite Coasean market connecting all potential assets and actors was critical to generating the view that increased, rather than reduced, commodification of the environment was the key to defending the planet as a site of habitation. And a particular financialised vision of the economic individual provided the backdrop against which a solution to the problem of providing a social safety net in an economically globalising world was presented.

These new visions of marketised social protection sought to assimilate the opposition between habitation and improvement in complex theoretical ways, but ways which were nevertheless as utopian as the *laissez-faire* economism that Polanyi railed against. 'The market' was still understood in simplistic terms, as a self-contained system of prices which people and firms would respond to predictably and straightforwardly, a view which seriously underestimated the complexity and perversity of market behaviours in the real world and seriously overestimated the ability of governments to dictate and direct those behaviours. To think that self-interest could so easily be steered to produce social goods is a type of economism different to, but every bit as fallacious as, the type that Polanyi identified. Why expect modern banks to behave in the interests of structural economic stability when their *raison d'être* centres on the production of private profit and the avoidance of private loss? Why expect individuals to produce a system of social insurance through their consumption practices when the consumer economy is geared to produce diametrically opposed results? Why assume that a select set of artificial price signals could form the basis of a meaningful challenge to anthropogenic climate change?

Any serious response to the visions of marketised social protection needs to face up to the intractability of these issues. Visions of a population of fully self-reliant rational individuals, of banks naturally working for the common good and of global corporations meekly internalising their environmental externalities and accepting lower profit rates all reflect a denial of the need to make difficult choices between policy goals that are in opposition with one another. The problem is that difficult choices like these are often difficult to articulate in political practice: as we have observed repeatedly in the last three chapters, hopeful narratives of win-win outcomes and squared circles sold policies well in public discourse, realistic appraisals of costs and benefits of different types, less so. The abnegation of difficult choices between habitation and improvement often proved to be the best strategy rather than explicit choices between them. In 2008, however, this would all change. From then on, economic ideologies were increasingly pitched in terms that consciously prioritised improvement over habitation or *vice versa*.

Improvement versus habitation after 2008

It was often remarked on how little economic ideological change occurred in response to the 2008 financial crisis. In the immediate aftermath, mainstream economics was widely discredited for its over-reliance on neoclassical, market-centric methodology, which was seen as a reason why the discipline was blind to the role of financial innovation in driving the potential for crisis (*e.g.* Concerned Students of Economics 10 2011), but in the lecture halls and the seminar rooms, it continued to be taught in largely the same way as it had been before (see Coyle 2012b). Without any new paradigms to take its place, neoclassical economics lived on, if only in 'zombie' form (Quiggin 2010). Keynes's work was briefly fashionable, with famous economists such as Paul Krugman, Joseph Stiglitz and Robert Skidelsky all popularising Keynesian readings of the crisis which did indeed challenge the neoclassical economic worldview. But to the extent that the ideas of 'the master' (Skidelsky 2010) made it into policy programmes, it was in the shape of limited financial stimulus measures – including quantitative easing – designed to support existing financial market practices, rather than the kinds of strong Keynesian governmental rule-enforcing which might challenge them (see contributions to Tily 2010). In any case, what stimulus packages that were developed in Europe quickly became swamped by the all-embracing logic of austerity (Blyth 2013).

If anything, the financial crisis appeared to have been a useful opportunity for the improvement rationality to re-organise itself, strengthening its grip on the mechanisms of governance rather than relinquishing it. The sub-prime mortgage crisis was immediately conceptualised in public policy as a problem of insufficient liquidity, with solutions oriented solely towards restoring profitability in the financial sector (Langley 2010). If one looked hard, one could find a few innovative ideas and approaches to the question of how to govern financial markets (Baker 2013; Brassett and Holmes 2015) but debate was largely confined to the question of what precise blend of governmental intervention – state-sponsored bailouts, traditional monetary policy, regulation *etc.* – or market discipline – the removal of taxpayer guarantees for banks – offered the best opportunity to make financial markets profitable again, leaving the dominating power of financial professionals over the fortunes of all unchallenged. The imposition of austerity policies across Europe reflected the same outlook. In the wake of the eurozone crisis – which was triggered in part by the drying up of credit in the aftermath of the sub-prime crisis – the European Union was explicit in prioritising defence of the financial sector and of the principle of 'sound money', happily allowing the costs of the crisis to fall on the side of fiscal expenditure, with massive cutbacks on all types of social provisioning in debtor nations the result (Holmes 2014a).

This could be seen as a simple continuation of neoliberalism, 'Terminator-like' (Dale 2016b: 2) in its ability to re-assemble the power of markets over society in response to economic crisis. But something really did change in 2008: after this point, the conflict between the goals of economic improvement and the goals of economic habitation was baldly visible. In contrast to the win-win outlook of the marketised social protection paradigm, the politics of austerity has been positively defined by a clear narrative of costs, revolving around acceptable uses of public debt. On one hand, financial profitability *should* be prioritised, even if it means socialising private bank debt via bailouts, whilst on the other, the social safety net provided by the state *should* be cut back in order to reduce public debt. Whether one agrees with it or not, austerity is an ideology that makes its choices very clear: rather than selling the idea that the needs of habitation would be met through the means of improvement, the ideology of austerity willingly admits that it is sacrificing the former in defence of the latter. But in exhibiting that choice so clearly, the ideology of austerity also inadvertently made it clear that other possible choices could be made, and so there was a profusion of innovative economic thought in public discourse.

For example, whilst scholars have been debating the nature and purpose of money and finance in human affairs for centuries, this debate became very visible in the wake of the crisis. One particularly interesting example was the Greek system of bartering credits known as the TEM (Τοπική Εναλλακτική Μονάδα), which emerged as a popular way of exchanging goods and services in towns ravaged by the eurozone crisis. The TEM was an innovative, if marginal and problematic, solution to a pressing problem: a shortage of cash in order to use as means of payment in everyday transactions, but it was played upon in the European press in terms of its ability to sustain livelihoods and social relations in a way that the euro could not. In the UK, the post-crisis mood of public distrust in the financial sector was also captured by the businessman Dave Fishwick, who, in 2011 set up a small-scale savings and loan organisation based in Burnley which celebrated the possibility of a finance which supported the community and which operated through personal relationships between savers, staff and borrowers. Whilst it was only one small bank, the traction that the story achieved was notable, provoking advocacy from a number of politicians and regulators (Brassett and Holmes 2015).

The volume of commentary on Bitcoin was another good example. It is easy to dismiss the cryptocurrency as a flash in the pan, perhaps as the Dutch tulips of our time, but again the extent to which it caught the public imagination in the time since 2008 was the interesting thing. As Maurer *et al.* discuss,

> The point is not whether Bitcoin 'works' as a currency, but what it promises: solidity, materiality, stability, anonymity, and, strangely, community. Indeed, in its endeavor to cut out intermediaries with the capacity to direct or limit the flow of funds among users and instead build a networked world of individual nodes able to exchange directly and 'freely' with one another, Bitcoin combines a practical materialism with a politics of community and trust that puts the code front and center.
> (Maurer et al 2013: 263)

No doubt, the vision of community at work in the self-image of the Bitcoin community is very different to the one present in local currency initiatives, or in Fishwick's crusade, but like them, it suggested a public mood in which financial relationships were being thought about in ways that eschewed the language of profitability, capital adequacy and moral hazard, and instead in ways that emphasised the social nature of money.

Of course none of these alternative models of finance was ever likely to replace current financial orders any time soon. Persistent questions over the use of Bitcoins to fund criminal activities often dominated its discussion on news agendas, whilst local currencies were often criticised on the basis that they were the preserve of the farmers'-market-loving middle classes rather than of the poor and unemployed who might genuinely stand to benefit from the types of social solidarity that they sought to embody. Nevertheless, systems like these at least foregrounded a newly popular sense that money and financial systems carry values about the type of society and economy in which we wish to live.

Another good example was the idea of a 'basic income' as a way to provide for welfare. Again this was an idea which had again been around for a long time, but one that became much more visible in public economic discourse after the financial crisis. Although there are many different names for such a policy (universal income, demogrant, citizen's income, social dividend, basic income guarantee) and many different individual policy proposals, they all centre on one fundamental policy principle as outlined by the Basic Income Earth Network: 'an income granted unconditionally to all individuals in a society without any means test or work requirement' (Basic Income Earth Network 2017). In most proposals, such an income would replace all existing means tested allowances, which are to a great extent the norm in modern welfare states. On one hand, it has been argued that this would eliminate the need for the huge bureaucracies required to administer means tested benefits. On the other, it is suggested that it would partially overcome the work disincentivisation problem commonly said to pertain to the provision of welfare, because it is not withdrawn as a recipient takes on employment.

On these politically ambiguous bases, basic income gathered a wide constituency of advocates in the post-2008 era, including economists and political interest groups of all ideological persuasions, from libertarians, neoclassicists and Silicon Valley billionaires through to socialists, post-Marxists and everything in between. Debate about basic income was increasingly to be found across all major press outlets, in television documentaries and in popular social science books (*e.g.* Bregman 2016; Murray and Pateman 2012; Standing 2017), and a variety of pilot schemes were run in countries as diverse as the United States, Namibia, India and the Netherlands. In the UK, the Green Party became a strong advocate of the idea of a basic income, their most recent proposal suggesting an income of £80 per week for all working age adults, a figure which is just higher than the current Jobseeker's Allowance level of £73.10 (Green Party 2015: 4), with different levels set for pensioners and children.

This is not the place for an examination of the pros and cons of a basic income. Suffice to say, critics on the right worry that such schemes will require increased taxation and will incentivise laziness despite their universality, whilst those on the left worry that it will excuse low pay and precipitate a decline in other forms of welfare provision; a wide political constituency of advocates has been matched by a wide constituency of detractors. But it has clearly been an example of growing support for economic policy visions focused on the provision of habitation. The economic 'problem' that basic income seeks to address is not a lack of productivity or profitability, but insecure working conditions, especially in light of the automation of jobs via technological progress (Standing 2017). Vaunted basic income schemes vary from those which would be entirely cost neutral once the abolition of existing benefits are factored in, to those which propose higher taxation of one form or another (income, wealth, pollution, financial transactions *etc.*), but all start from the basic idea that the state has obligations to citizens in terms of providing for habitation that are unique and which cannot be described in terms of market failure. As Anthony Atkinson, a long-time defender of the basic income idea notes, it [reaffirms] the principle that societies have a duty to provide social protection ... We can argue about what constitutes 'decent', and about the conditions attached to the social minimum, but everyone should have a right to resources, over which they have control.

(Atkinson 2011: 1)

The visibility of basic income in public debate demonstrated a new tone to public debate in which, to borrow Cerny's words (1994), the *character* of welfare, state and economy was increasingly up for debate.

The problem is that, whilst all this was indeed indicative of a new public visibility of innovative thought about the purposes of the economy, and of a new emphasis on the ends of habitation, none of it has been successful in policy terms as of yet. The only time that a basic income policy came close to nationwide implementation was in Switzerland where it was presented to the populace in the form of a plebiscite in 2016, but was rejected by 77% of voters. Innovative financial ideas generated a lot of column inches, but did not alter the direction of public economic management. More generally, anti-austerity protests came in all shapes and sizes from 2010 onwards, including the global *Occupy* movement, the Greek and Spanish *Indignados* protests and the anti-tuition fees marches in the UK, but none were successful in securing change. Tuition fees were pushed through, the EU continued to pursue austerity policy prescriptions, and all governments acquiesced sooner or later to those prescriptions. The collapse of Syriza's attempt to negotiate concessions on the EU's programme of structural adjustment was emblematic in this regard.

In sum, the question of how to secure habitation had now been unambiguously raised, first by the experience of financial crisis and then by the effects of austerity, but public policy appeared unable or unwilling to answer that question. But this would all change again in 2016. If financial crises since 2008 had provoked a pivot towards improvement at the expense of habitation in public policy, with ideologies of habitation forming the ineffective resistance, the rise of Donald Trump and Britain's referendum vote to leave the European Union signalled a complete about turn, with habitation ascendant in ways that could not be addressed or understood through the language of improvement.

Habitation versus improvement in 2016

Many viewed the case for Brexit and various aspects of Trump's manifesto as economically illiterate and, in terms of the likelihood of generating growth and productivity, they had a point. It was demonstrated in study after study that the migrants which both Brexit and Trump campaigns promised to refuse entry to drove higher productivity in the British and American economies, and further that they contributed more to the public purse in taxation than they took out via benefits and entitlements (Travis 2016). Similarly, it was unarguable that access to the EU single market drove stronger British trade and that all the trade deals that Trump professed a desire to 'rip up' were designed to secure better access to foreign markets for US firms, boosting private sector productivity. But all of these arguments played on an imaginary of improvement only. Such appeals spoke to 'the economy' understood in aggregate terms, as a machine to increase productivity and GDP output. By contrast, the Brexit and Trump campaigns appealed, in different ways, to an imaginary of habitation and livelihood.

Consider the way in which each side of each debate handled the perennial electoral issue of jobs. With the appropriate theoretical mix, it is straightforward to argue that protectionism, restrictions on immigration, the abandonment of free trade deals and the general instability provoked by the election of Trump or the departure from the European Union would reduce material welfare in a general sense and 'cost jobs' in aggregate across the economy (the mix being comparative advantage, Keynesian multiplier, new monetary consensus and a pinch of decision theory). But, even if we accept the veracity of those arguments on their own terms – and there is plenty of good economic theory which calls attention instead to the those who might make material losses from international economic integration (Rodrik 2017) – they are abstract and difficult to identify with in an everyday sense. As David Yarrow has argued, the problem is that such arguments 'conceive of "economic benefits" and, by implication, "economic drawbacks" in reductionist terms: typically, the overall effects of migration on GDP growth, tax receipts or job creation figures mark the limits of the discussion' (Yarrow 2017). As he continues to note, this meant that '[f]actors such as reduced job security, diminished voice and autonomy in the workplace, restricted opportunities for self-development, or generalised work intensification ... are posited as "non-economic" or "cultural factors"' (Yarrow 2017).

By contrast, Trump and Brexit played on a different vision of the economy which did speak to these factors directly within an imaginary of economy as livelihood. Trump's campaign promises often centred on specific jobs done by specific people in specific communities, communities marginalised economically by processes of improvement. For example, promises to 'get coal miners back to work' figured heavily. These promises were often pro-market and anti-state, focusing on the reduction of subsidies to green energy suppliers and the elimination of 'devastating anti-coal regulation' (Trump cited in Fears 2017). A report by staff at the Centre on Global Energy Policy at Columbia found that such factors were in fact a small part of the reason for the decline of coal in the US, with issues such as decreased demand due to higher energy efficiency, increased competition from natural gas and the effects of a slow-down in Chinese coal demand on global prices having played much more significant roles (Houser et al. 2017). And in terms of the jobs themselves, coal is an industry marked by increasing automation – digging by explosives, increasingly powerful drilling systems, driverless haulage *etc*. Between 2000 and 2015, the coal industry lost over half of its workforce, but productivity grew to such a degree that output increased by 8% over the same period (Saha and Liu 2017).

Such arguments suggest the benefits of a relaxed policy attitude to the decline of the industry, but only within the context of an imaginary of improvement. Although it was rooted in a faith in the free market, Trump's was nevertheless a rhetoric of direct action to defend the livelihoods of people who had lost out due to wider processes of economic improvement, whatever the effects on total output or productivity.

The Brexit campaign was fought primarily on the issue of immigration, but evidence of a correlation between support for leaving the EU and local influx of migrants was at best mixed (Goodwin and Heath 2016). Stronger was the correlation with levels of relative deprivation in the UK, particularly in those areas which were marked by the highest degrees of economic insecurity (Bell 2016; see also Becker et al. 2017). Areas which recorded the highest levels of support for Brexit were most likely to be traditional working-class communities – Doncaster, Great Yarmouth and Boston, for example – all areas which have suffered the brunt of de-industrialisation, the shrinking of labour markets and unemployment in the UK over the past quarter century (Goodwin and Heath 2016). These are long-term trends associated with Britain's shift away from manufacturing and manual labour-intensive work, in which it no longer retains a competitive advantage, towards a model of growth rooted in financial and corporate services primarily clustered in London, in which it does. Although there were various other types of Brexit voter – those with entirely justifiable concerns about the democratic deficits that undermine the EU's claims to legitimacy as well as misty-eyed patriots – these economically 'left behind' voters, as they became known, were decisive, having reasonable cause to reject the status quo (Yarrow 2017), and the Brexit campaign was successful in pitching itself in those terms.

There was strong evidence that departing from the EU would harm such voters' interests even on issues we might think of in habitation terms. Promises to curb immigration were mixed with other promises to reduce employment regulation, including the EU working time directive and laws requiring equal treatment of full- and part-time employees (Joseph Rowntree Foundation 2016), changes that would likely *increase* labour market insecurity. Even on immigration itself, most economic studies concluded that restrictions would have little or no effect on wage or employment levels (Joseph Rowntree Foundation 2016). But, like Trump, Brexit campaigners talked in terms of direct action to defend livelihood. The plausibility of such promises – the 'fake news' issue – is pertinent here. The very fact that the campaigns appealed to voters in terms of livelihood and habitation meant that they could not be disproved by opposed appeals rooted in the language of improvement. The battle was over competing visions of the nature of the economy, not empirical knowledge which could be verified as 'non-fake'. The appeal of these ideologies lay in the promise to defend people's livelihoods directly, rather than in promising a better life indirectly through generalised processes of economic improvement. The former speaks in terms of legislation and action, the latter in terms of statistical proof and abstract notions of growth. However right or wrong the economics of Brexit or Trumpism may have been, it is that direct discursive orientation to questions of habitation that underlined a big part of their electoral appeal.

Can the language of habitation be rescued from the divisive rhetoric evinced in the Brexit and Trump campaigns? Does a commitment to the defence of livelihood necessarily come packaged with hostility to the already weak and marginalised, particularly the weakest and most marginalised of all: migrants? As James Scott argued, the ideology of economic growth grew more and more politically appealing over the twentieth century 'due to its promise as a technological "fix" for class struggle' (1998: 99). As long as material welfare rose in an unbroken manner, profits and wages could rise at the same time, displacing more difficult debates about the most just distribution of wealth amongst the classes. By this account, economic improvement is a palliative for social conflict. If conflict – whether along class, race, or other lines – is the result of the slowdown of economic improvement, then should we be simply seeking to restore growth and profitability with the hope that greater social co-operative sentiments will follow behind?

The problem is that the underlying costs to habitation seem unlikely to fall away and perhaps are getting worse. The case for increased labour market flexibility will still be made on efficiency and profit grounds. More and more jobs will be automated out of existence and there is no guarantee that, in contrast to the classic Schumpeterian ideal of creative destruction, this time the destruction of jobs will not outpace the creation of new ones. For most people, so much of one's livelihood still depends on having 'a job' – the pay, the stability of livelihood, but also the benefits and the psychological sense of self-worth, and while this is the case, the disruptive effects of automation and technology are deeply problematic. On top of this, whether due to inflation, protectionism, consumer debt overhang or the same collapse of confidence in financial markets that triggered the crisis in 2008, further financial crises look likely (Bank for International Settlements 2017), and our knowledge of the damage economic growth causes to the viability of the planet as an ecosystem is only increasing. The tension between improvement and habitation is not disappearing any time soon.

Instead of resigning ourselves to these apparently interminable contradictions, a more optimistic, and Polanyian, route is to think about how we might make room for a plurality of human needs in the way in which we think about the economy. The social value of habitation and improvement are, in Polanyi's account, both great. Material progress and the need for some security of livelihood are presented as being fundamental to the condition of humanity in market societies, so neither can be rejected outright. But, critically, each is of fundamentally different type: one does not lead to the other in any automatic way, and neither can be substituted for by the other, and so we must bargain, debate and trade-off between them.

In some senses, one could make the case that we are in fact in the process of such bargaining now. As I have argued, much public debate about the economy for at least two decades before the financial crisis was set within the post-ideological pretensions of third way thought, which hinged on the idea that all that had been opposed in previous political philosophies of either the right or left could either be forgotten or reconciled (Mouffe 2000: 108). The brashness with which austerity prioritised improvement damaged this way of thinking, and Brexit and Trump have now upset it altogether. The disagreements between each side of each debate do not hinge on different methods to secure the same economic goals, but rather on different goals, each set within different imaginaries of the nature of the economy and its purpose. If that pluralism bleeds out beyond the campaigns themselves and sets the tone for a value-laden, normatively driven political economic debate in which choices and the costs of choices have to be justified more openly, rather than swept under the technocratic carpet or assumed away theoretically, then that may be a good thing: perhaps an economic version of Mouffe's vision of politics 'not as the search for an inaccessible consensus ... but as an "agonistic confrontation" between conflicting interpretations' (2000: 20). Although this is a long way from the thoroughly *antagonistic* politics of Brexit and Trump as we have experienced it so far, from such a perspective, the more numerous and diverse imaginaries of the economy are, the stronger that debate about it can be.

The direction of the political projects of Brexit and Trump in themselves remains to be seen. As the negotiations over Brexit rumble on, Labour and Conservative parties both express a desire to end freedom of movement in the name of curbing immigration, but also to retain access to the single market. This fence-sitting is an understandable position for parties wishing to seek power as it can be sold to those who voted for Brexit and against, but such an outcome has been ruled out by EU leaders, and so it seems likely that, if not all one way or the other, some explicit trade-off will have to be made between the two goals. Trump has lived up to his manifesto on some economic points – withdrawal from TPP and the Paris Climate Agreement for example, but failed on others – notably the Mexican border wall and promises of massive infrastructure spending. As for the miners, one coal mine opened in June 2017, with around 100 full time jobs – a not-very-convincing fulfilment of his pledges to them. In any case, Trump's bizarre ways and the possibility of impeachment make prediction impossible. The outcomes of his presidency and of British departure from the EU are unpredictable in general, but it seems likely that appeals to visions of improvement and of habitation will continue to form the dividing lines of political economic discourse for some time to come, for better or worse.

Concluding comments

In this book, I have argued that Polanyi's work *The Great Transformation*, offers a lot of potential to help us understand the direction of capitalism in terms of the 'great debates' that underpin it. Rather than isolating particular conceptual tools and applying them to this or that specific policy issue, I have attempted to engage in the same expansive mode of analysis that Polanyi evinced in *TGT* in the belief that, beyond its content, it is the form of that book which comprises a substantial part of its appeal. In Polanyiological terms, my aim has been to demonstrate that his thesis is in part a reflection of an attitude to modernist tropes of abstract reason and universalism which were common to other scholars during the time at which Polanyi wrote. This attitude manifested in *TGT* as a critique of the marginalism of Carl Menger and his contemporaries, but it was clearly a worldview which permeated Polanyi's approach to liberalism in general as well as to fascism and certain strands of Marxism and socialism. It was an attitude to the epistemological false securities offered by any ideology which professed to contain complete, universal solutions to humanity's economic problems.

I have agreed with critics that the way in which Polanyi mapped this critique on to the history of economic ideas in *TGT* is problematic, but by isolating the argumentative root of his thesis, I have sought to present a more nuanced history which extends Polanyi's approach beyond the critique of *laissez-faire* economism. My main conclusion has been that, in Western political economic thought in which the economy has been identified as a distinct sphere of human engagement, the structure of argument has often been presented in terms of logical contradiction, whether between divine and earthly order, between the freedom and the power that private property affords, between the benefits of competition and the costs of monopoly, or between the need for habitation and the desire for improvement. Sometimes, theorists have been happy to live with such contradictions and simply appeal to our sense of judgment to find ways to navigate between each pole. More often, the very presentation of the nature of the economy in terms of contradiction has led theorists to find ways to conceptually transcend each contradiction in one way or another.

For Polanyi, the tension between habitation and improvement is generic to capitalism, but it is only in the time since he wrote that it has assumed a role as new master contradiction in public discourse on the economy, whether manifest in the perceived contradiction between the benefits of globalisation and its effects on the welfare state, the benefits of financial innovation and its effects on economic stability, or the benefits of economic growth in general and its effects on the biosphere. In the second half of the book we have seen how economic theory sought to deal with these tensions over the twentieth century, finding new ways to transcend each contradiction, instead of admitting that we need to judge the balance between ends that cannot be perfectly reconciled. The end result was a series of more or less utopian schemes to secure habitation via improvement through systems of marketised social protection.

Although this transcendent mindset had its roots in economic theory, my analysis has suggested that it is pointless to blame economists for the rise of these ideas. Economic ideas don't get very far if no-one likes them, and in arenas of finance, environment and welfare alike, I have sought to demonstrate that the win-win world of marketised social protection was one which was often lapped up by politicians and one which could be sold to electorates and business interests with relative ease. Visions of perfectibility sold well because they promised a world without contradiction, and that is a very appealing promise indeed.

If the marketised social protection mindset really has been killed off by a decade of financial crisis and austerity and the explosive events of 2016, if this really is a transformational juncture in the history of economic ideas, then I would hope that the future trajectory of debate evinces some of the doubt, the lack of assuredness and the openly ethical nature of argument that I have shown to characterise various previous junctures in the history of economic ideas. The metaphor of the fall from grace in the natural law approach to property, the Enlightenment concern over the balance between freedom and power and the wrangling over the moral status of market competition in the early activities of the Mont Pelerin Society all showed something of this spirit. Today, in a time when the tensions between habitation and improvement have come to a head on so many fronts, basic questions like 'what do we want the economy to do for us?', 'what different values do we want it to embody?', 'how do we decide on the relative value of growth and stability?' *etc.* need to become a feature of public debate. Indeed, as I have discussed in this chapter, to some degree they already have.

If future answers to those questions slowly become compressed and simplified down to a series of as yet unknown universalised, abstract maxims in the same way that Locke's conception of property, Smith's notion of competition, and the moral economy of the early MPS did, then, by the argument of this book, that will be an unfortunate thing. By engaging in such a broad history of ideas, I hope to have shown that the desire to use theory to attempt to transcend economic contradiction is a very basic and widespread impulse in political economic thought, so there is no reason to think that it will vanish any time soon. But that is looking a long way in the future. For the time being, whilst there is great uncertainty as to the future direction of economic ideas in public discourse, and no clear successor paradigm to that of marketised social protection, it is clear that we have entered a period in which economic values and priorities have to be defended, rejected, argued for or against. With a bit of luck, the economic debate surrounding Trump and Brexit will prove to mark only an early waypoint in this period rather than its end.

Bibliography

Abdelal, R. (2009) 'Constructivism as an approach to international political economy', in *Routledge handbook of international political economy (IPE): IPE as a global conversation*, ed. M. Blyth (Oxford: Routledge) pp.62–76.

Agamben, G. (2011) *The kingdom and the glory: For a theological genealogy of economy and government* (Stanford, CA: Stanford University Press).

Andrews, E.L. (2008) 'Greenspan concedes error on regulation', *The New York Times* 23/10/08:B1.

Aquinas, T. (1920 [1274]) *Summa theologiae of St. Thomas Aquinas*, second revised edition (London: Burns Oates and Washbourne) [Accessed on 24/08/17 at: www.newadvent.org/summa/index.html].

Armitage, D. (2004) 'Introduction' in *The free sea*, Grotius, H. (Indianapolis, IN: Liberty Fund).

Arrow, K.J. (1969) 'The organisation of economic activity: Issues pertinent to the choice of market versus non-market allocation' in *The analysis and evaluation of public expenditures: The PBS system*, ed. US Congress: Joint Economic Committee (Washington, DC: US Government Printing Office) pp.1–16.

Atkinson, A.B. (2011) 'Basic income: Ethics, statistics and economics', unpublished paper [Accessed on 23/08/17 at www.nuff.ox.ac.uk/users/atkinson/Basic_Income%20Luxembourg%20April%202011.pdf].

Atkinson, D. and Elliott, L. (2007) *Fantasy Island: Waking up to the incredible economic, political and social illusions of the Blair legacy* (London: Constable).

Bäckstrand, A. and Lövbrand, E. (2006) 'Planting trees to mitigate climate change: Contested discourses of ecological modernization, green governmentality and civic environmentalism', *Global Environmental Politics* 6:1 pp.50–75.

Baker, A. (2013) 'The new political economy of the macroprudential ideational shift', *New Political Economy* 18:1 pp.112–139.

Bank for International Settlements (2017) *87th annual report, 1 April 2016–31 March 2017* (Basel: Bank for International Settlements).

Basic Income Earth Network (2017) 'About basic income' [Accessed on 23/08/17 at http://basicincome.org/basic-income/].

Battye, F., Bishop, B., Harris, P., Murie, A., Rowlands, R. and Tice, A. (2006) *Evaluation of key worker living: Final report* (London: Department for Communities and Local Government).

Baum, G. (1996) *Karl Polanyi on ethics and economics* (Montreal and Kingston: McGill-Queen's University Press).

Baumol, W. (2002) 'Towards microeconomics of innovation: Growth engine hallmark of market economics', *Atlantic Economic Journal* 30:1 pp.1–12.
BBC (2009) 'Pensions safety net shows strain' [Accessed on 23/08/17 at http://news.bbc.co.uk/1/hi/business/8344415.stm].
Bean, J.M.W. (1963) 'Plague, population and economic decline in England in the later Middle Ages', *The Economic History Review* 15:3 pp.423–437.
Becker, S.O., Fetzer, T. and Novy, T. (2017) 'Who voted for Brexit? A comprehensive district-level analysis', *Centre for Competitive Advantage in the Global Economy* working paper No.305, Oct. 2016, resubmitted Apr 2017.
Bell, T. (2016) 'The referendum, living standards and inequality', Resolution Foundation website [Accessed on 04/06/17 at www.resolutionfoundation.org/media/blog/the- referendum-living-standards-and-inequality/].
Bentham, J. (1978[1802]) 'Security and equality of property' in *Property: Mainstream and critical positions*, ed. C.B. Macpherson (Oxford: Basil Blackwell) pp.39–56.
Berlin, I. (1969) *Four essays on liberty* (Oxford: Oxford University Press).
Bernstein, S. (2001) *The compromise of liberal environmentalism* (New York: Columbia University Press).
Best, J. (2003) 'From the top-down: The new financial architecture and the re-embedding of global finance', *New Political Economy* 8:3 pp.363–384.
Best, J. and Paterson, M. (2010) 'Understanding cultural political economy' in *Cultural political economy*, eds. J. Best and M. Paterson (New York: Routledge) pp.1–25.
Birchfield, V. (1999) 'Contesting the hegemony of market ideology: Gramsci's "good sense" and Polanyi's "double movement"', *Review of International Political Economy* 6:1 pp.27–54.
Black, F., Jensen, M.C. and Scholes, M. (1972) 'The capital asset pricing model: Some empirical tests' in *Studies in the theory of capital markets*, ed. M.C. Jensen (New York: Praeger) pp.79–121.
Blackburn, R. (2006) 'Finance and the fourth dimension', *New Left Review* 39 pp.39–70.
Blackstone, W. (1959) *Ehrlich's Blackstone (Commentaries)* (San Carlos, CA: Nourse Publishing Company).
Blair, T. (2003) 'The third way: New politics for a new century' in *The new labour reader*, eds. A. Chadwick and R. Heffernan (Cambridge: Polity Press) pp.28–33.
Blanchard, I. (1970) 'Population change, enclosure, and the early Tudor economy', *The Economic History Review* 23:3 pp.427–445.
Blaney, D.L. and Inayatullah, N. (2010) *Savage economics: Wealth, poverty, and the temporal walls of capitalism* (London: Routledge).
Bleiker, R. (1998) 'Retracing and redrawing the boundaries of events: Postmodern interferences with international theory', *Alternatives: Global, Local, Political* 23:4 pp.471–497.
Block, F. (2007) 'Understanding the diverging trajectories of the United States and Western Europe: A neo-Polanyian analysis', *Politics & Society* 35 pp.3–33.
Block, F. and Somers, M. (2003) 'In the shadow of Speenhamland: Social policy and the old poor law', *Politics & Society* 31:2 pp.283–323.
Block, F. and Somers, M. (2014) *The power of market fundamentalism* (Cambridge, MA: Harvard University Press).
Blyth, M. (2002) *Great transformations: Economic ideas and institutional change in the twentieth century* (Cambridge: Cambridge University Press).
Blyth, M. (2013) *Austerity: The history of a dangerous idea* (Oxford: Oxford University Press).

Bohannan, P. (1955) 'Some principles of exchange and investment among the Tiv', *American Anthropologist* 57:1 pp.60–71.
Bookstaber, R. (2007) *A demon of our own design: Markets, hedge funds and the perils of financial innovation* (Hoboken, NJ: John Wiley & Sons).
Boulding, K. (1966) 'The economics of the coming spaceship Earth' in *Environmental quality in a growing economy*, ed. H. Jarrett (Baltimore, MD: Johns Hopkins University Press) pp.3–14.
Boyson, N.M., Stahel, C.W. and Stulz, R.M. (2006) 'Is there hedge fund contagion' in *The NBER working papers series* (Cambridge, MA: National Bureau of Economic Research).
Brassett, J. and Holmes, C. (2010) 'International political economy and the question of ethics', *Review of International Political Economy* 17:3 pp.425–453.
Brassett, J. and Holmes, C. (2015) 'Building resilient finance? Uncertainty, complexity, and resistance', *British Journal of Politics and International Relations* 18:2 pp.370–388.
Braun, M. (2009) 'The evolution of emissions trading in the European Union – The role of policy networks, knowledge and policy entrepreneurs', *Accounting, Organizations and Society* 34 pp.469–487.
Bregman, R. (2016) *Utopia for realists* (Amsterdam: De Correspondent).
Buckle, S. (1991) *Natural law and the theory of property* (Oxford: Clarendon Press).
Buick, A. (2011) 'Non-market socialism' in *Life without money: Building fair and sustainable economies*, eds. A. Nelson and F. Timmerman (London: Pluto Press) pp.139–160.
Burawoy, M. (2003) 'For a sociological Marxism: The complementary convergence of Antonio Gramsci and Karl Polanyi', *Politics & Society* 31:2 pp.193–261.
Burgin, A. (2012) *The great persuasion: Reinventing free markets since the depression* (Cambridge, MA: Harvard University Press).
Burke, E. (1795) *Thoughts and details on scarcity* (London: Rivington).
Callinicos, A. (2001) *Against the third way* (Cambridge: Polity Press).
Camus, A. (2005) *The myth of sisyphus* (London: Penguin).
Cangiani, M. (2012) 'Freedom in a complex society', *International Journal of Political Economy* 41:4 pp.34–53.
Capoor, K. and Ambrosi, P. (2009) *State and trends of the carbon market 2009* (Washington, DC: World Bank).
Caporaso, J.A. and Tarrow, S. (2009) 'Polanyi in Brussels: Supranational institutions and the transnational embedding of markets', *International Organization* 63:4 pp.593–620.
CDM Executive Board (2004) *Methodological tool: Tool for the demonstration and assessment of additionality* (Bonn: UNFCCC).
Cerny, P.G. (1994) 'The dynamics of financial globalization: Technology, market structure, and policy response', *Policy Sciences* 27:4 pp.319–342.
Chandler, D. (2014) 'Beyond neoliberalism: Resilience, the new art of governing complexity', *Resilience* 2:1 pp.47–63.
Chang, M. (2012) 'Understanding the rules of European economic governance: Economics, politics, and wishful thinking', *Journal of European Integration* 34:3 pp.297–303.
Changzheng, Z. (2010) 'China responds to US criticism of yuan policy', in *Caixin online* (Bejing: Caixin Online).
Chantrill, C. (2017a) 'UK public spending since 1900' [Accessed on 23/07/17 at www.ukpublicspending.co.uk/past_spending].
Chantrill, C. (2017b) 'Public spending on pensions since 1994' [Accessed on 23/08/17 at www.ukpublicspending.co.uk/spending_chart_1994_2020UKb_17c1li111mcn_00t].

Clapp, J. and Dauvergne, P. (2005) *Paths to a green world: The political economy of the global environment* (London: The Massachusetts Institute of Technology Press).
Clark, T.D. (2014) 'Reclaiming Karl Polanyi, socialist intellectual', *Studies in Political Economy* 94:1 pp.61–84.
Coase, R. (1960) 'The problem of social cost', *Journal of Law and Economics* 3 pp.1–44.
Coggan, P. (2008) *Guide to hedge funds: What they are, what they do, their risks, their advantages* (London: The Economist in association with Profile Books).
Comninel, G.C. (2000) 'English feudalism and the origins of capitalism', *The Journal of Peasant Studies* 27:4 pp. 1–53.
Concerned Students of Economics 10 (2011) 'An open letter to Greg Mankiw, 03/11/11', [Accessed on 23/08/17 at https://mronline.org/2011/11/03/harvard031111-html/].
Connolly, W.E. (2007) 'Pluralization', in *William E. Connolly: Democracy, pluralism and political theory*, eds. S.A. Chambers and T. Carver (London: Routledge) pp.37–60.
Copeland, B.R. and Taylor, M.S. (2005) 'Free trade and global warming: A trade theory view of the Kyoto protocol', *Journal of Environmental Economics and Management* 49:2 pp.205–234.
Council of the European Union, The (2005) *Climate change: Medium and longer term emission reduction strategies, including targets* (Brussels: The Council of the European Union).
Coyle, D. (2012a) 'Are economics graduates fit for purpose?', *VoxEU.org* [Accessed on 04/06/17 at http://voxeu.org/article/are-economics-graduates-fit-purpose].
Coyle, D. [ed.] (2012b) *What's the use of economics: Teaching the dismal science after the crisis* (London: London Publishing Partnership).
Cramer, R. (2007) 'Asset based welfare policy in the UK: Findings from the Child Trust Fund and Saving Gateway Initiatives' paper delivered at the Research Conference of the Association for Public Policy Analysis and Management, November 9–11, Washington, DC.
Credit Suisse/Tremont (2008) 'Benchmark performance summary' [Accessed on 14/10/08 at www.hedgeindex.com/hedgeindex/en/default.aspx?cy=USD].
Crouch, C. (2009) 'Privatised Keynesianism: An unacknowledged policy regime', *British Journal of Politics & International Relations* 11:3 pp.382–399.
Dale, G. (2008) 'Karl Polanyi's *The Great Transformation*: Perverse effects, protectionism and Gemeinschaft', *Economy and Society* 37:4 pp.495–524.
Dale, G. (2010) *Karl Polanyi: The limits of the market* (Cambridge: Polity Press).
Dale, G. (2011) 'Positivism and "functional theory" in the thought of Karl Polanyi 1907–1922', *Sociology Compass* 5:2 pp.148–164.
Dale, G. (2016a) *Karl Polanyi: A life on the left* (New York: Columbia University Press).
Dale, G. (2016b) *Reconstructing Karl Polanyi* (London: Pluto).
Dales, J.H. (1968a) *Pollution, property and prices: An essay in policy-making and economics* (Toronto: University of Toronto Press).
Dales, J.H. (1968b) 'Land, water and ownership', *The Canadian Journal of Economics* 1:4 pp.791–804.
Davies, W. (2014) *The limits of neoliberalism authority, sovereignty and the logic of competition* (London: SAGE Publications).
de Goede, M. (2003) 'Beyond economism in international political economy', *Review of International Studies* 29:1 pp.79–97.
de Goede, M. (2005) *Virtue, fortune and faith: A geneaology of finance* (Minneapolis, MN: University of Minnesota Press).

Dent, M. (2006) 'Patient choice and medicine in health care – Responsibilization, governance and proto-professionalization', *Public Management Review* 8:3 pp.449–462.

Department for Communities and Local Government (2012) 'Table 1300: Number of outstanding mortgages, arrears and repossessions, United Kingdom, from 1969' [Accessed on 23/08/17 at www.gov.uk/government/statistical-data-sets/live-tables-on-repossession-activity].

Department of Social Security (1998) *A new contract for welfare* (London: HMSO).

Diamond, J. (1997) *Guns, germs, and steel* (New York: W.W. Norton).

Directgov UK (2010) 'Savings Gateway – what it is and who qualifies' [Accessed on 23/08/17 at http://webarchive.nationalarchives.gov.uk/20090204012953/http://www.direct.gov.uk/en/MoneyTaxAndBenefits/ManagingMoney/SavingsAndInvestments/DG_10010450].

Dolphin, T. and Prabhakar, R. (2010) *Asset-based welfare and child poverty: Next steps for the Welsh assembly* (London: Institute for Public Policy Research).

Dreshner, M. (1961) *The mathematics of games of strategy: Theory and applications* (Englewood, NJ: Prentice Hall).

Druckman, A. and Jackson, T. (2009) 'The carbon footprint of UK households 1990–2004: A socio-economically disaggregated, quasi-multi-reqional input-output model', *Ecological Economics* 68 pp.2066–2077.

Economist, The (1997) 'Disappearing taxes' *The Economist* (London edition) 31/05/97 pp.17–23.

Economist, The (2013) 'ETS, RIP?' *The Economist* (US edition) 20/04/13 [Accessed on 23/08/17 at www.economist.com/news/finance-and-economics/21576388-failure-reform-europes-carbon-market-will-reverberate-round-world-ets].

Edmonds, D. and Eidinow, J. (2007) *Rousseau's dog* (London: Faber).

Egenhofer, C. (2007) 'The making of the EU emissions trading scheme: Status, prospects and implications for business', *European Management Journal* 25:6 pp.453–463.

Eichengreen, B.J. (2008). *Globalizing capital: A history of the international monetary system* (Princeton, NJ: Princeton University Press).

Elliott, L. (2017) 'Crash course: what the Great Depression reveals about our future' in *The Guardian* (online edition) 04/03/17 [Accessed on 04/08/17 at www.theguardian.com/society/2017/mar/04/crash-1929-wall-street-what-the-great-depression-reveals-about-our-future].

Engelen, E., Erturk, I., Froud, J., Leaver, A. and Williams, K. (2010) 'Reconceptualizing financial innovation: Frame, conjuncture and bricolage', *Economy and Society* 39:1 pp.33–63.

European Commission (2009) 'Towards a comprehensive climate change agreement in Copenhagen', *SEC (2009)101/102*. (Brussels: European Commission).

European Commission (2015) *EU ETS handbook* (Brussels: European Union).

European Commission (2017) 'The EU emissions trading system' [Accessed on 04/06/17 at https://ec.europa.eu/clima/policies/ets_en].

European Union (2003) *Directive 2003/87/EC of the European Parliament and Council* (Brussels: European Union).

European Union (2009) 'Emissions trading: Member states approve list of sectors deemed to be exposed to carbon leakage', *Press briefing ref. IP/09/628*.

Evans-Pritchard, A. (2008) '1930s beggar-thy-neighbor fears as China devalues' in *The Telegraph* (online edition) [Accessed on 23/08/17 at www.telegraph.co.uk/finance/economics/3546471/Chinese-economy-1930s-beggar-thy-neighbour-fears-as-China-devalues.html].

Ezrati, M. (2006) 'Portable alpha: A glimpse of the future', *The Journal of Investing* 15:3 pp.119–123.

Fama, E. (1970) 'Efficient capital markets: A review of theory and empirical work', *The Journal of Finance* 25:2 pp.28–30.

Fears, D. (2017) 'Donald Trump promises to bring back coal jobs but experts disagree', in *The Independent* 29/03/17 [Accessed on 23/08/17 at: www.independent.co.uk/news/world/americas/donald-trump-coal-mining-jobs-promise-experts-disagree-executive-order-a7656486.html].

Financial Services Authority (1998) *Promoting public understanding of financial services: a strategy for consumer education* (London: Financial Services Authority).

Financial Services Authority (2004a) *Building financial capability in the UK* (London: Financial Services Authority).

Financial Services Authority (2004b) *Consumer understanding of financial risk* (London: Financial Services Authority).

Financial Services Authority (2004c) *Young people and financial matters* (London: Financial Services Authority).

Financial Services Authority (2005) 'Hedge funds: A discussion of risk and regulatory engagement', *Financial Services Authority discussion paper 05/4*, June 2005 (London: Financial Services Authority) [Accessed on 04/06/17 at www.fsa.gov.uk/pubs/discussion/dp05_04.pdf].

Financial Times (2008) 'Regulating short selling' in *Financial Times* 24/09/08: p.32.

Finlayson, A. (2008) 'Characterizing New Labour: The case of the child trust fund', *Public Administration* 86:1 pp.95–110.

Finlayson, A. (2009) 'Financialisation, financial literacy and asset-based welfare', *British Journal of Politics & International Relations* 11:3 pp.400–421.

Foster, D.P. and Peyton Young, H. (2008a) 'The hedge fund game: Incentives, excessive returns and piggy-backing', *Department of economics discussion paper series* (Oxford: University of Oxford, Economics department).

Foster, D.P. and Peyton Young, H. (2008b) 'Hedge fund wizards', *Economists' Voice* 5:2 pp.1553–3832.

Foucault, M. (2002 [1970]) *The order of things: An archaeology of the human sciences* (London: Routledge).

Foucault, M. (1984) 'Polemics, politics and problematizations', interview conducted by P. Rabinow in May 1984, [Available at http://foucault.info/foucault/interview.html].

Foucault, M. (1988) *Madness and civilization* (London: Vintage Books).

Foucault, M. (2008) *The birth of biopolitics: Lectures at the collège de france 1978–79*, eds. M. Senellart, F. Ewald and A. Fontana (Basingstoke: Palgrave Macmillan).

Freeden, M. (2003) 'The ideology of New Labour' in *The New Labour Reader*, eds. A. Chadwick and R. Heffernan (Cambridge: Polity Press) pp.43–48.

Friedman, M. (2002 [1962]) *Capitalism and freedom* (Chicago, IL: University of Chicago Press).

Friedman, T.L. (1999) *The lexus and the olive tree* (New York: Farrar, Straus and Giroux).

Fung, W.K.H. and Hsieh, D. (1997) 'Empirical characteristics of dynamic trading strategies: The case of hedge funds', *Review of Financial Studies* 10: pp.275–302.

Fung, W.K.H. and Hsieh, D. (2001) 'The risk in hedge fund strategies: Theory and evidence from trend followers', *Review of Financial Studies* 14: pp. 313–341.

Fung, W.K.H. and Hsieh, D. (2006) 'Hedge funds: An industry in its adolescence', *Economic Review – Federal Reserve Bank of Atlanta* 91:4 pp.1–34.

Fung, W.K.H., Hsieh, D., Naik, N.Y. and Ramadorai, T. (2008) 'Hedge funds: Performance, risk and capital formation', *The Journal of Finance* 63:4 pp.1777–1803.

Gamble, A. and Wright, T. (2004) 'Introduction' in *Restating the state?*, eds. A. Gamble and T. Wright (Oxford: Blackwell) pp.1–10.

Geuss, R. (2008) *Philosophy and real politics* (Princeton, NJ: Princeton University Press).

Giddens, A. (1991) *Modernity and self-identity: Self and society in the late modern age* (Cambridge: Polity Press).

Giddens, A. (2002) *Where now for New Labour?* (Cambridge: Polity Press).

Gieve, J. (2006) 'Hedge funds and financial stability', in *HEDGE 2006* (London: Bank of England).

Gifford, S. (2009) 'UK personal debt exceeds UK GDP for second year running – says Grant Thornton' [Accessed on 01/02/10 at www.grant-thornton.co.uk/press_room/uk_personal_debt_exceeds_uk_gd.aspx].

Goodwin, M. and Heath, O. (2016) 'Brexit vote explained', *Joseph Rowntree Foundation/Solve UK poverty report*, August 2016 [Accessed on 23/08/17 at https://www.jrf.org.uk/report/brexit-vote-explained-poverty-low-skills-and-lack-opportunities].

Gordley, J. (1991) *The philosophical origins of modern contract doctrine* (Oxford: Clarendon Press).

Gough, J.W. (1966) 'Introduction' in *The second treatise of government*, J. Locke (London: Barnes and Noble).

Graeber, D. (2015) *The utopia of rules: On technology, stupidity, and the secret joys of bureaucracy* (Brooklyn, NY: Melville House).

Granovetter, M. (1985) 'Economic action and social structure: The problem of embeddedness', *The American Journal of Sociology* 91:3 pp.481–510.

Gray, J. (2002) *Straw dogs: Thoughts on humans and other animals* (London: Granta Books).

Green Party, The (2015) 'Basic income: A detailed proposal', *Consultation paper*, April 2015. [Accessed on 04/07/17 at https://policy.greenparty.org.uk/assets/files/Policy%20files/Basic%20Income%20Consultation%20Paper.pdf].

Greener, I. (2009) 'Towards a history of choice in UK health policy', *Sociology of Health and Illness* 31 pp.309–324.

Grotius, H. (1916 [1609]) *The freedom of the seas, with introductory note by James Brown Scott* (London: Oxford University Press).

Habermas, J. (2006) *Time of transition* (London: Polity).

Hahn, R. and Hester, G. (1989) 'Where did all the markets go? An analysis of EPA's Emissions Trading Program', *Yale Journal on Regulation* 6:1 pp.109–153.

Hall, K.L., Finkelman, P. and Ely Jr., J.W. (2005) *American legal history: Cases and materials* (Oxford: Oxford University Press).

Hardie, I. and MacKenzie, D. (2007) 'Assembling an economic actor: The agencement of a hedge fund', *The Sociological Review* 55:1 pp.57–80.

Hardin, G. (1968) 'The tragedy of the commons', *Science* 162: pp.1243–1248.

Hardin, G. (1993) *Living within limits: Ecology, economics and population taboos* (New York: Oxford University Press).

Harmes, A. (2001) 'Institutional investors and Polanyi's double movement: A model of contemporary currency crises', *Review of International Political Economy* 8:3 pp.389–437.

Hart, K. and Hann, C. (2009) 'Learning from Polanyi 1' in *Market and society*, eds. K. Hart and C. Hann (Cambridge: Cambridge University Press) pp.1–16.

Harvey, B.F. (1991) 'Introduction: The 'crisis' of the early fourteenth century' in *Before the Black Death: Studies in the 'crisis' of the early fourteenth century*, ed. B.M.S. Campbell (Manchester: Manchester University Press) pp.1–24.
Hay, C. (2002) *Political analysis: A critical introduction* (London: Palgrave).
Hay, C. (2009) 'Good inflation, bad inflation: The housing boom, economic growth and the disaggregation of inflationary preferences in the UK and Ireland', *British Journal of Politics & International Relations* 11:3 pp.461–478.
Hayek, F.A. (1948) *Individualism and economic order* (Chicago, IL: Chicago University Press).
Hayek, F.A. (1978) *Law, legislation and liberty* (Chicago, IL: University of Chicago Press).
Hayek, F.A. (1994[1944]) *The road to serfdom* (Chicago, IL: University of Chicago Press).
Hedge Fund Intelligence (2008) 'Press release: Hedge fund assets rise 27% to $2.6 trillion' [Accessed on 03/09/08 at www.hedgefundintelligence.com/images/594/55599/Global%20hedge%20fund%20assets%20$2%206tn%20April%202008.pdf].
Hegel, G.W.F. (1930 [1807]) *The phenomenology of the mind* (London: Allen and Unwin).
Hejeebu, S. and McCloskey, D. (1999) 'The reproving of Karl Polanyi', *Critical Review: A Journal of Politics and Society* 13:3 pp.285–314.
Hettne, B. (2006) 'Re-reading Polanyi: Towards a second great transformation?' in *Karl Polanyi in Vienna: The contemporary significance of The Great Transformation*, eds. K. McRobbie and K. Levitt (Montreal and London: Black Rose) pp.60–72.
Hillenkamp, I., Lapeyre, F. and Lemaître, A. (2013) *Securing livelihoods: Informal economy practices and institutions* (Oxford: Oxford University Press).
Hills, J. (1998) *Thatcherism, New Labour and the welfare state* (London: Centre for Analysis of Social Exclusion, London School of Economics).
Hirsch, F. (1977) *Social limits to growth* (London: Routledge).
Hobsbawm, E. (1988) *The age of revolution: Europe 1789–1848* (London: Abacus).
Holmberg, J. and Sandbrook, R. (1992) 'Sustainable development: what is to be done?' in *Policies for a small planet*, ed. J. Holmberg (London: Earthscan) pp.1–48.
Holmes, C. (2009) 'Seeking alpha or creating beta? Charting the rise of hedge fund-based financial ecosystems', *New Political Economy* 14:4 pp.431–450.
Holmes, C. (2014a) '"Whatever it takes": Polanyian perspectives on the Eurozone crisis and the gold standard', *Economy and Society* 43:4 pp.582–606.
Holmes, C. (2014b) 'Introduction: A post-Polanyian political economy for our times', *Economy and Society* 43:4 pp.525–540.
Hont, I. (2015) *Politics in commercial society: Jean-Jacques Rousseau and Adam Smith* (Cambridge, MA: Harvard University Press).
Hood, A. and Oakley, L. (2014) 'The social security system: Long-term trends and recent changes', *Institute for Fiscal Studies briefing note BN156* [Accessed on 04/07/17 at www.ifs.org.uk/publications/7438].
Houser, T., Bordoff, J. and Marsters, P. (2017) 'Can coal make a comeback?', *Columbia Centre on Global Energy policy report*, April 2017 [Accessed on 04/07/17 at http://energypolicy.columbia.edu/sites/default/files/Center%20on%20Global%20Energy%20Policy%20Can%20Coal%20Make%20a%20Comeback%20April%202017.pdf].
Hume, D. (1766) *A concise and genuine account of the dispute between Mr. Hume and Mr. Rousseau* (London: T. Beckert and P.A. de-Hondt) [Accessed on 04/06/17 at https://archive.org/details/concisegenuineac00hume].
Hume, D. (1888 [1740]) *A treatise of human nature* (Oxford: Clarendon Press).

Bibliography

Hume, D. (1902 [1777]) *Enquiries concerning the human understanding and concerning the principles of morals* (Oxford: Oxford University Press).

Inayatullah, N. and Blaney, D. (1999) 'Towards an ethnographic understanding of Karl Polanyi's double critique of capitalism', *Millennium – Journal of International Studies* 28:2 pp.311–340.

Ineichen, A.M. (2003) *Absolute returns: Risk and opportunities of hedge fund investing* (Hoboken, NJ: John Wiley & Sons).

Insolvency Service, The (2010) 'Historic insolvency statistics' [Accessed on 01/02/10 at www.insolvency.gov.uk/otherinformation/statistics/historicdata/HDmenu.htm].

International Financial Services London (2008) *Hedge funds 2008 datasheet* (London: International Financial Services London).

Ismail, E. *et al.* (2007) 'The democratization of finance? Promises, outcomes and conditions', *Review of International Political Economy* 14:4 pp.553–575.

Jacobs, B.I. and Levy, K.N. (2007) '20 myths about enhanced active 120–120 strategies', *Financial Analysts Journal* 63:4 pp.19–26.

Jaeger, R.A. (2003) *All about hedge funds: The easy way to get started* (London: McGraw-Hill).

Jagger, S. (2007) 'Sub-prime lender says problems are on scale of Great Depression' in *The Times* 31/08/07.

Jameson, F. (1992) *Postmodernism, or, the cultural logic of late capitalism* (Durham, NC: Duke University Press).

Jessop, B. (2001) 'Regulationist and autopoieticist reflections on Polanyi's account of market economies and the market society', *New Political Economy* 6:2 pp.213–232.

Jevons, W.S. (1865) *The coal question: An inquiry concerning the progress of the nation, and the probable exhaustion of our coal-mines* (London: Macmillan).

Jiang, X. (2014) 'The rise of carbon emissions trading in china: A panacea for climate change?', *Climate and Development* 6:2 pp.111–121.

Jones, E. (2003) 'Idiosyncrasy and integration: Suggestions from comparative political economy', *Journal of European Public Policy* 10:1 pp.140–158.

Jones, G. (1973) *The sovereignty of the law* (Toronto: University of Toronto Press).

Jones, R. (2010) 'Why it takes an age to pay for this' in *The Guardian* 04/03/10, 'Money' Section: 5.

Jopson, B. and Crooks, E. (2014) 'US states consider carbon trading schemes', in *Financial Times* 09/06/14 [Accessed on 23/08/17 at www.ft.com/content/e4356328-ee7c-11e3-95f9-00144feabdc0].

Joseph Rowntree Foundation (2016) 'The EU referendum and UK poverty, briefing paper' 24/05/16 [Accessed on 23/08/17 at: www.jrf.org.uk/report/eu-referendum-and-uk-poverty].

Judis, J.B. (2016) *The populist explosion: How the great recession transformed American and European politics* (New York: Columbia Global Reports).

Kagan, J. (2009) *The three cultures: Natural sciences, social sciences, and the humanities in the 21st century* (Cambridge: Cambridge University Press).

Kambhu, J., Schuermann, T. and Stiroh, K.J. (2007) 'Hedge funds, financial intermediation and systemic risk', *Federal Reserve Bank of New York Economic Policy Review* 13:3 pp.1–18.

Kay, J. (2004) 'The state and the market' in *Restating the state?*, eds. A. Gamble and T. Wright (Oxford: Blackwell) pp.35–69.

Karmin, C. (2007) 'Market's ride: Hedge funds do about 30% of bond trading, study says' in *The Wall Street Journal* (Eastern edition) 30/08/07: C3.

Kerr, J., Foley, C., Chung, K. and Jindal, R. (2006) 'Reconciling environment and development in the clean development mechanism', *Journal of Sustainable Forestry* 23:1 pp.1–18.

Kim, W. (2010) 'Polanyi's double movement and neoliberalization in Korea and Japan', *Journal of Social, Cultural and Political Protest* 9:4 pp.373–392.

Kirby, P. (2002) 'The World Bank or Polanyi: Markets, poverty and social well-being in Latin America', *New Political Economy* 7:2 pp.199–217.

Klein, N. (2007) *The shock doctrine* (Montreal: Knopf Canada).

Knafo, S. (2005) 'The gold standard and the origins of the modern international monetary system', *Review of International Political Economy* 13:1 pp.78–102.

Kneese, A. and Schultze, C. (1978) *Pollution prices and public policy* (Washington, DC: The Brookings Institution).

Kollmuss, A., Schneider, L. and Zhezherin, V. (2015) 'Has joint implementation reduced GHG emissions? Lessons learned for the design of carbon market mechanisms' *Stockholm Environmental Institute policy brief 2015–2007* [Accessed on 04/06/17 at www.sei-international.org/mediamanager/documents/Publications/Climate/SEI-WP-2015-07-JI-lessons-for-carbon-mechs.pdf].

Konings, M. (2015) *The emotional logic of capitalism: What progressives have missed* (Stanford, CA: Stanford University Press).

Krugman, P. (2010) 'Chinese rumbles' in *The New York Times* (online edition) 04/02/10.

Labour Party, The (1997) *The Labour Party manifesto: New Labour because Britain deserves better* (London: The Labour Party).

Lacher, H. (1999) 'The politics of the market: Re-reading Karl Polanyi', *Global Society* 13:3 pp.313–326.

Langdell, C. (1880) *A summary of the law of contracts* (Boston, MA: Little, Brown and Company).

Langley, P. (2006) 'The making of investor subjects in Anglo-American pensions', *Environment and Planning D: Society and Space* 24:6 pp.919–934.

Langley, P. (2007) 'Uncertain subjects of Anglo-American financialization', *Cultural Critique* 65 pp.67–91.

Langley, P. (2010) 'The performance of liquidity in the subprime mortgage crisis', *New Political Economy* 15:1 pp.71–89.

Laski, H.J. (1962) *The rise of European liberalism: An essay in interpretation* (London: Unwin Books).

Latouche, S. (2009) *Farewell to growth* (Cambridge and Malden, MA: Polity Press).

Le Grand, J. (2007) *The other invisible hand: Delivering public services through choice and competition* (Princeton, NJ: Princeton University Press).

Leake, S. (1867) *The elements of the law of contracts* (London: Stevens and Sons).

Levy, J.D. (2006) 'The state also rises' in *The state after statism: New state activities in the age of liberalization*, ed. J.D. Levy (Cambridge, MA: Harvard University Press) pp.1–29.

Lewis, M. (1991) 'The age demanded: The rhetoric of Karl Polanyi', *Journal of Economic Issues* 25:2 pp.475–483.

Lie, J. (1991) 'Embedding Polanyi's market society', *Sociological Perspectives* 34:2 pp.219–230.

Lindgren, H. (2007) 'Long-short story short', *New York Magazine* 16/04/10 [Accessed on 23/08/17 at http://nymag.com/news/features/2007/hedgefunds/30345/].

Lloyd Thomas, D.A. (1995) *Locke on government* (London: Routledge).

Locke, J. (1966 [1689]) *The second treatise of government* (London: Barnes and Noble).

Locke, J. (1967 [1689]) *The two tracts on government* (Cambridge: Cambridge University Press).
Louis, E. (2007) 'The guilty parties', *New York Daily News* 11/12/07.
Lukes, S. (2006 [1973]) *Individualism* (Essex: Basil Blackwell).
Lysandrou, P. (2012) 'The primacy of hedge funds in the subprime crisis', *Journal of Post-Keynesian Economics* 34:2 pp.225–253.
Macaulay, M. and Wilson, J. (2008) 'Hobson's choice? Meaning, manner and merits of choice in public services', *International Journal of Public Sector Management* 21 pp.674–686.
MacKenzie, D. (2007) 'The political economy of carbon trading', in *London Review of Books* 29:7 pp.29–31 [Accessed on 23/08/17 at www.lrb.co.uk/v29/n07/donald-mackenzie/the-political-economy-of-carbon-trading].
Mackintosh, J. (2008) 'New York hedge fund revealed as biggest short seller of UK banks' *Financial Times* 24/09/08: p.23.
Mance, H. (2016) 'Britain has had enough of experts, says Gove' in *Financial Times* (Online edition) 03/06/16 [Accessed on 04/08/17 at www.ft.com/content/3be49734-29cb-11e6-83e4-abc22d5d108c].
Manne, A.S. and Richels, R.G. (1999) 'The Kyoto Protocol: A cost-effective strategy for meeting environmental objectives?' *Energy Journal* 20 pp.1–23.
Mansfield, H.C. (1979) 'On the political character of property in Locke' in *Powers possessions and freedom*, ed. A. Kontos (London: University of Toronto Press) pp.23–38.
Markowitz, H. (1952) 'Portfolio selection', *The Journal of Finance* 7:1 pp.77–91.
Martin, R. (2002) *Financialization of daily life* (Philadelphia, PA: Temple University Press).
Marx, K. (1963a [1843]) 'On the Jewish question' in *Karl Marx: Early writings*, ed. T.B. Bottomore (London: C.A. Watts & Co.).
Marx, K. (1963b [1844]) 'Contribution to the critique of Hegel's philosophy of right' in *Karl Marx: Early writings*, ed. T.B. Bottomore (London: C.A. Watts & Co.).
Marx, K. (1963c [1844]) 'Economic and philosophical manuscripts (I, II and III)' in *Karl Marx: Early writings*, ed. T.B. Bottomore (London: C.A. Watts & Co.).
Marx, K. (1973 [1848]) *Grundrisse* (London: Penguin).
Marx, K. (1995 [1887]) *Capital* (Oxford: Oxford University Press).
Masters, R.D. and Kelly, C. (1994) 'Introduction: Rousseau's *Social Contract*' in *The collected writings of Rousseau, vol.4*, eds. R.D. Masters and C. Kelly (London: University Press of New England) pp.xi–xxvi.
Maurer, B., Nelms, T.C. and Swartz, L. (2013) 'When perhaps the real problem is money itself!: The practical materiality of bitcoin', *Social Semiotics* 23:2 pp.261–277.
McCloskey, D. (2006) *The bourgeois virtues: Ethics for an age of commerce* (Chicago, IL: Chicago University Press).
McLean, I. (2008) 'Climate change and UK politics: From Brynle Williams to Sir Nicholas Stern', *Political Quarterly* 79:2 pp.184–193.
Medema, S.G. (1994) *Markings on a long journey* (London: Macmillan).
Medrano, J.D. (2012) 'The limits of European integration', *Journal of European Integration* 34:2 pp.191–204.
Mehrling, P. (2005) *Fischer Black and the revolutionary idea of finance* (Chichester: John Wiley & Sons).
Mendell, M. (2007) 'Karl Polanyi and instituted process of economic democratisation' in *Karl Polanyi: New perspectives on the place of the economy in society*, eds. M. Harvey, R. Ramlogan, and S. Randles (Manchester: Manchester University Press).

Mendell, M. and Salée, D. (1991) 'Introduction' in *The legacy of Karl Polanyi: Market, state and society at the end of the twentieth century*, eds. M. Mendell and D. Sallee (Basingstoke: Macmillan).
Migone, A. (2007) 'Hedonistic consumerism: Patterns of consumption in contemporary capitalism', *Review of Radical Political Economics* 39 pp.173–200.
Mill, J. (1963 [1844]) *Elements of political economy* (New York: Augustus M. Kelley).
Mill, J.S. (1915 [1848]) *Principles of political economy* (New York: Longmans, Green and Co.).
Mill, J.S. (1874 [1863]) 'On the definition of political economy, and on the method of investigation proper to it' in *Essays on some unsettled questions of political economy*, 2nd ed. (London: Longmans).
Mirowski, P. and Plehwe, D. (2009) *The road from Mont Pèlerin the making of the neoliberal thought collective* (Cambridge, MA: Harvard University Press).
Mises, L. von (1949) *Human action: A treatise on economics* (New Haven, CT: Yale University Press).
Mitchell, T. (2008) 'Rethinking economy', *Geoforum* 39:3 pp.1116–1121.
Montgomerie, J. (2006) 'Giving credit where it's due: Public policy and household debt in the United States, the United Kingdom and Canada', *Policy and Society* 25:3 pp.109–142.
Montgomerie, J. (2013) 'America's debt safety-net', *Public Administration* 91:4 pp.871–888.
Montgomerie, J. and Büdenbender, M. (2014) 'Round the houses: Homeownership and failures of asset-based welfare in the United Kingdom', *New Political Economy* 20:3 pp.386–405.
Barker, N. and Healey, M. (2004) *Saving retirement* (London: MORI).
Mouffe, C. (2000) *The democratic paradox* (London, New York: Verso).
Mudde, C. and Rovira Kaltwasser, C. (2017) *Populism: A very short introduction* (Oxford: Oxford University Press)
Munck, R. (2006) 'Globalization and contestation: A Polanyian problematic', *Globalizations* 3:2 pp.175–186.
Murray, M. and Pateman, C. (2012) *Basic income worldwide: Horizons of reform* (Basingstoke: Palgrave Macmillan).
National Association of Pension Funds (2007) *Institutional investment in the UK six years on* (London: National Association of Pension Funds).
Navarro, P. (2008) 'China plays beggar thy neighbor' in *Asia Times Online* 23/07/08 [Accessed on 25/08/17 at www.atimes.com/atimes/China_Business/JL09Cb01.html].
Notermans, T. (2000) *Money, markets, and the state: Social democratic policies since 1918* (Cambridge: Cambridge University Press).
Obstfeld, M. (2017) 'Foreword' in *World economic outlook April 2017: Gaining momentum?* (Washington, DC: International Monetary Fund).
O'Malley, P. (1996) 'Risk and responsibility' in *Foucault and political reason: Liberalism, neo-liberalism and rationalities of government*, eds. A. Barry, T. Osborne and N. Rose (Chicago, IL: University of Chicago Press) pp.189–213.
Open University/BBC (2009) 'The love of money', documentary as part of the *Open University/BBC collaboration series*.
Orth, J.V. (1998) 'Contract and the common law' in *The state and freedom of contract*, ed. H.N. Scheiber (Stanford, CA: Stanford University Press) pp.44–65.
IPCC (2014) *Climate change 2014: Synthesis report. Contribution of Working Groups I, II and III to the fifth assessment report of the Intergovernmental Panel on*

Climate Change, eds./core writing team, R.K. Pachauri and L.A. Meyer (Geneva: Intergovernmental Panel on Climate Change).
Pachauri, R.K. and Reisinger, A. (2007) *Climate change 2007: Synthesis report* (Geneva: IPCC).
Palaciaos, J. (2001) 'Globalisation's double movement: Societal responses to market expansion in the 21st century' paper given at the Eighth Karl Polanyi International Conference: 'Economy and Democracy', November 14–16, Mexico City.
Parsons, C. and Welsh, P. (2006) 'Public sector policies and practice, neoliberal consumerism and freedom of choice in secondary education: A case study of one area in Kent', *Cambridge Journal of Education* 36 pp.237–256.
Paxton, W. (2003) *Equal shares? Building a progressive and coherent asset-based welfare policy* (London: Institute for Public Policy Research).
Peck, J. (2012) *Constructions of neoliberal reason* (Oxford: Oxford University Press).
Pigou, A.C. (1932) *The economics of welfare* (Indianapolis, IN: Liberty Fund Inc.).
Pitt-Watson, D. (2009) *Pensions for the people: Addressing the savings and investment crisis in Britain* (London: Royal Society for the Encouragement of Arts).
Plehwe, D. (2009) 'Introduction' in *The road from Mont Pèlerin the making of the neoliberal thought collective*, eds. P. Mirowski and D. Plehwe (Cambridge, MA: Harvard University Press).
Polanyi, K. (1935) 'The essence of fascism' in *Christianity and the social revolution*, eds. J. Lewis, K. Polanyi and D.K. Kitchin (London: Gollancz).
Polanyi, K. (1947) 'Our obsolete market mentality', *Commentary* 3:2 pp.109–117.
Polanyi, K. (1966) *Dahomey and the slave trade: An analysis of archaic economies* (Seattle, WA: University of Washington Press).
Polanyi, K. (1968 [1957]) *Primitive, archaic and modern economies: Essays of Karl Polanyi* (New York: Doubleday Anchor).
Polanyi, K. (1977) *The livelihood of man* (New York: Academic Press).
Polanyi, K. (2001 [1944]) *The great transformation: The political and economic origins of our time* (Boston, MA: Beacon).
Polanyi, K. (2014) *For a new West: Essays, 1919–1958* (Cambridge: Polity Press).
Polanyi-Levitt, K. (2005) 'Keynes and Polanyi: The 1920s and the 1990s', *Review of International Political Economy* 13:1 pp.152–177.
Polanyi-Levitt, K. (2006) 'The great transformation from 1920 to 1990' in *Karl Polanyi in Vienna: The contemporary significance of The Great Transformation*, eds. K. McRobbie, K. Levitt (Montreal, London: Black Rose) pp.3–12.
Polanyi-Levitt, K. and Mendell, M. (1987) 'Karl Polanyi: His life and times', *Studies in Political Economy* 22:1 pp.7–39.
Posner, R. (2009) *A failure of capitalism: The crisis of '08 and the descent into depression* (Cambridge, MA: Harvard University Press).
Poundstone, W. (1992) *Prisoner's dilemma* (New York: Doubleday).
Power, M. (2017) 'Has Western-style democracy become too expensive for capitalism?', *Financial Times* (Online edition) 14/06/17 [Accessed on 25/08/17 at www.ft.com/content/d0a5c460-5044-11e7-a1f2-db19572361bb].
Prabhakar, R. (2009) 'The development of asset-based welfare: the case of the Child Trust Fund in the UK', *Policy & Politics* 37 pp.129–143.
Press Association. (2016) 'David Cameron: leaving European Union would be "act of self-harm"' in *The Guardian* (online edition) 05/04/16 [Accessed on 04/08/17 at www.theguardian.com/politics/2016/apr/05/david-cameron-leaving-european-union-would-be-act-of-self-harm].

Pryke, M. and Allen, J. (2000) 'Monetized time-space: Derivatives – money's "new imaginary"?', *Economy and Society* 29:2 pp.264–284.
Pufendorf, S. (1994) *The political writings of Samuel Pufendorf*, ed. C. Carr, trans. M.J. Seidler (Oxford: Oxford University Press).
Quiggin, J. (2010) *Zombie economics: How dead ideas still walk among us* (Princeton, NJ: Princeton University Press).
Raffer, K. (2011) 'Neoliberal capitalism: A time warp backwards to capitalism's origins?', *Forum for Social Economics* 40:1 pp.41–62.
Randles, S. (2003) 'Issues for a Neo-Polanyian research agenda in economic sociology', *International Review of Sociology: Revue Internationale de Sociologie* 13:2 pp.409–434.
Rasmussen, D.C. (2008) *The problems and promise of commercial society: Adam Smith's response to Rousseau* (University Parks, PA: Penn State University Press).
Regan, S. (2001) *Assets and progressive welfare* (London: Institute for Public Policy Research).
Repetto, R. (2013) 'Cap and trade contains global warming better than a carbon tax', *Challenge* 56:5 pp.31–61.
Ricardo, D. (1963 [1817]) *The principles of political economy and taxation* (Homewood, IL: Richard D. Irwin Inc.).
Righter, R. (2009) 'Obama's lethal game of beggar-thy-neighbour' in *The Sunday Times* (online edition) 30/01/09 [Accessed on 23/08/17 at www.thetimes.co.uk/article/obamas-lethal-game-of-beggar-thy-neighbour-0w0vklcjv2z].
Robbins, L. (1932) *An essay on the nature and significance of economic science* (London: Macmillan & Co.).
Robinson, H. and O'Brien, N. (2007) *Europe's dirty secret: Why the EU emissions trading scheme isn't working* (London: Open Europe).
Robison, R. [ed.] (2006) *The neo-liberal revolution: Forging the market state* (Basingstoke: Palgrave Macmillan).
Rodrik, D. (2017) 'Populism and the economics of globalization', Online working paper [Accessed on 29/09/17 at: https://drodrik.scholar.harvard.edu/files/dani-rodrik/files/populism_and_the_economics_of_globalization.pdf].
Rosner, P. (1990) 'Karl Polanyi and socialist accounting' in *The Life and Work of Karl Polanyi*, ed. K. Polanyi-Levitt (New York: Black Rose Books) pp.55–65.
Rothbard, M. (1961) 'Down with primitivism: a thorough critique of Polanyi', Volker Fund, *von Mises Institute working paper* [Accessed on 23/08/17 at https://mises.org/library/down-primitivism-thorough-critique-polanyi].
Rothbard, M. (2004 [1962]) *Man, economy, and state: A treatise on economic principles* (Auburn, AL: Ludwig von Mises Institute).
Rousseau, J.-J. (1755) *A discourse on political economy* [Accessed on 23/08/17 at www.constitution.org/jjr/polecon.htm].
Rousseau, J.-J. (1984 [1754]) *A discourse on inequality* (London: Penguin).
Rousseau, J.-J. (1994) *The collected writings of Rousseau, Vol. 4* (London: University Press of New Zealand).
Ruggie, J. (1982) 'International regimes, transactions and change: Embedded liberalism in the postwar economic order', *International Organization* 36:2 pp.379–415.
Ryan-Collins, J., Greenham, T., Werner, R. and Jackson, A. (2016) *Where does money come from?: A guide to the UK monetary and banking system* (London: New Economics Foundation).
Saha, D. and Liu, S. (2017) 'Increased automation guarantees a bleak outlook for Trump's promises to coal miners', Brookings: The Avenue website [Accessed on 23/08/17

at www.brookings.edu/blog/the-avenue/2017/01/25/automation-guarantees-a-bleak-outlook-for-trumps-promises-to-coal-miners/].

Sandbrook, R. (2011) 'Polanyi and post-neoliberalism in the global south: Dilemmas of re-embedding the economy', *New Political Economy* 16:4 pp.415–444.

Sandor, R.L., Bettelheim, E.C. and Swingland, I.R. (2002) 'An overview of a free-market approach to climate change and conservation', *Philosophical Transactions: Mathematical, Physical and Engineering Sciences* 360 pp.1607–1620.

Scharpf, F. (1999) 'The viability of advanced welfare states in the international economy: Vulnerabilities and options', *MPFiG Working Papers* 99/9.

Scharpf, F. and Schmidt, V. (2000) *Welfare and work in the open economy, Vol. 1: From vulnerability to competitiveness* (Oxford: Oxford University Press).

Schimmelfennig, F. (2014) 'European integration in the euro crisis: The limits of postfunctionalism', *Journal of European Integration* 36:3 pp.321–337.

Schneewind, J. B. (1998) *The invention of autonomy: A history of modern moral philosophy* (Cambridge: Cambridge University Press).

Schor, J. (1993) *The overworked American: The unexpected decline of leisure* (New York: Basic Books).

Schwager, J.D. (2001) *The new market wizards: Conversations with America's top traders* (London: Harper Business).

Scott, J.C. (1998) *Seeing like a state: How certain schemes to improve the human condition have failed* (New Haven, CT: Yale University Press).

Sen, A. (1999) *Development as freedom* (New York: Oxford University Press).

Serricchio, F., Tsakatika, M. and Quaglia, L. (2013) 'Euroscepticism and the global financial crisis', *Journal of Common Market Studies* 51:1 pp.51–64.

Sharpe, W. (1970) *Portfolio theory and capital markets* (New York: McGraw-Hill).

Sharpe, W. (1992) 'Asset allocation: Management style and performance measurement', *The Journal of Portfolio Management* 18:1 pp.7–19.

Sharpe, W. (2007) *Investors and markets* (Princeton, NJ: Princeton University Press).

Sharpe, W. (1963) 'A simplified model for portfolio analysis', *Management Science* 9:2 pp.277–293.

Shen, W. (2014) 'Chinese business at the dawn of its domestic emissions trading scheme: Incentives and barriers to participation in carbon trading', *Climate Policy* 15:3 pp.339–354.

Sherraden, M. (1991) *Assets and the poor: A new American welfare policy* (New York: M E Sharpe).

Shiller, R.J. (2008) *Subprime solution: How today's global financial crisis happened and what to do about it* (Princeton, NJ: Princeton University Press).

Shrimpton, A. (2008) 'Interview on Newsnight', on *Newsnight*, (London: British Broadcasting Corporation.

Sidiropoulos, M., Trabelsi, J. and Karfakis, C. (2005) 'Has the "franc fort" exchange rate policy affected the inflationary dynamics? Theory and new evidence', *International Economic Journal* 19:3 pp.379–395.

Sijm, J.P.M., Kuik, O.J., Patel, M., Oikonomou, V., Worrell, E. and Lako, P. (2004) *Spillover of climate policy – An assessment of the incidence of carbon leakage and induced technological change due to CO_2 abatement measures* (Amsterdam: Netherlands Research Programme on Climate Change).

Silva, E.C.D. and Zhu, X. (2009) 'Emissions trading of global and local pollutants, pollution havens and free riding', *Journal of Environmental Economics and Management* 58:2 pp.169–182.

Silver, B. and Arrighi, G. (2003) 'Polanyi's "double movement": The Belle Époques of British and U.S. hegemony compared', *Politics and Society* 31:2 pp.325–355.

Singer, J.W. (2000) 'Property and social relations: From title to entitlement' in *Property and values: Alternatives to public and private ownership*, eds. C. Geisler and G. Daneker (Washington, DC: Island Press) pp.3–20.

Skidelsky, R.J.A. (2010) *Keynes: The return of the master* (London: Penguin).

Slater, D. (1997) *Consumer culture and modernity* (Oxford: Polity Press).

Smith, A. (1891 [1776]) *An inquiry into the nature and causes of the wealth of nations* (London: Ward, Lock, Bowden & Co.).

Smith, A. (1976 [1759]) *The theory of moral sentiments* (Oxford: Clarendon Press).

Smith, A. (1980) *Essays on philosophical subjects*, ed. W.P.D. Wightman (Indianapolis, IN: Liberty Fund).

Solomon, S.D., Qin, M., Manning, Z., Chen, M., Marquis, K.B., Avery, M., Tignor, H.L. and Miller, D. (2007) *Summary for policymakers* (Cambridge: Cambridge University Press).

Spash, C.L. (2010) 'The brave new world of carbon trading', *New Political Economy* 15:2 pp.169–195.

Sreenivasan, G. (1995) *The limits of Lockean rights in property* (Oxford: Oxford University Press).

Standing, G. (2011) *The precariat: The new dangerous class* (London: A&C Black).

Standing, G. (2017) 'Universal basic income is becoming an urgent necessity' in *The Guardian* (online edition) 12/01/17 [Accessed on 23/08/17 at www.theguardian.com/commentisfree/2017/jan/12/universal-basic-income-finland-uk].

Starr, M.A. (2007) 'Saving, spending, and self-control: Cognition versus consumer culture', *Review of Radical Political Economics* 39 pp.214–229.

Stewart, H. (2008) 'IMF says US crisis is "largest financial shock since Great Depression"' *The Guardian* (online edition) [Accessed on 23/08/17 at www.theguardian.com/business/2008/apr/09/useconomy.subprimecrisis].

Stiglitz, J. (2001) 'Foreword' in *The great transformation*, K. Polanyi (Boston, MA: Beacon).

Streeck, W. (2011) 'The crises of democratic capitalism', *New Left Review* 71: Sept/Oct pp.5–29.

Strong, T.B. (2012). *Politics without vision: Thinking without a banister in the twentieth century* (Chicago, IL: University of Chicago Press).

Swain, W. (2015) *The law of contract 1670–1870* (Cambridge: Cambridge University Press).

Taylor-Gooby, P. (2003) 'Open markets versus welfare citizenship: Conflicting approaches to policy convergence in Europe', *Social Policy & Administration* 37:6 pp.539–554.

Taylor-Gooby, P. and Taylor, E. (2015) 'Benefits and welfare: Long-term trends or short-term reactions?', *British Social Attitudes* 32 pp.1–28.

Thaler, R.H. and Sunstein, C.R. (2008) *Nudge: Improving decisions about health, wealth and happiness* (London: Penguin).

Tietenberg, T.H. (1985) *Emission trading: An exercise in reforming pollution policy* (Washington, DC: Resources for the Future).

Till, H. (2004) 'On the role of hedge funds in institutional portfolios', *The Journal of Alternative Investments* 6:4 pp.77–89.

Tily, G. [ed.] (2010) *Keynes betrayed* (Basingstoke: Palgrave Macmillan).

Timmins, N. (2009) 'Action urged to save final salary pensions', in *Financial Times* 27/11/09: 3.

Tisdell, C. (2001) 'Globalisation and sustainability: environmental Kuznets curve and the WTO', *Ecological Economics* 39 pp.185–196.

Tomasberger, C. (2003) 'Freedom and responsibility: Karl Polanyi on freedom', 9th International Karl Polanyi Conference, 11/03, Montreal.

Toporowski, J. (2003) 'Finance and political economy' delivered at the Economics for the Future Conference, 26/09/17, Cambridge: Cambridge University.

Toussaint, J. and Elsinga, M. (2009) 'Exploring asset-based welfare: Can the UK be held up as an example for Europe?', *Housing Studies* 24:5 pp.669–692.

Travis, A. (2016) 'Are EU migrants really taking British jobs and pushing down wages?' *The Guardian* 20/05/16 [Accessed on 23/08/17 at www.theguardian.com/politics/2016/may/20/reality-check-are-eu-migrants-really-taking-british-jobs].

Treasury, H.M. (2008) *The Saving Gateway: operating a national scheme* (London: HM Customs and Excise).

Trenchard, J. and Gordon, T. (1723) *Cato's letters* [Accessed on 23/08/17 at http://classicliberal.tripod.com/cato/].

Tribe, K. (2015) *The economy of the word: Language, history, and economics* (Oxford: Oxford University Press).

Triffin, R. (1960) *Gold and the dollar crisis* (New Haven, CT: Yale University Press).

Tucker, R.C. (1961) *Philosophy and myth in Karl Marx* (Cambridge: Cambridge University Press).

Tully, J. (1980). *Discourse on property: John Locke and his adversaries* (Cambridge: Cambridge University Press).

Tully, J. (1991) 'Introduction' in *On the duty of man and citizen according to natural law*, ed. J. Tully (Cambridge: Cambridge University Press) pp.xiv–xxxvii.

Turner, A. (2009) *The Turner Review: A regulatory response to the global banking crisis* (London: Financial Services Authority).

Tveitdal, S., Stuhlberger, C., Heberlein, C. and Kirby, A. (2009) *Climate in peril: A popular guide to the latest IPCC reports* (Nairobi: United Nations Environment Programme).

UK Department for Work and Pensions (2006) *Security in retirement: Towards a new pensions system* (London: Department for Work and Pensions).

UK Department for Work and Pensions (2009) *Saving for retirement: Implications of pensions reforms on financial incentives to save for retirement* (London: Department for Work and Pensions).

UK Department of Trade and Industry (1998) 'Modern markets: confident consumers', *UK government white paper*. (London: HMRC).

UK Financial Inclusion Taskforce (2006) *Treasury committee inquiry on financial inclusion: Submission from the Financial Inclusion Taskforce* (London: HM Treasury).

UK Government (2007) *Pensions Act* (United Kingdom: Houses of Parliament).

UK Office for National Statistics (2008) *Pension Trends 1: Pensions legislation – An overview* (London: Office for National Statistics).

UK Office for National Statistics (2009) *Pension Trends 6: Private pensions* (London: Office for National Statistics).

UK Parliament (1956) *Clean Air Act* (London: UK Government Papers).

UK Pensions Commission (2004) *Pensions: Challenges and choices* (Norwich: The Stationery Office).

UK Pensions Commission (2005) *A new pension settlement for the twenty-first century: The second report of the pensions commission* (London: UK Pensions commission).
UK Treasury (2003) *The budget* (London: HM Treasury).
UK Treasury (2008) *The Saving Gateway: Operating a national scheme* (London: HM Treasury).
Underhill, G.R. (2000) 'State, market, and global political economy: Genealogy of an (inter-?) discipline', *International Affairs* 76:4 pp.805–824.
UNFCCC [United Nations Framework Convention on Climate Change] (1998) *Kyoto Protocol to the United Nations Framework Convention on Climate Change* (Bonn: UNFCCC).
UNFCCC [United Nations Framework Convention on Climate Change] (2006) *Report of the Subsidiary Body for Scientific and Technological Advice on its twenty-fourth session FCCC/SBSTA/2006/5*, 13 September 2006 (Bonn: UNFCCC).
UNFCCC [United Nations Framework Convention on Climate Change] (2015) *Paris agreement, UNFCCC agreement* [Accessed on 23/08/17 at http://unfccc.int/paris_agreement/items/9485.php].
US Congress (2009) 'American Recovery and Reinvestment Act' in *Pub.L. 111–115* (Washington, DC: US Congress).
Valdés, J.G. (1995) *Pinochet's economists: The Chicago School of Economics in Chile* (Cambridge: Cambridge University Press).
van Apeldoorn, F. and Horn, L. (2007) 'The marketisation of European corporate control: A critical political economy perspective', *New Political Economy* 12:2 pp.211–235.
van der Pijl, K. (2009) 'A survey of global political economy, Version 2.1, October 2009' [Accessed on 18/08/17 at https://libcom.org/files/A%20survey%20of%20global%20political%20economy.pdf].
Van Horn, R. (2009) 'Reinventing monopoly and the role of corporations: The roots of Chicago law and economics' in *The road from Mont Pelerin: The making of the neoliberal thought collective*, eds. P. Mirowski and D. Plehwe (Cambridge, MA: Harvard University Press) pp.204–237.
Vincent-Jones, P., Hughes, D. and Mullen, C. (2009) 'New Labour's PPI reforms: Patient and public involvement in healthcare governance?', *Modern Law Review* 72 pp.247–271.
Volker, P. (2011) 'Financial reform: unfinished business', in *The New York Review of Books* 24/11/11 [Accessed on 23/08/17 at www.nybooks.com/articles/2011/11/24/financial-reform-unfinished-business/].
Walzer, M. (1983) *Spheres of justice: A defence of pluralism and equality* (New York: Basic Books).
Warde, A. (1994) 'Consumption, identity formation and uncertainty', *Sociology* 28:4 pp.877–898.
Watson, M. (2007) 'Trade justice and individual consumption choices: Adam Smith's spectator theory and the moral constitution of the fair trade consumer', *European Journal of International Relations* 13 pp.263–288.
Watson, M. (2008) 'The split personality of prudence in the unfolding political economy of New Labour', *Political Quarterly* 79:4 pp.578–589.
Watson, M. (2009a) '"Habitation vs. improvement" and a Polanyian perspective on bank bail-outs', *Politics* 29:3 pp. 183–192.
Watson, M. (2009b) 'Investigating the potentially contradictory microfoundations of financialization', *Economy and Society* 38:2 pp.255–277.

Watson, M. (2009c) 'Planning for a future of asset-based welfare? New Labour, financialized economic agency and the housing market', *Planning Practice and Research* 24:1 pp.41–56.
Watson, M. (2014) 'The great transformation and progressive possibilities: The political limits of Polanyi's Marxian history of economic ideas', *Economy and Society* 43:4 pp.603–662.
Weber, M. (1979) 'Freedom and coercion' in *The economics of contract law*, eds. A.T. Kronman and R.A. Posner (Toronto: Little, Brown and Company) pp.230–233.
Weber, M. (2001 [1904]) *The protestant ethic and the spirit of capitalism* (London: Routledge).
West, A. and Pennell, H. (2005) 'How new is New Labour? The quasi-market and English schools 1997 to 2001', *British Journal of Educational Studies* 50:2 pp.206–224.
Wight, M. (2005) *Four seminal thinkers in international theory* (Oxford: Oxford University Press).
Wilson, E. (2009) 'Making the world safe for Holland: "De indis" of Hugo Grotius and international law as geoculture', *Review (Fernand Braudel Center)* 32:3 pp.239–287.
Wood, E.M. (2002) *The origin of capitalism: A longer view* (London: Verso).
Wood, E.M. (2008). *Citizens to lords: A social history of Western political thought from antiquity to the middle ages* (London and New York: Verso).
Yarrow, D. (2017) 'Responses to populism: A Polanyian critique of liberal discourse', *Political Quarterly*, forthcoming.
Zapfel, P. and Vainio, M. (2002) 'Pathways to European greenhouse gas emissions trading: History and misconceptions', *FEEM Working Paper, Milan No 85/2002* [Accessed on 04/07/17 at www.feem.it/en/publications/feem-working-papers-note-di-l avoro-series/pathways-to-european-greenhouse-gas-emissions-trading-history-and-mi sconceptions/].
Zelizer, V. (1988) 'Beyond the polemics on the market: Establishing a theoretical and empirical agenda', *Sociological Forum* 3:4 pp.614–634.
Zelizer, V. (1989) 'The social meaning of money', *American Journal of Sociology* 95:2 pp.342–377.

Index

acquisition, labour theory 51–54
agricultural improvement 26–28
alienation 67
alpha returns 89–91, 94, 95
'America First' 5–6
American Declaration of
    Independence 54
American Revolution 55
Aquinas, Thomas 45–47, 50, 65
Aristotle 46
Arrow, Kenneth 105
Asian financial crisis (1997) 87, 93
asset-based welfare 122–129
austerity 140, 143, 147
Austrian School economics 69–72
automation 11, 142, 144, 146

Bank of England 84, 87, 95, 119
banking: central 84, 86, 96;
    community 141
basic income 141–143
Basic Income Earth Network 142
Bawerk, Eugen Böhm von 69
benevolence, opposition to
    self-interest 59
Bentham, Jeremy 34, 36, 66
Berlin, Isaiah 19, 36–37, 74, 76
Bernanke, Ben 95
beta returns 89–92, 93, 94
Bitcoin 141
Blackstone, William 54–56, 66, 75
Blair, Tony 120
Brexit campaign 5–8, 13,
    16, 143–147
British Social Attitudes Survey 118
Brundtland Report (UN) 110
Burke, Edmund 33, 34
buy-to-let mortgage
    lending 127–128

Cameron, David 6
Camus, Albert 37–38, 39
Capital (Marx) 67
Capital Assets Pricing Model (CAPM)
    89–90, 101–102
'capital flight,' and state
    spending 117–118
capitalism: arguments for 53–54; debates
    underpinning 147–149; disruption 7;
    industrial 30–31, 99; Keynesian
    welfare 22–23; Marxist critique 24–25;
    price mechanism for resolving tensions
    137; social legitimacy 88
carbon leakage 111
carbon trading 107–115
catallaxy 71–72
central banking 84, 86, 96
Certified Emission Reduction Units
    (CERs) 108, 111, 113
Chicago School economics 72–74,
    88, 91, 92
China: carbon trading 112, 114;
    currency manipulation 85;
    protectionism 85
City of London 118
Clean Development Mechanism (CDM)
    108, 110, 112–114
climate change: and globality 100–102;
    and pollution trading 107–110;
    strategies 114, 115
coal industry 144–145
Coase, Ronald 104–106, 108, 112, 115
Cold War, and economic thought 73
Commentaries on the Laws of England
    (Blackstone) 54–56
commercial society: fall from grace 15,
    53, 58, 60, 65–66, 67, 149; freedom 61;
    and natural law tradition 49–50,
    57–58; and property 50–56, 58–59,

Index

61–62, 65–67; transition from subsistence economy 52–53
commodification, critique of 24–25
common law: English 54–56; European 100
communism 14, 73, 137
community banking 141
competition: and climate change 101–102; and consumer choice 120–122; and consumer credit 126–127; and financial markets 97; and monopoly 64, 69–72, 76–77
Conservative party (UK) 147
consumer choice: and pensions 132; and public services 120–122
consumer credit 125–129
consumerism, and welfare provision 123–129
contract: concept 55–56; moral justification 66; notion 49–50
credit *see* consumer credit
currencies: floating exchange rates 86; manipulation 85; speculation 87

Dales, J.H. 106–107
debt *see* consumer credit
defined benefit schemes (DB) 129–132
defined contribution schemes (DC) 129–132
deregulation: financial markets 87–88, 92; hedge funds 96
A Discourse on Inequality (Rousseau) 60, 62
A Discourse on Political Economy (Rousseau) 60–61
disembedded market 24
Dissertation on the Poor Laws (Townsend) 32–34
diversification, investment 88
divine order, and property 45–50
'double movement' 19–25

ecological politics 99–102
economic crisis, protectionist response 85
economic cycle, new phenomenon 31
economic debates, underpinning capitalism 147–149
economic formalism 34, 43–44, 66
economic growth: and defence of livelihood 145; and environment 99–102; and finance 78, 96; Polanyi's view 28–40; tension with habitation 10–11, 16, 26, 29–33, 118, 140, 146
economic ideas, disembedding of 74–77

economic liberalism: failure 4, 10–12; faith in 34–35; Marx's rejection 67–68, 69; Polanyi's view 10–12, 84 *see also* neoliberalism
economic problematisation: and Enlightenment 45, 61–62, 63, 65, 66; and natural law tradition 44–45, 47–48, 50–51, 52–54, 56, 65; and neoliberalism 45, 69–71, 72, 76–77; Polanyi's view as history of 14–15; and property 44–45, 63; and transcendence 74, 96, 138
economics: 'catallactic' science 71–72; discipline 10, 12, 32, 67, 87, 102, 139
The Economics of Welfare (Pigou) 102–103
economism: and monetary politics 83–88; and neoliberalism 74; Polanyi's critique 10–14, 14–15, 18–25, 30, 31–33, 35, 37–38, 43–44, 74
economy: bifurcation of political 65–68; complexity 12–13; and Enlightenment 57, 61–62; and environment 99–102; and finance 83–84, 86, 90–92, 98; independence 34; and livelihood 27, 144–145, 147; logical contradictions 148–149; natural law tradition 44–48, 51–53, 59; neoclassical definition 10; and neoliberalism 69–77; notion 47–49; Polanyi's definition 10–11, 23–25; Polanyi's view 14–15, 19–25; political 9–10, 32, 65–68, 77; and politics 17; transcendence 148–149; transition to commercial society 52–53
education, league tables 121–122
efficient markets hypothesis (EMH) 91–92, 95, 96, 98, 102
Elements of Universal Jurisprudence (Pufendorf) 49–50
embedded liberalism 21, 22
Emission Reduction Units (ERUs) 108, 113
emissions trading *see* pollution trading
enclosures movement 28, 99
Encycloédie (Diderot and d'Alembert) 60–61
Enlightenment: and economic problematisation 15, 45, 61–62, 63, 65, 66; property and justice 57–62; and understanding of property 65–66
An Enquiry Concerning the Principles of Morals (Hume) 59

environment: and common law 100; and economy 99–102; and legislation 100, 101; and marketised social protection 78–79, 104–106, 110; and 'Pigovian taxes' 103–104
environmental degradation, and globality 100–101
environmental protection, market-based approaches 78–79, 104–106, 110
equilibrium theory 105
'The Essence of Fascism' (Polanyi) 14
ethics, Kant's system of 36
European Central Bank 87
European Union: austerity 143; Brexit campaign 145; defence of financial sector 140; Emissions Trading Scheme (ETS) 108–109, 111–112, 113, 115; pollution trading 107–109; single market 143, 147
euroscepticism 86
eurozone crisis 85–86, 140
exchange: derived from nature 49; free 64–65; price formation 50
Exchange Rate Mechanism (ERM) 87, 93
exchange rates 40, 84, 86
externalities 102–106, 112

Fall of Man 15, 37, 53, 58, 60, 65–66, 67, 149
Fama, Eugene 91
far right, rise of 86
fascism 14, 137
'fictitious commodities' 16
finance: deregulation 87–88; growth model 4–5; and marketised social protection 77–78; and money 83–93, 96–98, 140–143
financial crises 4–5, 11, 21–22, 87, 92, 97–98, 139–143, 146–147, 149
financial innovation 92–96, 97
financial markets: deregulation 92; efficiency 88–92; government intervention 140; innovation 92–96, 97; sector 86–87
Foucault, Michel 14, 138
freedom: based upon economic freedom 71; and economic problematisation 15; of movement 6–7, 147; opposition with power 59–61, 63; Polanyi on 37–39; and power 72–74, 76; of the seas 48–49
Friedman, Milton 72–74, 75

global financial crisis (2008) 4–5, 87, 92, 97–98, 139–140
globalisation 20, 117
globality, and environmental degradation 100–101
Gold Standard monetary system 3–5, 10–11, 20, 35, 40, 83–86
government: intervention 137, 140; power 71; power to protect property 63 see also state
Great Depression 4, 20
The Great Transformation (TGT) (Polanyi): and the 1930s 3–4, 6–8; breadth and scope 9, 14; and capitalism 147–149; concepts and ideas 8–10; critique of economism 35; critique of modernity 30–34; importance 16–17; insights 8; and IPE 3; on money 83; and the nature of freedom 38–39; and welfare provision 116
Grotius, Hugo 48–49, 50
guild socialists 29

habitation: and Brexit campaign 145–146; as improvement 125; need for 10–11; state spending on 117; tension with economic growth 29–33, 118, 140; tension with improvement 16, 18, 25–31, 33, 39, 77, 79, 92, 96, 97–98, 100–103, 137–149; and Trump campaign 145–146; underlying costs 146
Hayek, F.A. 71, 72, 73, 75
hedge funds 92–96
Hegel, G.W.F. 67
history: of economic ideas 7, 8, 32–33, 43, 44–45, 77–78, 148–149; and marketisation 19–20
home equity, as source of income 127–128
home repossessions 129
housing schemes 124, 125, 129
Human Action (Mises) 70–71
Hume, David 45, 57, 61–63, 65, 66, 67, 71, 74, 83

immigration 6, 145, 147
improvement: agricultural 26–28; habitation as 125; ideology of 53; and legislation 102; tension with habitation 16, 18, 25–31, 33, 39, 77, 79, 87, 92, 96, 97–98, 100–103, 137–149 see also economic growth

Index

individualism, and property 55–56
industrial capitalism 30–31, 99
Industrial Revolution 30–33, 66
industrial transformation 26, 28, 116
inequality, injustice of 60
innovation, financial 92–96, 97
insularity, rise of 85–86
Intergovernmental Panel on Climate Change (IPCC) 107, 112, 114
international political economy (IPE): Polanyi's view 19–25; post-Polanyi 18; teaching 7–8; and *TGT* 3–4
international trade 4, 20, 48–49
investment: alpha returns 89–91, 94, 95; beta returns 89–92, 93, 94; diversification 88; hedge funds 92–96; portfolio selection theory 89–92

Jefferson, Thomas 55
Jevons, Stanley 66, 113
jobs, Trump campaign 144
Jobseeker's Allowance 142
John of Paris 47
Joint Implementation (JI) programme 108, 112–113, 114
justice: private property and claims for 54–56; and property 57–62, 63

Kant, Immanuel, system of ethics 36
Key Worker Living policy 124
Keynesian theory: embedded liberalism 7; popular 139; privatised 126–127; welfare capitalism 22–23
Konings, M. 23–25
Kyoto Protocol (1997) 107–110, 111

labour markets: benefits of free movement 6–7; Brexit campaign 145; future 146; insecurity 11, 116–118, 145; theory of acquisition 31, 51–53; wages 31
Labour Party government (UK) 118–125, 129–132, 147
laissez-faire economic theory: analysis of 12–14, 21–22, 34, 43–44, 122; collapse of liberalism 137
land: appropriation 53; commodity and function 99–100; enclosures movement 28, 99
law: English 54–56; European 100
Le Mythe de Sisyphe (Camus) 37–38
legislation: and English workers 116–117; and environment 100, 101; and improvement 102 *see also* common law
Lippmann, Walter 70, 73
livelihood: and Brexit campaign 145–146; economy as 10–11, 27–28, 144; insecurity 31, 83–84, 116; tension with improvement 26, 29, 38; and Trump campaign 145–146
Locke, John 50–56, 57–60, 65, 74, 75; influence of 54–56
London, City of 118

Macron, Emmanuel 5
Malthus, Thomas 19, 34, 39
Mare Liberum (Grotius) 48–49
market efficiency, financial 88–92
marketised social protection 16–17, 21, 129–133, 137–139, 148–149; environment 102, 104–105, 106, 110; financial markets 85, 88–92; welfare provision 129–133
market/markets: concept 88–90, 96–97; disembedded 24; and economy 10–12; environmental protection 104–106, 110; failure 12; fundamentalism 38–39; history 19–20; hybridity with state 22–23; ideology 34; as medium 105; Misesian understanding 96–97; Polanyi's definition 23–25; self-regulation 10–11; state functions 12, 118; tension with society 20–21, 38–39; welfare provision 119–124, 130–132
Markowitz, Harry 88–89
Marx, Karl 24–25, 61, 67–68, 69
Marxism 24–25, 36
Menger, Carl 19, 20, 66, 148
Merkel, Angela 4, 5
migration 6, 143
Mill, James 66
Mill, John Stuart 66
Mises, Ludwig von 69, 70–71, 73, 75
modernity, Polanyi's critique 18–19, 30–34
monetary politics 83–88
money, and finance 83–93, 96–98, 140–143
monopoly, and competition 64, 69–72, 76–77
Mont Pelerin Society (MPS) 45, 69–74, 75
morality: and consumer choice 121–122; and economic problematisation 15; individual 14; and power 65–66, 72;

and property 65–66; and proximity 59; suppression 66–67, 73–75
mortgage markets 126–128

nationalism, rise of 85–86
natural law tradition: approach 15, 44; and economic problematisation 44–45, 47–48, 50–51, 52–54, 56, 65; and labour theory of acquisition 51–54; notion of economy 47–50; and private property 44, 47–50, 51–54
natural philosophy 46
nature, and climate change 99–115
neoliberalism: continuation 140; and economic problematisation 45, 69–71, 72, 76–77; and economism 74; and the economy 69–77; and marketisation 21–23; moral crisis 75; and power 77; view on price and order 69–74
neo-Polanyian narrative 18, 21–25
New Deal 137
New Labour 129–131, 132
non-economic behaviour 39–40
non-market institutions 11

Obama, Barack 112
Obstfeld, Maurice 7
On the Law of Nature and of Nations (Pufendorf) 49
opportunity costs, and externalities 105–106
ownership *see* property

Paris Climate Agreement (2015) 107, 111, 147
pensions: and consumer choice 132; and hedge funds 94; Pension Protection Fund 130–131; in practice 129–132; public spending 130
perfectibility *see* visions of perfectibility
personal finances, in practice 124–129
personal insolvency 129
Pigou, Arthur 102–105
'Pigovian taxes' 103–105
Polanyi, Karl: on complexity of society 38–39; critique of economism 10–14, 18–25, 31–33, 35, 37–38, 43–44, 74; critique of modernity 30–34; 'double movement' 19–25; ecological politics 99–102; on economic growth 28–40; on freedom 37–39; on the Gold Standard 3–4; influences and experiences 8, 24–25, 36; on livelihood 27–28; on money 83–84; thesis as postmodern 34–40; visions of perfectibility 13–17, 38–39, 76, 92
Polanyi, Michael 8
political economy *see* economy
'Political Ideas in the Twentieth Century' (Berlin) 36
political theory: comparisons 6–8, 13; influece of Locke 54–56; rejection of religion 57
pollution trading 106–114
poor relief 32–34, 43
populism 5
portfolio selection theory 89–92, 95
Posner, Richard 105
postmodern thesis, Polanyi's 34–40
post-Polanyian scholarship 18
poverty: and industrial capitalism 30–31; and philosophical outlook 35; relief 31–34, 43
power: and economic problematisation 15; and freedom 59–61, 63, 72–74, 76; and neoliberalism 77; and price 63–65; and property 63
price: in commerical society 53; derived from value 50; and externalities 105; formation 50; function 63–64; monopoly 72; and neoliberalism order 71–74; and power 63–65; pure faith in 75, 76; resolving tensions 87, 137
Private Finance Initiative model 118
private property *see* property
privatisation 118
product, private and social 103–105
profitability, tension with habitation 16
property: and commercial society 50–56; as despotic dominion 54–56; and divine order 45–50; and economic problematisation 44–45; and justice 54–56, 57–62, 63; and labour theory of acquisition 51–54; meaning 63; and moral problematisation 65–66; natural law tradition 44, 47–50, 51–54; opposition between freedom and power 59–61; rights 105–106, 115; *status quo* 54–55; uneven distribution 59
protectionism: arguments against 6–7; and economic crisis 85
'protestant ethic' 45
Protestantism 44–45
'prudentialism' 122–123, 125, 130
public service provision, and consumer choice 120–122

public spending: on pensions 130; on social security 118; on welfare 117–118
public-private partnership 22
Pufendorf, Samuel 48, 49–50, 52

quantitative easing 139

Rawls, John 36
regulation, and environment 103–104
religion: and economic liberalism 34–35; and economic thought 15; rejection 57
Ricardo, David 19, 34, 66
The Road to Serfdom (Hayek) 71, 73
Rothbard, Murray 72
Rousseau, Jean-Jacques 45, 59–63, 65, 66, 67, 74
Rutte, Mark 5

self-identity, and consumption 127
self-interest: individual 55, 57–59, 62; opposition to benevolence 59; and social justice 59
self-regulation 40
Sen, Amartya 76
Smith, Adam 32, 33, 45, 62–65, 66, 69, 71–72, 74, 75, 76–77
social cost: and externality 102–106; of welfare economics 115
social embeddedness, Polanyi's view 23–25
social justice, based on self-interest 59
social protection: and financial markets 85, 88–92; marketised 11, 16, 21, 39–40, 77–79, 137–139; marketised and environment 102, 104–105, 106, 110
social security, public spending 118
society: complexity 38–39; marketisation 19, 20, 21, 38–39
Soros, George 93
Speenhamland system of poor relief 31, 43; Speenhamland Act (1834) 116
Spheres of Justice (Walzer) 29–30
state: expenditure 117–118; and externalities 103–104; and livelihood 116–117; and markets 12, 20, 21–22, 22–23, 118 *see also* government
stock market crash (1929) 4–5
sub-prime mortgage crisis 85, 93, 95–96, 140
subsistence economy, transition to commercial society 52–53

substantivist economics 23, 27–28
sulphur dioxide trading 107, 109
Summa Theologiae (Aquinas) 45–47
A Summary of the Law of Contracts (Langdell) 56
sustainable development 110
Switzerland, basic income 143
Syriza party (Greece) 5

TEM credit bartering system 140–141
TGT see The Great Transformation (TGT) (Polanyi)
theocentric knowledge, decline 34
third way ideology 119–121, 123–124, 132, 147
totalitarian ideology 14, 70–71
Townsend, Joseph 32–34, 39, 43
trade unions, formal recognition 116
transcendence: contradiction between habitation and improvement 92, 96; of economic ideas 74–77; and economic problematisation 15, 74, 96, 138; and the economy 148–149; and marketised social protection 138–139; through policy design 138–139
transformation, tension with security of livelihood 25–28
Treatise on Human Nature (Hume) 57
Trump, Donald 5, 6
Trump campaign 6–8, 13, 16, 143–147
tuition fees 143
Turner report 127–128, 131
Two Treatises of Government (Locke) 50–53

United Kingdom: basic income 142; Building Societies Act (1986) 126; carbon footprint 112; Child Trust Fund (CTF) 123, 125; Clean Air Act (1956) 102; community bank 141; Consumer Credit Act (1974) 126; Department for Work and Pensions (DWP) 124; and the ERM 87; Financial Inclusion Taskforce (2006) 124; Financial Services Act (1986) 126–127; Financial Services Authority (FSA) 93, 96, 123; National Health Service (NHS) 120–121; National Pensions Saving Scheme (NPSS) 131–132; pensions *see* pensions; Pensions Act (2007) 130; The Savings Gateway 125; Social Security Act (1986) 129–130

United States: carbon trading 112; Clean Air Act Amendments (1990) 107; coal industry 144–145; Federal Reserve 96; pensions 131; protectionism 85; Securities and Exchange Commission (SEC) 93
universities, league tables 121–122
unsecured lending 129
utilitarianism 10, 66

value theory 50
visions of perfectibility 13–17, 38–39, 76, 92

wages, and labour markets 31
Walras, Léon 66
Walzer, M. 29–30
The Wealth of Nations (Smith) 33, 63

Weber, Max 44–45, 61
welfare provision: in the 20th century 116–119; argument against 32–34; asset-based 122–129; and consumerism 123–129; individuals personally accountable 119; linked to prices rather than earnings 129; marketisation 78–79, 119–124, 130–132; people and 116–133; social cost 115; tension with economic growth 117–118
welfare state model 117
Wilders, Geert 5
World Economic Outlook April 2017 (IMF) 7

xenophobia, rise of 85–86